10/15

NO SUCH THING AS A FREE GIFT

The Gates Foundation and the Price of Philanthropy

NO SUCH THING AS A FREE GIFT

The Gates Foundation and the Price of Philanthropy

Linsey McGoey

VERSO

London • New York

First published by Verso 2015

1 3 5 7 9 10 8 6 4 2

Parts of Chapter 3 previously appeared in 'The Philanthropic State: Market-State Hybrids in the Philanthrocapitalist Turn', *Third World Quarterly*, vol. 35, no. 1, (2014), 109–25.

Verso
UK: 6 Meard Street, London W1F 0EG
US: 20 Jay Street, Suite 1010, Brooklyn, NY 11201
www.versobooks.com

Verso is the imprint of New Left Books

ISBN-13: 978-1-78478-083-8 (HB)
eISBN-13: 978-1-78478-119-4 (US)
eISBN-13: 9781-78478-120-0 (UK)

British Library Cataloguing in Publication Data
A catalogue record for this book is available from the British Library

Library of Congress Cataloging-in-Publication Data
A catalog record for this book is available from the Library of Congress

Typeset in Minion by Hewer Text UK Ltd, Edinburgh, Scotland
Printed in the US by Maple Press

Contents

What thoughtful rich people call the problem of poverty, thoughtful poor people call with equal justice the problem of riches.

– R. H. Tawney

Winning Paradise Economically

The year is 2012. John E. Mahama drinks a Star beer at a café in East Legon, a wealthier area of central Accra populated by foreigners from the dozens of aid agencies operating in Ghana.

It is mid-April. Ghana's wet season is almost upon the country – clouds gather and linger without breaking; the sky flits between clear and overcast. For a city with two million residents, the streets in richer boroughs such as Cantonments and East Legon are strikingly quiet in the early evening.

There's a flat-screen TV inside the café. In a short while, the football will be on: Chelsea are playing Barcelona. A pair of lanky, teenaged boys walk with a swagger to the patio of the café. They pull up two chairs and position themselves close to the window, inches from the pane, prepped to watch the game from outside, peering through the glass. They know that venturing inside is bound to be costly: sandwiches at the café are an eye-opening fifteen Ghanaian cedis, about five British pounds – no cheaper than in central London.

It's the same with rental properties. One- or two-bedroom flats in Cantonments or East Legon rent for $1,500 to $2,000 a month, on a par with areas of London, New York, or Chicago. Many Ghanaians who work in Accra, Ghana's capital city, don't live there – they can't afford to. Cleaners, nannies, and office personnel wake at 4.30 a.m. to arrive at work by 7.30 or 8.00 a.m., riding in cramped Tro-Tros – rusted mini-vans that form a makeshift transport system, their insides stripped clean and crammed with benches holding eighteen to twenty passengers at a time. Locals blame the vibrant aid industry for driving up rental costs.

Seen for years as one of Sub-Saharan Africa's golden economic performers, Ghana earned middle-income status in 2011. The World Bank determines a country's ranking according to a decades-old (many say outdated) classificatory scheme based on gross national income per capita. Boosted by a commodities boom in gold, diamonds, and recently discovered oil deposits, many Ghanaians have grown wealthier in recent years. Inequality has widened dramatically.[1]

While richer Ghanaians ready themselves for watching the football match, staff from the Ghana Health Service battle a recent outbreak of cholera in the capital. Eighteen people have died in Accra during the first days of April. More are dying as I sit across from John Mahama in the quiet shade of the café patio.

'Just about the same time last year there was also a cholera outbreak in Accra', Mahama says. 'Sanitation in Ghana is one of the worst in Africa. Only about 13 per cent of Ghanaians have access to approved latrines.' He pauses, emphasizing his words: 'Only one–three per cent.'

Mahama is young, polite, and more privileged than most. His calm demeanour is something of a performance. He is far angrier and more tired than he'll admit. Until recently, he worked at the Ghana AIDS Commission, a job he took up after completing an MSc in International Health at University College, London. Before leaving for England, he hadn't appreciated just how isolated Ghana's academic community was from the latest scientific research into the health burdens affecting most Ghanaians.

His biography is almost a metaphor for the nation itself. A high-achiever, Ghana's vibrant private sector has helped the nation to climb the global economic indices, inviting more and more foreign investment. Yet many of the country's poorest citizens watch from the peripheries, their lives unchanged by the proclamations of progress issued from Washington, DC or Geneva. 'Middle-income status' means little to those who have no income at all.

Much like Mahama's clearer-eyed appreciation of Ghana's lack of academic resources after returning from his year abroad, the nation's newfound wealth simply illuminates its frustratingly absent basic amenities: the lack of latrines; the dearth of safe water pumps. There are parts of Accra where ten or twelve family members sleep side by side in rambling, one-room shanties with corrugated iron roofs. Most of Jamestown, a cripplingly poor borough just fifteen minutes away from East Legon by car, has uncovered sewers and no latrines – defecation and urination take place openly in the street.

'We seem to be doing well on some fronts', says Mahama. 'The private sector in Ghana is quite huge now. Gold mining, for example. There are a lot of private companies in the extractive industry. Gold – and quite recently oil and gas. If these organizations were interested in filling the infrastructure gap for water and sanitation, we would have come a long way by now.'

On a separate continent, a century earlier, the accumulation of an unprecedented oil fortune raised similar questions to those asked by Mahama: who benefits the most from rises in national income? What's the best way to make sure that the poor have a share in a country's growing wealth: Regulation? Taxes? Philanthropy?

John D. Rockefeller was convinced that the best approach to combating poverty was less regulation and more philanthropy. He fought for years to secure a charter that would permit him to establish the Rockefeller Foundation. Time and again, the US Congress rejected his overtures, citing concern for the public welfare and objections over the manner in which Rockefeller had amassed his fortune. Published in *McClure's Magazine* in the early 1900s, a series of articles by the journalist Ida Tarbell exposed decades of corporate espionage, price-fixing, bribery, and the creation of bogus companies to disguise illegal activities. In 1909, the Department of Justice launched an anti-trust suit against Rockefeller's Standard Oil. Senator Robert La Follette denounced Rockefeller as the 'greatest criminal of our age'.[2]

Philanthropic foundations at this time were viewed as mere outposts of profit-seeking empires, only cosmetically different from the corporations that had spawned them, a convenient way for business magnates to extend their reach over domestic and foreign populaces. They were a 'scheme for perpetuating vast wealth', the US Attorney General George Wickersham said, one 'entirely inconsistent with the public interest'.[3]

But Rockefeller was determined to establish a trust that would help him scale up his philanthropic giving, something he embarked upon long before the Department of Justice launched its suit against Standard Oil. In 1901, partly at the urging of his son, he established the Rockefeller Institute for Medical Research, housed on a vast stretch of disused farmland bordering what came to be called York Avenue, on Manhattan's Upper East Side, bought for $700,000. The Institute soon emerged as a global centre for medical excellence.[4]

Rockefeller's own three-year-old grandson had died from Scarlet fever just months earlier, compelling him to invest more heavily in biomedical research. Thanks to advances underway in Europe, the 'germ theory' of disease – the idea that infections were caused by tiny organisms invisible to the human eye but discoverable under the lens of a microscope – had begun to supplant miasma theories. Miasma theories, from the Greek for 'pollution', suggested that 'bad air' was often a cause of ill-health, and so contained, as scientists might later have punned, a small germ of truth.

Researchers at the Koch and Pasteur Institutes, set up in Berlin and Paris in 1891 and 1887 respectively, had been cultivating a better understanding of germ theory for nearly two decades. The Rockefeller Institute became the first centre in the United States to follow in their path.

Hideyo Noguchi, a Japanese-born bacteriologist who rose from deep poverty to a senior position at the Rockefeller Institute, grew confident that he had isolated the cause of yellow fever – a scourge transmitted by the bite of a female mosquito. Based on his findings, the Rockefeller Foundation began distributing vaccines and anti-serums throughout Central and South America and the French African colonies. Noguchi was convinced of the vaccine's value – but others were not. He travelled to Accra, epicentre of the British-controlled Gold Coast, determined to prove he was right. He was struck down with yellow fever himself, and died in hospital. Quietly, the Rockefeller Foundation ceased distributing the useless vaccine.[5]

The year is 2013. Wearing a neatly pressed blue Oxford shirt and beige chinos unnoticed by many in the room, Bill Gates stands among patients and nurses in a health clinic in Ahentia, a village one hour's drive north of Accra. Vaccines are being administrated throughout the clinic, a small, tin-roofed structure. Gates listens while local nurses describe the vaccination procedures. Mothers carry booklets to track the vaccinations received by each of their children. Each immunization is jotted down in a large registry book. Once a month, the district director of health services in the region gathers together different sub-district heads to validate their vaccination records. Slowly, the data percolates through chains of command so that, district by district, Ghana's National Health Service has a clear picture of immunization coverage across the country. The system has worked well. Ghana has been polio-free for ten years, and there have been no recorded child deaths from measles since 2002.[6]

A journalist at the scene points out that not many of the nurses or patients at the Ahentia health clinic seem to know who Gates is.

'These are the countries where I'm the least known. I mean, nobody knows me here', Gates says to a reporter. 'Maybe in the capital', he adds, 'but that has nothing to do with why we do the work.'[7]

Why does he do the work? It's a question that's emerged time and again as the Bill and Melinda Gates Foundation, the most powerful philanthropic organization in the world, outspends the donations that Rockefeller, adjusted for today's dollars, made over his entire lifetime. Today, unlike Rockefeller facing sceptical members of Congress 100 years ago, the Gates Foundation commands considerable public support, fuelled by celebrity accolades from, at times, unlikely sources.

Take an encounter between Gates and P. Diddy. Gates, of course, made his billions revolutionizing the world of computing. P. Diddy – otherwise known as Sean Combs or Puff Daddy, the rap star turned fashion impresario – first made his fortune in the music industry. Gates and P. Diddy don't tend to run in the same social circles. Legend has it their first meeting was a memorable one.

It took place, reportedly, in New York, where Gates had been hanging out at the back of a bar with Bono and other friends when P. Diddy approached their table. He stood before Gates and nodded.

'You are a motherfucker.'

Gates's eyes darted at the man. It's doubtful the world's most generous philanthropist hears comments like this too often – at least not to his face.

Diddy continued his train of argument: 'You are a motherfucker. What you are doing on immunization in Botswana? Motherfucker.'

Gates leaned back in his chair. He realized that Diddy was offering him a high compliment.

The encounter is reported by Matthew Bishop and Michael Green in their book *Philanthrocapitalism: How the Rich Can Save the World*. The book has become something of a bible for a new breed of philanthropist vowing to reshape the world by running philanthropic foundations more like for-profit businesses. In this world, Gates is hailed as the 'MacDaddy' of the new philanthropy. Bishop and Green offer a quote from Bono on the appeal of Gates's charitable work: 'Jay-Z, all of the hip-hop guys, kind of adore him. Because he is not seen as a romantic figure – well, maybe romantic in the sense that Neil Armstrong is romantic, a scientist but not a poet. He gets shit done.'[8]

Getting shit done. You might hear other phrases for it. The new philanthrocapitalists claim to be more results-oriented and more efficient than earlier philanthropic donors. They want to revolutionize the last realm untouched by the hyper-competitive, profit-oriented world of financial capitalism: the world of charitable giving. In place of bureaucratic quagmires, they plan to get shit done.

How? What exactly is philanthrocapitalism? What makes the 'new' philanthropy any different from earlier approaches? Bishop and Green define philanthrocapitalism in two main ways. First there's a micro-level definition. Philanthrocapitalism is a novel way of doing philanthropy, one that emulates the way business is done in the for-profit capitalist world. Second, at the macro level, philanthrocapitalism describes the way that capitalism itself can be naturally philanthropic, driving innovation in a way 'which tends to benefit everyone, sooner or later, through new products, higher quality and lower prices.'[9]

Powerful individuals have embraced Bishop and Green's concept of philanthrocapitalism. Former President Bill Clinton wrote a foreword for the book's paperback edition, stressing that the concept is what drives his own approach at the Clinton Foundation. 'You can also see the same approach', he adds, 'taking hold throughout the world. Nobel Peace Prize–winner Muhammad Yunus pioneered with the Grameen Bank's microcredit loans, which have helped lift more than 100 million people out of poverty across the world. The Gates Foundation has used it to save countless lives from malaria, to search for better ways to prevent HIV/AIDS, and to improve education in poor communities in the United States.'[10]

New trends such as philanthrocapitalism, microfinance, impact investing, and social entrepreneurship fall within the 'business-oriented' rubric that Bishop, Green, and Clinton hail for lifting individuals out of poverty, saving lives and improving education. In just a couple of decades, these trends have launched curriculum shake-ups at leading business schools, where students want more and more modules on social entrepreneurship; introduced pressure for more flexible tax codes for for-profit businesses that have a social mission; and inspired investors and entrepreneurs across North America, Europe, and emerging markets to shift their attitude about what constitutes a bottom line.

Nevertheless, even as enthusiasm for philanthrocapitalism continues to win hearts in Davos and Silicon Valley, there are growing challenges to the power of the small group of private donors playing an outsized role in national and global policy-making.

Critics of philanthrocapitalism raise three main concerns. The first centres on the accountability and transparency of private philanthropic players – or lack thereof. Take the Gates Foundation. It provides 10 per cent of the World Health Organization's overall budget. In 2013 it emerged as the largest single donor to the UN health agency, donating more than the US government.[11] According to its charter, the WHO is meant to be accountable to member governments. The Gates Foundation, on the other hand, is accountable to no one other than its three trustees: Bill, Melinda, and Berkshire Hathaway CEO Warren Buffett. Many civil society organizations fear the WHO's independence is compromised when a significant portion of its budget comes from a private philanthropic organization with the power to stipulate exactly where and how the UN institution spends its money.

The second concern is that philanthropy, by channelling private funds towards public services, erodes support for governmental spending on health and education. Outspoken observers such as Michael Edwards, a former executive at the Ford Foundation, point out that private philanthropy is no substitution for hard-fought battles over labour laws and social security, in part because philanthropy can be retracted on a whim, while elected officials, at least in theory, have citizens to answer to.[12] The tension between private philanthropy and public spending has become clear in recent battles over public education in the United States. Often working in collaboration, three powerful 'mega-foundations' – the Gates Foundation, the Walton Family, and the Broad Foundation – are helping to build one of the fastest-growing industries in the United States: secondary and primary schools run on a for-profit basis.

The third major concern is that many philanthropists, both today and in the past, earned their fortunes through business strategies that greatly exacerbate the same social and economic inequalities that philanthropists purport to remedy. The great industrialists of the late nineteenth and early twentieth centuries were dubbed robber barons due to the widespread condemnation of their predatory business tactics. Today, some of the world's most celebrated philanthropists, from Gates to George Soros, earned billions through business tactics that have compounded financial instability, eroded labour protections, and entrenched global economic inequalities.

In Gates's case, Microsoft's business practices have been deemed illegal in a number of anti-trust legal suits in the US and Europe. Mitch Kapor, the billionaire co-founder of Lotus Software and a long-time business rival of Gates throughout the 1980s and 1990s, has emphasized this point. As he stated to me: 'It's incontestable that under Gates's leadership Microsoft exercised its monopoly power to unfairly stifle competition. This was the main finding of fact in the US Department of Justice anti-trust case against Microsoft. The resulting Gates fortune, the majority of which is now being distributed by the Bill and Melinda Gates Foundation, was accumulated in some measure through ill-gotten means.'[13]

*   *   *

What might nineteenth-century observers have made of today's philanthropists? Chances are, many would have cast a cynical eye over the largesse of individuals such as Gates.

One of the most influential early philanthropists was Andrew Carnegie. He helped to create America's vast system of public libraries, and gave vast sums to inhabitants of Dunfermline, Scotland, the town where he was born and spent his early years. He was also one of the earlier benefactors of the Tuskegee Institute, founded by Booker T. Washington to advance African American education. And his donations divided people, then and now.

Carnegie published his first 'Wealth' essay, a short piece extolling the importance of charity, in 1889. Three years later, he presided over one of the bloodiest labour standoffs in US history. In the early spring months of 1892, a labour contract expired at Carnegie's Homestead Plant. Workers, enraged at the suggestion of a 35 per cent wage cut, voted to strike. Carnegie was travelling in Europe at the time, an absence helping him to deflect blame for the bloodshed that soon unfolded at Homestead.

He left his business ally Henry Clay Frick in charge of quelling the workers' rebellion. As tensions with the striking workers became more heated, Frick built a fence three miles long and twelve feet high, lined it with barbed wire – including peepholes for the muzzles of rifles – and hired the Pinkerton Detective Agency to guard strike-breakers who were ferried in to bust the union. He later called on the US National Guard to quell the strike. Eight thousand state militia arrived. Men on both sides of the dispute were killed in the stand-off that followed. The strike held for months before the defeated workers were forced back to work.[14]

Frick sent a short one-word telegram to Carnegie, then travelling in Italy: 'Victory!' Carnegie's reply was immediate: 'Cables received. First happy morning since July. Congratulate all around.' Frick added in a follow-up telegram: 'Our victory is now complete and most gratifying. Do not think we will ever have any serious labor trouble again.' Carnegie's response was again immediate: 'Life worth living again. Now for long years of peace and prosperity. I am now interested in Art matters, until your cable my mind was always running away with me to Pittsburgh.'[15]

Deep mistrust between American workers and industry tycoons like Carnegie hardly created a receptive atmosphere for the latter's philanthropic overtures. Scores of novelists wrote satires of the 'generosity' of benefactors such as Carnegie, Rockefeller, and – later on – Henry Ford, who was more reluctant about parting with his wealth. First published in 1914, Robert Tressell's *The Ragged-Trousered Philanthropists* extended the label of 'philanthropists' to a group of house painters who, as Tressell saw it, acceded meekly to the demands of their bosses. With sly wit, Tressell suggested that their willingness to surrender their labour cheaply was the ultimate philanthropic act.

William Jewett Tucker, a theologian who would later serve as the ninth president of Dartmouth College, wrote an eviscerating review of Carnegie's first 'Wealth' essay, suggesting, 'I can conceive of no greater mistake most disastrous to the end of religion if not to society than that of trying to make charity do the work of justice.'[16]

Tucker's views bear a trace of the earlier writings of Ralph Waldo Emerson, who, in essays such as 'Self-Reliance', spurned what he saw as the infantilizing effect of charity, the tendency for giving to entrench a relation of inequality between individuals where shared appreciation of their equality and individuality should flourish. In a stunning denunciation of Christian morality, Emerson scorns Samaritan notions of one's duty to strangers, to one's immediate brethren, to fellow countrymen. 'Are they my poor?' he asks, recalling a time when a 'foolish philanthropist' insists that he owes a duty to the less affluent. No, he asserts, they are not: he owes them nothing, and they owe him nothing. When people give, it's as if they are offering an apology, as if they must expiate themselves for the sin of living. That act of expiation is the true sin, an immoral renunciation of the gift of life, false penance for living and breathing to the fullest. 'I do not wish to expiate', he writes, 'but to live. My life is for itself and not for a spectacle.'[17]

Oscar Wilde, an admirer of Emerson, drew on these sentiments in his own denouncements of charity in his much-quoted essay 'The Soul of Man Under Socialism'. Wilde would apply Emerson's reservations about charity to the context of the 1890s, a time when an increasingly militant working class, incensed by rampant inequality and looming economic depression, derided the idea that hand-outs from the wealthy could appease their demands. 'The best among the poor', Wilde wrote, 'are never grateful. They are ungrateful, discontented, disobedient and rebellious. They are quite right to be so . . . Why should they be grateful for the crumbs that fall from the rich man's table? They should be seated at the board, and are beginning to know it.'[18]

Often, nineteenth-century attacks on charity were elitist in nature, dismissive of the capabilities of working men and women, if not outright cruel. 'The worst of charity', Emerson once wrote, 'is that the lives you are asked to preserve are not worth preserving.'[19]

Others were preoccupied less with the worthiness of recipients than with the motivations of the donors. A powerful short story from Charles Baudelaire recounted a fictional encounter between two unnamed main characters and a beggar in the street. In the very short piece, no longer than 1,000 words, Baudelaire manages to capture the unspoken tensions that can plague even the smallest and seemingly most inconsequential acts of charity. First there's the attitude of the beggar. Is he grateful for the handouts he receives? Or does he resent them? The narrator in Baudelaire's tale tries to put the poor beggar's ambivalence and helplessness into words: 'I know nothing more disquieting than the mute eloquence of those supplicating eyes that contain at once, for the sensitive man who knows how to read them, so much humility and so much reproach. He finds there something close to the depth of complicated feeling one sees in the tear-filled eyes of a dog being beaten.'

And then there is the ambivalence of the giver himself. As the narrator and his friend pass the beggar, both men dispense coins into the beggar's cap. The narrator's offering is much smaller than his friend's. He notices this and commends his friend for his generosity. 'It was the counterfeit coin', the friend replies calmly, without apology, in a matter-of-fact way, as if the fact that it was a fake coin helps to explain and justify the considerable size of the gift.

The narrator is flabbergasted. He stares at his friend in silence and realizes, appalled at the thought, that the man is being self-congratulatory, proud even, knowing that he has duped the poor beggar. His satisfaction lies in the fact that the beggar doesn't yet realize that he has been duped. The narrator sees clearly at that moment that his friend's 'aim had been to do a good deed while at the same time making a good deal; to earn forty cents and the heart of God; to win paradise economically; in short to pick up gratis the certificate of a charitable man.'

Duping the beggar is cruel in itself, the narrator tells himself. But what's *most* reprehensible about the 'gift' is that his friend is entirely taken in by his own actions. He *believes* himself to be the magnanimous man he appears to be to the beggar. The narrator offers a final musing: 'To be mean is never excusable, but there is some merit in knowing that one is; the most irreparable of vices is to do evil out of stupidity.'[20]

Is Baudelaire's story relevant to philanthropy today? Are today's philanthropists knowingly dispensing 'false coins'? Are they deliberately trying to pick up for free the imprimatur of charitable men?

In many cases, the answer is a resounding no. Charity is dispensed in good faith, with the aim to help rather than harm, and with a spirit of genuine self-sacrifice. And yet, within the growing trend of philanthrocapitalism, there is more than a strong whiff of the idea that it's possible to 'do a good deed while at the same time making a good deal'. Indeed, that very idea – of combining profit-making with good deeds – is widely hailed as *the* defining feature of the new philanthrocapitalism. And what's lacking today is any public censure for that very idea. Where are the individuals like William Jewett Tucker, who disparaged the idea that charity could ever replace the notion of social justice?

While a handful of critics of philanthrocapitalism do exist, their voices are drowned by the deafening chorus of philanthropy enthusiasts who I think of as 'TED Heads' – amiable entrepreneurs and executives who congregate at exorbitantly priced TED events around the world, flocking to headline events ('speaking innovation to power'; 'branding for good') with the earnestness of a Grateful Deadhead on his fifth tour.

Sometimes the motivations of TED Heads are genuinely charitable, in the sense of requiring no personal return or gain. Other times their intentions are outspokenly commercial, aimed at protecting the corporate brand or expanding market share in poor nations. Occasionally, as with Invisible Children's 2012 Kony video – a viral sensation which was quickly derided for, among other quibbles, implying that Joseph Kony's Lord's Resistance Army was dominant in Uganda when it had been largely forced out in 2006 – the campaigns of Generation TED Head seem, well, a little bit stupid.[21] Which, as Baudelaire suggests, may be the most dangerous kind of charity of all.

This book does two main things. First, I add historical nuance to the claims of today's philanthrocapitalists, pointing out the similarities between their approach and earlier philanthropists such as Carnegie and Rockefeller. Second, I explore the often unseen or unvoiced ramifications of how today's grant dollars are spent. What type of political influence is wielded by deep-pocketed benefactors? What are the pros and cons of private individuals, many with wealth greater than the GDPs of most nations, advocating more aggressively for the health, education, and agriculture policies they want to see implemented at home and abroad?

Proponents of philanthrocapitalism often claim that a business-like approach to philanthropy is something entirely new. For example, in 1999, the influential management scholars Mark Kramer and Michael Porter published an article in *Harvard Business Review* claiming that far too few foundations 'think strategically about how they can create the most value for society with the resources they have at their disposal. Little effort is devoted to measuring results. On the contrary, foundations often consider measuring performance to be unrelated to their charitable mission.'[22]

That comment is not true. In reality, a businesslike approach to charity has been dominant within large-scale organized philanthropy for at least 120 years, ever since industrialists such as Carnegie and Rockefeller vowed to apply business techniques to the realm of philanthropy. Just look at Rockefeller's main philanthropic advisor, a former Baptist clergyman named Frederick T. Gates. In 1888, Gates left the Baptist ministry to spend the following decades advising first Rockefeller and then his son, John D. Rockefeller Jr., on the best way to manage their vast philanthropic holdings. Gates was a major adherent of the Efficiency Movement, a school of thought that sought to apply Taylorist principles of management to all spheres of social and business life. Gates continually counseled Rockefeller to try to leverage his philanthropic spending in ways that would achieve the most observable good, such as tackling diseases that killed or crippled the most sufferers.

As the sociologist Nicolas Guilhot points out, both Rockefeller Sr. and Andrew Carnegie claimed 'to apply the rational methods of business to the administration of charitable deeds, which they considered to be outdated and deficient'.[23] William Schambra, director of the Hudson Institute's Bradley Center for Philanthropy and Civic Renewal, reiterated this to me in an interview: 'The notion that we should organize our philanthropies the way we organize our corporations – that was John D. Rockefeller's original idea. That we establish a kind of corporate structure with a bureaucracy and careful decision-making. [Philanthrocapitalism] is just more of that.'[24]

When proponents of philanthrocapitalism claim that the 'new' philanthropy is more impact-oriented or businesslike than the approaches of the past, they are brazenly ignoring the existence or legacy of movements like the Efficiency School, which was obsessed with measuring the impact of philanthropic giving. The historian Stanley Katz has made this point bluntly. 'Much of the current foundation promotional rhetoric', he writes, 'seems to me to bespeak a troubling lack of knowledge about the history of the great and large American foundations.'[25]

If you extend your historical gaze further back, to the eighteenth century, the parallels between today's philanthrocapitalists and earlier generations are even more striking.

A key claim of the 'new' philanthropy is that markets and morals are not distinct phenomena, but commensurate goods. By harnessing the power of the market, philanthrocapitalism inevitably contributes to the welfare of a wider community. This is a powerful idea, but it's hardly a new one. Quite the contrary, it echoes long-held assumptions about the societal advantages of private enterprise. Indeed, one might say it's the founding kernel of modern political economy, apparent at least since the writings of Bernard Mandeville, James Steuart, and Adam Smith, each of whom advanced the idea that individuals labouring to meet their own self-interested economic goals naturally contribute to the common good.[26] Bishop and Green's *Philanthrocapitalism* offers only two cursory references to Smith's work, neither developed in depth. Perhaps attempting to underscore the originality of their own argument, they gloss over the similarities between their own notion and Smith's concept of the invisible hand, the idea that 'by pursuing his own interest [the individual] frequently promotes that of the society more effectively than when he really intends to promote it'.[27]

Felix Salmon, a former Reuters journalist, has queried this

historical amnesia. Criticizing the purported novelty of the notion of philanthrocapitalism, Salmon points out that the 'realization that business has the capacity to create as well as destroy social value is known as "economics", and goes back at least as far as Adam Smith. There's nothing new about it, and nor is there anything new about economists using this insight to assuage the guilt of the rich.'[28] The philosopher Slavoj Žižek has also noted the strange déjà vu that pervades the rhetoric of philanthrocapitalism enthusiasts, suggesting that their maxims are like a 'postmodernized version of Adam Smith's invisible hand: the market and social responsibility are not opposites, but can be reunited for mutual benefit . . . their goal is not to earn money, but to change the world (and as a by-product, make even more money)'.[29]

Both Salmon and Žižek make witty and persuasive points. But two things *are* new about philanthrocapitalism. One is its scale; the other is its explicitness. On the matter of scale, while solid numbers are elusive, it is clear that global philanthropy is widely believed to be in a golden phase. Nearly half of the 85,000 private foundations in the United States alone were created in the past fifteen years. About 5,000 more philanthropic foundations are set up each year.

Experts differ over whether this flourishing of individual foundations represents a significant increase in overall charitable giving in comparison to earlier decades. Ray Madoff, a professor of law at Boston College, points out that within the US, overall charitable giving has remained at about 2 per cent of the gross domestic product since the 1970s, and that contributions from individuals have stayed relatively the same for forty years, amounting to about 2 per cent of disposable income.[30] Broadening the gaze beyond the US, clear-cut pronouncements about increases in global philanthropy are easier to make. David Moore and Douglas Rutzen of the International Centre for Not-for-Profit Law suggest that global philanthropy has dramatically increased in recent years, a growth that has 'corresponded with a rise of private wealth in Brazil, India, China, and other countries.'[31]

The surge in global philanthropy is rooted in growing wealth concentration, something that has enriched the ability to give away eye-popping sums. The global wealthy, of course, have had a remarkably 'good' financial crisis in the years since 2007, when growing recognition of pending financial catastrophe first threatened global markets. In the US, the incomes of the wealthiest 1 per cent rose by an impressive 31 per cent from 2009 to 2012, while the rest of the country saw their incomes rise by a woeful 0.4 per cent.[32] Many within the 1 per cent are using their financial windfalls to pad the endowments of their philanthropic foundations.

But to what end?

What's remarkable about the growing number of foundations over the past two decades is that they haven't had any effect on reducing economic inequality. In fact the opposite appears to be the case. What to make of the fact that growing philanthropy and growing inequality seem to go hand in hand? Does philanthropy actually make the rich richer and the poor poorer?

Straightforward assertions of causality are hard to make. But there are numerous reasons why increased levels of philanthropy may contribute to growing inequality and increased poverty. One is that charitable donations deprive treasuries of tax revenues that could be spent on redistributive welfare policies. The second is that the vast majority of charitable donations do not provide economic relief for low-income individuals. The annual 2012 *Giving USA* study reported that only 7 per cent of the previous year's overall charitable donations in the nation reached programmes defined as for 'public-society benefit' in contrast to much higher spending on religious and cultural pursuits. A report from the National Committee for Responsive Philanthropy found that 55 per cent of foundation arts grants in the United States go to organizations with budgets greater than $5 million, which represent less than 2 per cent of the more than 100,000 arts and culture non-profits in the nation. The primary audience for these large institutions tends to be white and upper-income.[33]

Another concern is that philanthropy is used to thwart demands for higher taxation, protecting and expanding assets rather than redistributing wealth. Philanthropy often opens up markets for US or European-based multinationals which partner with organizations such as the Gates Foundation in order to reach new consumers. Giving more is an avenue for getting more, helping to concentrate wealth in an ever-narrowing nucleus of power-brokers with growing influence over policy-setting at organizations such as the WHO or the UN's Food and Agriculture Organization (FAO).

Philanthropists themselves are often the first to admit that their philanthropy is aimed at preserving rather than redistributing wealth. Carlos Slim is, perhaps, the most candid about this fact, summarizing his own approach to charity with the comment, 'Wealth is like an orchard. You have to share the fruit, not the trees.'[34] His candour illustrates something else that's distinctive about the new philanthropists: their forthrightness about the personal advantages of philanthropy. What's novel today is the *outspoken* way that powerful donors admit and even champion the fact that gift-giving is a useful vehicle for preserving privilege, something that distinguishes them from earlier donors.

Social scientists have long been fascinated by philanthropy and gift-giving. Drawing on the writing of Marcel Mauss, Jacques Derrida suggested that gifts can be seen as a type of *pharmakon*: a Greek term with multiple meanings, including remedy, poison, talisman, remedy, and intoxicant.[35] Gifts are a double-edged offering. Recipients typically feel beholden to reciprocate the gift, while decorous silence over exactly how or when repayment should take place can make the gift *more* burdensome than a strictly economic exchange with clearly delineated stipulations for repayment, interest, and so on. As the sociologist Pierre Bourdieu suggests, this vagueness is what underlies the power of the gift. In his words:

The major characteristic of the experience of the gift is, without doubt, its ambiguity. On the one hand, it is experienced (or intended) as a refusal of self-interest and egoistic calculation, and an exaltation of generosity – a gratuitous, unrequited gift. On the other hand, it never entirely excludes awareness of the logic of exchange . . . No one is really unaware of the logic of exchange (it constantly surfaces in explicit form, when for example someone wonders whether a present will be judged sufficient) . . . but no one fails to comply with the rule of the game which is to act as if one did not know.[36]

Like Bourdieu, Antonio Gramsci also perceived large-scale giving as an economic strategy, one rendered all the more powerful for appearing apolitical. Philanthropy, he asserted, is a way for elites to pursue and legitimate their actions, ensuring the viability of economic and foreign policy interests abroad. Modern notions of soft power owe a debt to Gramsci's writing on philanthropy.

Bourdieu's and Gramsci's insights resonate with a common popular belief that philanthropists often have tacit ulterior motives for giving, from earning the tax write-off, to accumulating political favours, to advancing corporate or governmental economic interests in foreign regions. What's different today is that such motives are no longer tacit. They are widely voiced by philanthrocapitalists themselves. The new philanthropists are increasingly proud, triumphant even, about the private economic fortunes to be made through embracing philanthrocapitalism. Not only is it no longer necessary to 'disguise' or minimize self-interest, self-interest is championed as the best rationale for helping others. It is seen not as coexisting in tension with altruism, but as a prerequisite *for* altruism. I explore the ramifications of this ideological shift.

This book's structure is straightforward. In the first half, I investigate the rise of the philanthrocapitalism movement, exploring

its political implications and commercial goals. Today's philanthrocapitalists are remarkably fond of the word 'social'. They affix
the word to an ecumenical bounty of commercial endeavours,
implying that this renders their actions more socially progressive. But does it? What evidence do we have that new trends such
as social entrepreneurship, microfinance, and social investing are
helping to alleviate poverty, foster more educational opportunities, or access to better health services? The answer is: less than
you might think.

In the second half of the book I focus on the Bill and Melinda
Gates Foundation. I offer snapshots of the foundation's influence in
nations such as Ghana and the US, where health activists and parent
groups both praise and lament the foundation's presence. I examine
the remarkable way that the Gates Foundation has transformed US
public education in little more than a decade. I look at the foundation's role in global agriculture, where the effort to introduce
Monsanto seeds and fertilizers to African markets is fuelling protest
from African citizens and elected officials.

Why the focus on Gates, over, say, George Soros? Or the Koch
brothers? Or Carlos Slim? The answer is simple: there's a need for it.

Most foundations with influence on a par with the Gates
Foundation have received considerable scrutiny from academics
and journalists. And yet the Gates Foundation – indisputably the
most influential private foundation in the world today – hasn't
received much critical attention. While *positive* news stories appear
almost daily, only a small handful of media and academic articles
have suggested there may be a downside to the foundation's activities. They include an important report from the *LA Times* which
queried whether the foundation's extensive holdings in oil companies subvert its public health mission. A couple of years later, a
physician based in London, David McCoy, analyzed the foundation's
total grants in global health to date and found that a small percentage goes to researchers based outside Europe and North America,

exacerbating glaring inequalities in research and development capacity between the global north and the global south, and restricting the ability of southern researchers to develop homegrown technological solutions. Diane Ravitch, the noted education historian, has written critically about the Gates Foundation's role in US public education.

These are important criticisms. But they are scattered among a few newspapers and academic journals. Why the lack of attention? Timing is one reason. The speed at which the Gates Foundation has emerged as a significant power-player in US and global political arenas has, by and large, simply outrun academic scrutiny of its achievements and failures.

But speed alone is not the sole problem.

'A large amount of money completely surrounded by people who want some', is how the US activist and social critic Dwight Macdonald once described the Ford Foundation. The same epithet applies to the Gates Foundation. Philanthropic foundations are a lifeline for a startlingly high number of academic research teams and fledgling non-profit organizations. Often, it's simply safer to stay quiet than to openly voice discomfort with how the foundation spends its money.[37]

There's also the fact that the Gateses do considerable good. Like Melinda's willingness to speak out about the importance of contraception when the lingering effects of the US government's former Global Gag Rule continue to make it hard for foreign NGOs receiving US funds to offer planned parenting options to women in developing countries. Or Bill's support for raising the capital gains tax in the US. He has also voiced support for the campaign for a global tax on currency speculation in global financial markets, something that has raised billions for government treasuries in regions where it has been introduced. And while the vast bulk of Gates's giving wasn't ramped up until he was well into his mid-forties and fifties, there's ample evidence that many of the causes he supports today have been close to his heart for decades. His much-reported 2014 donation of $1 million to campaigners calling for tighter firearm controls in the state of Washington wasn't a whim donation; almost twenty years earlier Gates had offered $35,000 towards a 1997 state ballot initiative supporting stricter gun laws.

But the fact that the Gateses often fund initiatives that many people approve of should not insulate them from criticism. And to date, that's exactly what has happened: gaping silence over foundation activities where spirited discussion should flourish. Even individuals who are sceptical of the tax incentives motivating large-scale philanthropy, or who think that philanthropy is no substitute for state welfare support and labour protections, tend to salute the efforts of Bill Gates. Worse, they may idealize Gates as a corrective to more conservative philanthropists such as the Koch brothers or the Walton family, heirs of the Walmart fortune.

A typical article tends to read like this one, by Barry Ellsworth, in an op-ed for the online news bulletin Allvoices.com: 'Charles and David Koch are at it again', Ellsworth writes,

> this time using their wealth to back a creepy 'Carenival' complete with games, jugglers, knife throwers, and acrobats whose sole purpose is to scare people away from Obamacare . . . some billionaires like Microsoft founder Bill Gates and Facebook's Mark Zuckerberg use some of their vast riches to advance the cause of mankind through humanitarian donations. Then there are those like the coal-loving Koch brothers, who seem to delight in using their money to throw up roadblocks to programmes that would benefit the vast majority of Americans.[38]

The problem with this type of commentary is that it is a little like professing that you believe in democracy but only if your preferred party is the sole candidate. The same regulatory laxity and tax allowances that make it possible for the Koch brothers to exert considerable influence over US politics underpins the ability of Gates, Zuckerberg, or Soros to fund a pro-immigration platform or to overhaul US education, for better or for worse. To rein in the Kochs you must be willing to rein in Gates. Or Soros. Or Buffett. Or Zuckerberg.

Another reason for focusing on Gates and his foundation is that no other public figure has been more influential in shifting the global discourse on philanthropy in recent decades. Through initiatives like the Giving Pledge – Gates and Buffett's exhortation to their fellow billionaires to give at least 50 per cent of their fortunes to charity – Gates offers a powerful antidote to the mushrooming legions of economic doomsayers who suggest that growing wealth gaps are *the* biggest threat to global sustainability today. 'Back off', Gates and his fellow pledgers protest when faced with criticism from economists such as Thomas Piketty and James Galbraith. 'We're giving it away.'

Gates has made his rejection of Piketty's call for a wealth tax clear on a number of occasions, including during a widely reported conversation with Piketty which the latter recounted at a conference in London in early 2015. Piketty told his audience that Gates said to him, 'I love everything that's in your book, but I don't want to pay more tax.' Piketty added: 'I think he sincerely believes he's more efficient than the government, and you know, maybe he is sometimes.'

Is he? This is the first book to address that question in depth. Just how efficient is Gates's philanthropic spending? Are the billions he has spent on US primary and secondary schools improving education outcomes? Are global health grants directed at the largest health killers? Is the Gates Foundation improving access to affordable medicines, or are patent rights taking priority over human rights?

It's not easy to criticize philanthropy at a time when giving appears more necessary than ever. And it's particularly not easy to criticize an organization as widely lauded as the Gates Foundation. Other foundations are more obviously subject to criticism, such as the Walton Family Trust, which for years has been something of a philanthropic whipping boy for critics on the left and the right. Those on the left condemn the Waltons' tendency to fund causes that clearly help to sanitize Walmart's image as a tight-fisted, union-busting employer. 'Much of Wal-Mart's philanthropy', Liza Featherstone at *The Nation* notes, 'has been directed towards promoting anti-government politics, whether by lobbying against high taxes for the rich or contributing to Republican candidates, conservative think-tanks and efforts to privatize education.'[39]

Even conservative critics have chimed in with the criticism. *Forbes*, for example, recently ran an article featuring a report from the watch-dog group Walmart 1% which points out that living members of the Walton family have given surprisingly little of their personal fortunes to the Walton Family Foundation. With just under $2 billion in assets, the Walton Family Foundation is a power-player in philanthropic circles. It doesn't approach the Gates Foundation's enormous $42 billion endowment, but it appears on the top-forty list of US foundations when ranked by endowment size.[40] Remarkably, only a miniscule portion of that money comes from the personal wealth of the second generation of Walton heirs: Rob, Jim, Alice, and Christy. The foundation sustains itself almost entirely through 'tax-avoiding trusts established with assets provided by the late Sam, Helen, and John Walton or their estates'. Jim and Alice Walton have made zero contributions to the foundation during its twenty-three-year existence, while Christy and Jim have offered nominal sums.[41]

Those figures, based on twenty-three years of tax filings by the Walton Family Foundation, don't reflect private donations made by family members outside of their main foundation, estimated at about $5 billion to date. But the facts are still startling: a large and powerful foundation bearing the Walton family name has received less than *0.05 per cent* of the living Walton's heirs combined net worth of $139.9 billion. To observers on the left and the right, that figure seems downright cheap. The author of the *Forbes* piece, Clare O'Connor, does what a lot of journalists writing about stingy billionaires tend to do: she contrasts the Waltons with Gates and Buffett, commending the latter for giving 36.2 per cent and 26.9 per cent of their wealth to philanthropic causes respectively.

The problem is, this is a Manichean way to approach philanthropy, unreservedly reprimanding those who give the least, and unreservedly applauding those who give the most. It's true that both Gates and Buffett have relinquished far more of their personal fortunes. They have also, unlike the Waltons, spoken passionately about and invested in causes that do not coincide with their own business interests. In many ways, theirs is the opposite of the overtly self-serving philanthropic and lobbying efforts of the Waltons. Buffett's widely reported scorn for tax laws that left his secretary forking over more proportionately of her salary in taxes than he does is evidence of that.

But there are many grey zones where the separation between the Gateses' personal interests and the Gates Foundation's priorities are less clear. Perhaps the clearest example is the thorny area of global patent protections. For decades, health activists in the US and internationally have suggested that current patent laws are a significant obstacle to achieving worldwide access to affordable medicines. Bill Gates does not agree. And his outspoken views on patents, combined with enormous cash injections towards the health policies he prefers, may have single-handedly thwarted efforts to open pharmaceutical markets to more generic competition. The influential health scholar James Love has noted the problem concisely: '[The Gates Foundation] funds most of the journalism on this topic, and they have been hard-line advocates for strong patent protection, since the 1990s. This creates more problems than you might think, because they influence the Obama Administration, the WHO, and the Global Fund on these issues, not to mention the press coverage and most academics and NGOs working on global health issues.'[42]

Another concern is the Gates Foundation's philanthropic partnerships with Coca-Cola, a company that has spent millions lobbying against increased taxes on sugary beverages, something health advocates see as essential to battling the global obesity epidemic. And let's not get started here on the Foundation's collaborations with Monsanto. I'll leave that for Chapter 7. But my interest in the Gates Foundation goes beyond cataloguing a string of corporate partnerships that have surprised and inflamed health and environmental activists. It goes beyond the question of whether philanthropy still counts as philanthropy if it helps to line a benefactor's pockets. I'm interested in the mindset that has fuelled public receptiveness to Gates's donations, a receptiveness that is fostered in part through tax-deductible philanthropic marketing efforts, and in other, less tangible ways through vestiges of religious sensibility which stress the importance of Christian charity even among secularists. It is a mindset that restricts public debate surrounding philanthropy by making even the most judicious criticism appear petty or small-minded. The same happens with criticism of foreign aid schemes – criticism Gates has taken offence to. On numerous occasions he has suggested that it's misguided to question the value of foreign aid. Through his foundation, he's spent hundreds of millions in tax-deductible grants to convey the public message that aid 'works'.

Unfortunately, the belief that aid 'works' is a simplistic and, in many ways, misguided one. It's a notion that diverts attention away from the realities of misplaced research priorities by the world's most powerful pharmaceutical companies, blankets understanding of how trade laws infringe upon national manufacturing and importing capacity, and obscures the role that global financial markets play in creating worldwide food instability.

Public enthusiasm for clipping the philanthropic wings of large benefactors has ebbed and flowed throughout recent decades. The Gates Foundation's reshaping of the global health field and the US education sector mirrors earlier initiatives led by Carnegie and

Rockefeller. Their efforts helped to pioneer access to health services, to public education, and to cultural and artistic endeavours, domestically and abroad. But their influence bred as much resentment as praise. For many, even the application of the term philanthropy is an incongruity when it comes to the 'big three' foundations of the twentieth century: the Carnegie, Rockefeller, and Ford Foundations. As the cultural historian Francesca Sawaya points out, 'Philanthropy has traditionally been defined as the disinterested expression of a "love of mankind." So why associate that term with the Carnegie or Rockefeller Foundation, whose financial histories and activities have not been seen as disinterestedly beneficent by their critics on either the left or the right?'[43]

Today, despite the unparalleled global influence of the Gates Foundation, legislators are mostly silent about the negative repercussions of large-scale giving. In DC, as one of my sources said to me, the 'appetite for reform' of the philanthropic sector is weaker than it has been for decades. The philanthrocapitalists have silenced their critics. The question is how, and for how long.

CHAPTER ONE

Big Men

Treat your interns right, the popular adage goes. Because one day they will be writing your pay cheques. And if they're not writing your pay cheque, they may be cutting business deals that you either want in on, or need to flee as far away from as possible. Bill Clinton knows this well. Not when it comes to *that* intern, but when it comes to Doug Band, a long-time staff member of Clinton's team who spearheaded the former president's metamorphosis into one of the most revered philanthropic impresarios of the twenty-first century.

Band started working for Clinton at the age of twenty-seven, when he was hired as Clinton's personal aide – also known as the body man. A good body man, or body woman, needs to cultivate a curious mixture of obsequiousness and extreme self-confidence. He needs to fetch coffee with good-natured servility, while feeling at home swanning through a high-ceilinged ballroom hot on the heels of a powerful boss. As Clinton's personal assistant, Band was many things: amanuensis, porter, therapist, human traffic comptroller, helping Clinton to greet the well-connected by name while dodging the more unimpressive petitioners hovering like mayflies. It was often grunt work with few obvious benefits.

When he took the job as Clinton's aide, Band had an MA in liberal arts and a law degree under his belt, both from Georgetown University. Body men don't need law degrees to carry out their duties, and so when he snagged the job in 2000, there were some raised eyebrows. It seemed like a lowly post, and the timing was off. Clinton's second term was approaching the very end of its twilight, and within a year he had left the White House and opened an office in Harlem. The exact nature of post-presidency consultancy work was yet to be defined. Band stayed on as Clinton's counsellor, and at the time, 'the phones weren't ringing much'.[1]

Band's work with Clinton was profiled by Alec MacGillis in a recent investigative article in the *New Republic*. MacGillis suggests it was Band who had an epiphany about how to get the phones buzzing more. The idea reportedly hit him in Davos, at a meeting of the World Economic Forum, while billionaires and heads of state lingered for a chance to shake Clinton's hand. Eying the queues of adoring fans, Band realized that Clinton's star power could be leveraged for philanthropic good – albeit not in the traditional way.

Established in 2001, Clinton's philanthropic foundation was already up and running. The William J. Clinton Foundation dispensed money to numerous causes, with a focus on global health and economic development. Band's idea was something new. He saw the need for an annual event, similar to Davos, which could bring powerful elites into contact with each other to forge 'partnerships' aimed at solving global problems. The first meeting of the Clinton Global Initiative (CGI) was held in 2005 and the get-together has grown larger ever since. Organizations pay a membership fee of $20,000 each year ($19,000 of which is tax deductible). This fee includes attendance at the CGI annual meeting, held in New York, as well as what the Clinton Foundation describes as "media support and showcasing opportunities." The meeting is billed as a chance to publicize one's philanthropic efforts to the "nearly 1,000 members of the media [who] are on-site at the Annual Meeting each year to report on the accomplishments of CGI members." The $20,000 membership fee is just to get past the door. Corporate donors often spend hundreds of thousands extra in sponsoring the annual meeting. Once inside, the event is run a bit like a charity auction. But instead of bidding on donated prizes – a day at the spa, a weekend in Aspen – attendees vie to outspend each other on the philanthropic contributions they pledge to make in the future.[2]

In the decade since it was set up, the CGI claims to have secured pledges worth $103 billion. It's a gigantic sum, trebling the amount disbursed by the Gates Foundation to date. Whether or not you like how the Gates Foundation has spent its money, however, at least it has actually been spent.

The Clinton Global Initiative is a clearing house. It's an annual extravaganza permitting donors to announce vast donations secure in the knowledge that a promise is not exactly a binding commitment. There is no global cabal of philanthropic bounty hunters, making sure CGI attendees make good on their pledges. Consider a headline-grabbing announcement from Virgin CEO Richard Branson, who in 2006 made a CGI pledge to commit $3 billion to fighting climate change over the upcoming decade. We are now one year away from the end-date of his pledge, and so far he has spent a mere $300 million. As MacGillis has emphasized, the question of what happens once the famous guests leave the conference venue is not exactly Clinton's area of expertise.[3]

Published in 2013, MacGillis's *New Republic* article sent currents of unease through DC power circles. The questions he raised were at once simple and hard to answer: Who has benefited the most from Clinton's philanthropic empire? Grant recipients in poor nations? Clinton himself? Or Doug Band?

In 2009, Band co-founded Teneo, which brands itself as a public relations and corporate consulting firm. Staff inside the Clinton Foundation grew uneasy when Band began exploiting the contacts he'd made through CGI in order to hustle business for Teneo. The *New York Times* ran a lengthy, critical article detailing years of financial shortfalls at the Clinton Foundation despite its receiving lucrative contributions from supporters. The relationship with

Teneo was also a concern, as 'some Clinton aides and foundation employees began to wonder where the foundation ended and Teneo began.' Bill Clinton eventually stepped down as a paid advisor to Teneo, not long after the *New York Post* ran an article suggesting that Hillary Clinton was angry about negative Teneo publicity.[4]

The problem is larger than individual scandals. The bigger issue is whether the aims of a for-profit company such as Teneo are compatible with the objectives of a non-profit such as the Clinton Foundation. A recent working paper available on Teneo's website provides a good example. Titled 'Integrated Activist Defense', the paper lays out steps for mitigating shareholder activism, 'an increasing challenge for listed companies. There are more than 100 major proxy battles each year in the US alone. Actions mounted against incumbent CEOs and boards are increasing.'[5] At a time when many management scholars and frustrated main street investors suggest that executive management needs reining in – with CEO remuneration and the lack of separation between the CEO and Chairman roles one of the largest bugbears of shareholders – companies such as Teneo command vast sums to ensure that shareholder demands are kept at bay.

The fact that Band acquired a personal fortune while charging fees for introducing people to Clinton is hardly unprecedented. Five years earlier another philanthropic buddy of Clinton, Frank Guistra, pocketed a small fortune after accompanying Clinton on philanthropic junkets throughout South America and Kazakhstan. Guistra's biography offers a useful example of the new generation of philanthrocapitalist: those who bring business acumen to the realm of philanthropy, who are outspoken about the personal advantages of philanthropic investment, and who leverage well-connected social networks in order to achieve personal gain.

Born in Sudbury, a mining town in northern Ontario, Guistra's father, a former nickel miner, introduced him to a financial broker, spurring an early interest in the market. In the early 1980s, Guistra jumped from a position at Merrill Lynch to a riskier placement at the lesser-known Yorkton Securities, relocating to Europe to head up the brokerage's resource group. Under Guistra, the journalist Andy Hoffman reports, Yorkton developed innovative ways to help clients secure bids to exploit profitable mineral deposits He suggested, for example, that Yorkton should hire a former finance minister from Chile to help post-Soviet countries draft new mining laws. As he described to Hoffman: 'We did that in Africa; we did that in South America. It was a great way to look credible.' The world of junior mining finance was in its infancy, and Guistra enabled Yorkton to capitalize on the fast-growing industry.[6]

Guistra left Yorkton in 1995, just before a series of front-page Canadian scandals began plaguing the mining world, including Bre-X, a scandal involving false claims of gold deposits in Butang, Indonesia. After Bre-X's stock soared on hype surrounding mineral deposits, the claims were exposed as fraudulent. Canadian public sector investors lost hundreds of millions, including the Quebec Public Sector Pension fund ($70 million), and the Ontario Teachers' Pension Plan ($100 million). The controversy raised questions over why no one seemed to have noticed that no deposits actually existed, including Peter Munk, CEO of Barrick Gold, the world's largest gold mining company. (When gold fever in Butang first struck, Munk peevishly lobbied Suharto, then president of Indonesia, to force Bre-X to share exploitation rights with Barrick Gold once the exact site of the gold was pinpointed. Even George H. W. Bush, a Barrick board member, was enlisted to have a polite word with the Indonesian dictator. Later on, Munk was thankful that his efforts ended up in vain, saving him from losing any significant money on the venture. As he confessed to the Canadian news magazine *Maclean's*, 'I praise my Lord that I didn't succeed. Sometimes luck is more important than talent.')[7]

Guistra has a knack for good timing. His departure from Yorkton saved him from association with an industry mired in controversy. His hiatus did not last long. In 2001, he sensed that gold, by then trading below $300, was due for a price hike. With a colleague, he bought Wheaton River Minerals, valued at $20 million. Four years later, Wheaton merged with Goldcorp, making it one of the world's most valuable gold producers.

In 2007 Guistra was introduced to Bill Clinton. With impressive speed, the Clinton Guistra Sustainable Growth Initiative was launched, aimed at spurring economic development through market-driven partnerships between the private sector, governments, and local communities. At the time, one particular partnership – specifically, between Guistra's MD-87 jet and Clinton's travel needs – fuelled a firestorm of criticism. Clinton and Guistra first took a trip together on the jet in June 2005, after Clinton's associates wrote to Guistra informing him that the ex-president needed a jet for a planned trip through South America. Three months later, Clinton and Guistra embarked on another jaunt. The first country on the itinerary was Kazakhstan, which has more than 20 per cent of the world's oil reserves and an abundance of mineral wealth. The state-run mining company, Kazatomprom, had signalled interest in allowing foreign investors to buy some of its ventures. Fruitfully for Guistra, Kazakhstan happened to be the first stop of the Clinton Initiative–planned, three-country tour in support of health programmes for HIV/AIDS. Guistra and Clinton were invited to dinner with Nursultan Nazarbayev, president of the nation for the previous two decades. Over dinner, Guistra and Nazarbayev chatted informally, just 'in passing', about Guistra's mining interests in the nation. Three days later, Guistra's year-long negotiations with Kazatomprom came to an end. The company's uranium deposits were sold to Guistra's group for $450 million. Guistra's personal stake in the deal was valued at more than $45 million.

According to the *New York Times*, 'the monster deal stunned the mining industry, turning an unknown shell company into one of the world's largest uranium producers in a transaction ultimately worth tens of millions of dollars to Mr. Guistra'. A media frenzy ensued. Reporters were quick to point out that, as well as paving the way for

Guistra's meeting with Nazarbayev, Clinton introduced Guistra to Colombian president Álvaro Uribe shortly before a shell company linked to Guistra paid $250 million for control of a Colombian oil venture.[8]

Concern over whether Clinton's friends might be leveraging philanthropic donations in order to exploit lucrative business opportunities led to calls for Clinton to publicize his campaign contributions. He resisted at first and then, in 2008, relented and released a list of names. Beyond this, little has changed. There is nothing illegal in Guistra's actions, and the more generous a benefactor is, the more his public reputation tends to grow. 'The one thing that always worked for me is generosity', Guistra confessed in conversation with Hoffman. 'Generosity can be very profitable.' If he happens to profit from business deals in the countries where he's focusing his philanthropic dollars, 'why is that bad?'[9]

Ambiguity over whether or not Guistra's or Clinton's philanthropy stems from altruism, self-interest, or an ever-shifting mixture of both, makes them what might be called 'liminal pioneers'. From the Latin for 'threshold', liminality – the act of existing on two separate planes of consciousness or physical development, of being 'neither here nor there', as the anthropologist Victor Turner puts it – characterizes the uncertain nature of philanthropic acts that straddle the borders of public benefit and private gain. The difficulty of determining whose interests are *most* served through philanthropic gestures – the donor or the recipient – has been at the heart of anthropological efforts to understand the social and economic functions of charity and gift-giving throughout history. Guistra is part of a long line of what early twentieth-century anthropologists labelled 'Big Men', tribal leaders who used gift-giving to accumulate well-placed friends, expand trading jurisdictions, and increase the number of contacts who could be prevailed upon to return a gift in future. As the Big Men might have put it in the past, just as Guistra does today: What's wrong with that?

STUCK IN THE KULA WITHOUT AN EXIT AGREEMENT

The term 'Big Man' is a derivation of the phrase *bikpela man* – meaning 'prominent men' – which was common in different dialects of Tok Pisin, a creole language spoken throughout Papua New Guinea. The term became popular in anthropology following the First World War, when a number of anthropologists specializing in studies of Melanesia used the term to describe male leaders whose authority was linked to their skilful use of gift-giving as a means to increase their personal and their community's wealth.[10]

One of the first anthropologists to investigate big men was Bronisław Malinowski, a Polish-British anthropologist. In 1914, Malinowski took a field trip to Melanesia. Inconveniently for him, the War broke out soon after his arrival. Although a resident of Britain, Malinowski had Austro-Hungarian citizenship. Denied return to Britain, Malinowski had two choices: spend the war interned as a detainee or spend it exiled on the Trobriand Islands, an archipelago off the coast of New Guinea. He chose political exile and spent the time investigating the practices of the Trobriand Islanders, including an intricate form of gift exchange called the *kula*.

Spanning a cluster of eighteen islands, including the Trobriand Islands, the custom of kula was centred on the exchange of artful valuables: decorative things such as pearly, translucent red-shell necklaces and white-shell armbands. Participants travelled hundreds of miles to exchange valuables, a laborious, time-consuming process which underscored the importance of gift-giving as a politically useful tactic. Far from being a selfless gesture, unspoken rules ensured that the generosity of donors would be compensated through the tacit and yet widely known requirement to return or pass on a gift in future. 'Once in the Kula', Malinowski observed rather ominously, paraphrasing a native saying, 'always in the Kula.'[11]

The French anthropologist Marcel Mauss incorporated Malinowski's observations into his much-cited 1925 essay 'The Gift', a study of how, in the absence of economic markets, gifts serve as a form of power, increasing the prestige and reputation of pastoral or tribal leaders. Mauss's work has helped to shape modern clichés, such as the idea that there is no such thing as a 'free gift'. Even the most benevolent gesture comes with a set of social obligations that are difficult to refuse, obliging the recipient to repay a gift or risk losing honour. Examining a range of practices, from the kula to potlatch – gift-giving festivals practised by indigenous peoples of the North American Pacific Northwest coast – Mauss explored the ways gift-giving served profitable ends, helping to advance personal and communal interests.

He noted that attempts to reject a gift are often perilous. To decline an offering is to 'show that one is afraid of having to reciprocate, to being "flattened" [i.e. losing one's name] until one has reciprocated'. Refusing a gift is a breach of social etiquette and a threat to one's honour, embroiling recipients in a gift exchange whether they like it or not. 'Generosity', in Mauss's words, 'is an obligation.'[12]

'The Gift' illuminates the economic usefulness of seemingly selfless acts of charity and friendship. Whether in isolated regions such as the Trobriand Islands or in the dense enclaves of today's most cosmopolitan global cities, charity is a key source of both social and economic power. 'The gift cycle', the anthropologist Mary Douglas suggested, 'echoes Adam Smith's invisible hand: gift complements market in so far as it operates where the latter in absent. Like the market it supplies each individual with personal incentives for collaborating in the pattern of exchanges.'[13]

Work by Mauss, Douglas, and, more recently, the Oxford economic historian Avner Offer has underscored the economic usefulness of philanthropic gestures to the donors of gifts. In both pre-industrial and capitalist economies, wealth is often augmented through what Offer calls 'economies of regard': the ability to court favour through extending a network of exclusive political or social contacts; through knowing how to act, dress, and speak around such contacts; through sensitive adherence to duties of gift-giving and economic 'freebies' (the corporate box, the Wimbledon tickets, the conference goodie bags).[14] Attention to 'economies of regard' helps to underscore a rather obvious point. Often, people lament the rise of 'crony capitalism' as if cronyism is an aberration of good operating practices. In reality, crony capitalism is not a perversion of business as usual. It *is* business as usual. In Guistra's words, 'generosity can be very profitable'.

A curiosity noted by early anthropologists such as Malinowski is that gift-giving often increased the power of the *initiator* of a gift exchange more so than the recipient, augmenting a donor's ability to capitalize on an ever-growing number of dependents. 'The aim of the "big man" transactor', the anthropologist Chris Gregory writes, 'is to acquire a large body of people (gift-debtors) who are obligated to him.'[15] Malinowski emphasized that gift-giving rarely fostered more equality between a donor and recipient. Rather, the more gifts that leaders were in a position to give away, the more powerful they became. The 'gifts' they surrendered tended to embroil recipients in webs of dependency that *reduced* their power through gestures that appeared at first glance to augment it.

Similar concerns are heard today from those on the political right and the left who are critical of the unintended effects of large-scale philanthropic and governmental aid packages. A recent example is *Dead Aid*, the economist and former Goldman Sachs employee Dambisa Moyo's smash bestseller, which argues that aid from governments and philanthropic donors unintentionally impedes the economic growth of regions that it seeks to uplift. She suggests that aid disincentivizes governments from refusing funds; thwarts them from turning to capital markets for investment opportunities; legitimizes protectionist trade regimes in the west; and propagates the myth that recipients are unable to forge successful economic policies without philanthropic support. Reduce aid now, Moyo cautions, or developing regions will never prosper.[16]

Her advice has drawn blunt criticism from experts such as Jeffrey Sachs, a proselytizing champion of US aid to developing regions, who pointed out acidly that Moyo's own education – degrees at Harvard and Oxford – was supported through scholarships. Should all such forms of charitable aid be dispensed with, too?[17]

One of Moyo's key arguments is that four decades of attempts by western aid agencies to apply development policies that worked well during the post-war Marshall Plan in Europe have failed for one blindingly obvious and yet strangely ignored reason: Africa is not Europe. Policy-makers determined to apply 'universally' sound economic policies underestimated the comparative infancy of African economic infrastructures. African nations did not yet have the mechanisms in place to benefit from the type of infrastructure-building underway in the north.

Observers on the left have suggested that this seeming 'problem' has been strategically useful for western donors: a convenient imbalance that has been economically advantageous for western countries to the detriment of developing regions. An exhaustive body of literature has documented the economic and political advantages of less sophisticated markets over more advanced ones. Theorists writing under the broad rubric of dependency theory have pointed out that the economic immaturity of poorer regions makes it easy for wealthier nations to capitalize on the advantages of globalization while bearing less of the cost. Cheap imports, widening labour pools, expanded markets for exports, and lenient health and environmental regulations are just a few of the areas where the 'underdevelopment' of regions such as Africa has been economically advantageous for richer countries. Other people's inequality is just as economically fruitful for some countries as it is hurtful to those who suffer from it.[18]

The dependency theory literature is vast, controversial, and, some say, outdated. Stalwarts who defend it tend to agree on a common intellectual forebear for their insights: Karl Marx, and particularly his views on the need for capitalist economies to dominate new markets in a quest for labour pools and raw materials. In the *Communist Manifesto*, Marx and Engels famously suggest that capitalism is a mode of economic production that 'compels all nations, on pain of extinction, to adopt the bourgeois mode of production; it compels them to introduce what it calls civilization into their midst, i.e., to become bourgeois themselves. In one word, it creates a world after its own image.' Their work illuminates the ways in which global capitalism can create global chains of dependency as obligatory and intractable as the chains of dependency depicted in anthropological studies of Big Men.

George Orwell describes the problem succinctly in *The Road to Wigan Pier*: 'Under the capitalist system, in order that England may live in comparative comfort, a hundred million Indians must live on the verge of starvation – an evil state of affairs, but you acquiesce in it every time you step into a taxi or eat a plate of strawberries and cream.' Aid and philanthropic organizations that purport to remedy this problem often manage, whether inadvertently or not, to perpetuate it. 'Put crudely', as the journalist Andy Beckett observes, 'the super-rich need to stay super-rich in order for their charitable enterprises to function.'[19]

THE BIG THREE

'There are no second acts in American lives', F. Scott Fitzgerald famously quipped. He was quite wrong. The most beloved second act in America is the rebirth of financiers and industrialists as the benefactors of humanity, vowing to improve humankind through ever more impressive charitable gifts. In the historian Jackson Lears's words, 'We are still fascinated – almost pornographically so – by success stories.' Few things shout success louder than the exuberant awakening of a wealthy man's philanthropic conscience.[20]

Organized philanthropy is not at all new or unique to America. But the birth of the early twentieth-century American philanthropic foundation led to radical shifts in the nature and aims of organized giving, helping to reshape global philanthropy, to borrow a phrase from Marx and Engels, 'after its own image'. In the process, widespread public mistrust of some of the industrial and labour practices of early industrialists shifted into a growing regard for their benevolence.

Although the late nineteenth century witnessed the establishment of a few small foundations, the major philanthropic foundations didn't emerge until the start of the twentieth century, when Carnegie and Rockefeller chose, within a few years of each other, to set up trusts. They were pioneers in their time, a period when parsimony among wealthy Americans prevailed over a sense of philanthropic duty. Before Carnegie began championing the virtues of giving away one's wealth, the idea that the wealthy should voluntarily part with their hard-won dollars was, to say the least, not in vogue. Some early industrialists even devised plans to keep their heirs from using their inheritance for philanthropic purposes, intent on ensuring that the money would be kept in the family rather than spent charitably.[21]

Carnegie's enlightenment is described in his 'Wealth' essays, manifestos on giving that inspired peers such as Rockefeller and admirers today like Gates. Suggesting that it would be 'better for mankind that the millions of the rich were thrown into the sea than so spent as to encourage the slothful, the drunken, the unworthy', Carnegie proclaimed that the only form of philanthropy worth its name was money spent on carefully policed causes.[22]

He explicitly divorced his own model of giving from acts of Christian almsgiving which saw charity as a virtue regardless of its practical effect. Carnegie felt that philanthropy enabled wealth to be re-invested in communities through channels that philanthropists were best placed to devise and to oversee. In his words:

> Thus is the problem of Rich and Poor to be solved. The laws of accumulation will be left free; the laws of distribution free. Individualism will continue, but the millionaire will be but a trustee of the poor, intrusted for a season with a great part of the increased wealth of the community, but administering it for the community far better than it could or would have done for itself.[23]

Carnegie's own steel fortune was amassed thanks to the advice and offer of a loan given by his employer. Born in a weaver's cottage in Dunfermline, Scotland, Carnegie's mother moved the family to Pennsylvania when he was a child. It was there that he began work at age thirteen as a bobbin boy and later as a boiler attendant at a cotton mill. Eventually hired on as a telegraph operator for the Pennsylvania Railroad, Carnegie quickly perceived the value of investing in the market. With borrowed money, he bought ten shares at $50 each in Adams Express Company, an upstart venture poised to benefit from the railway boom. Dividends from the company reached $10 a month. His first dividend check was, as Lears writes, 'a revelation' for Carnegie, a startling realization of the power of capital investment: the sheer magic of the easy ability to capitalize from something that he 'had not worked for with the sweat of my brow'.[24]

As Carnegie's steel fortune grew, he began to harbour a staunch belief: his own wealth *was* his workers' wealth. Given that he reinvested his money in community projects, he felt that his workers would, and should, appreciate that his financial expansion and profits were instrumental to their own welfare. Accordingly, whenever the price of steel fell in the market, he would lower his worker's wages, confident that 'he embodied, as always, the interests of the broader community: by keeping labor costs down, he kept prices down for all'.[25]

Carnegie thought that the chief duty of a philanthropist was to build ladders enabling the less well-off to climb up, while at all times exercising caution over which *sort* of people should be helped. As he saw it, a 'true reformer' was someone who was as careful 'not to aid the unworthy as he is to aid the worthy'. The unworthy were those who might exploit philanthropic generosity, engaging in vices such as drink or gambling. The worthy were those who would avail themselves of 'free libraries, parks, and means of recreation, by which men are helped in body and mind'.[26]

Carnegie's business empire expanded by cultivating useful political allies and alliances with fellow industrialists, including Frick, who Carnegie took on as a business partner in 1882. Over the next decade, they honed labour policies that were fiercely resisted by their workers. American labourers were sceptical of the idea that the growing wealth of business magnates would inevitably enrich their own lives. In 1892, as Howard Zinn describes, a wave of strikes ignited across the US: a general strike in New Orleans; a coal miners' strike in Tennessee; a copper miners' strike in Coeur d'Alene, Idaho. The strikes were often bloody affairs: the conflict in Coeur d'Alene resulted in five dead and sixteen in hospital.[27]

The Homestead strike began early in the summer months of 1892 and lasted until the air grew chill. Frick and Carnegie's decision to draw on both Pinkertons and the National Guard to quell the workers was widely condemned in the press. Despite criticism from Illinois governor John Altgeld, who sympathized deeply with labour and opposed the deployment of federal troops, thousands of national militia were ferried to the site of the strike. The People's Party, a short-lived political party first established in 1891, made up mostly of white cotton farmers based in Southern states, condemned the 'hireling standing army, unrecognized by our laws, which is established to shoot them [the workers] down'.[28]

The strike held for four months before the strikers admitted defeat. After the stand-off reached its whimpering close, the strike leaders were charged with murder, but each was acquitted by sympathetic jury members. The entire Strike Committee was then arrested for treason against the state. Once again, they were acquitted. But sympathy alone can't feed families: suffering from the deaths of lost friends, desperate to feed their families, the fight for fair working conditions was vanquished. Carnegie and Frick's triumph is widely thought to have kept unionization out of the Carnegie plants until deep into the twentieth century. In the following years workers had little choice but to take 'wage cuts and increases in hours without organized resistance'.[29] The crushing of the strike ushered in an era of fabulous profits for Carnegie Steel, while wages for unskilled workers remained stagnant or declined. At one time, Carnegie had been a vocal supporter of a 'sliding scale' remuneration system: labourer's wages would be raised in times of high profits, and lowered during bear seasons. As his wealth grew he changed his mind. 'At the very least', the historian Kevin Phillips points out, 'Carnegie made a calculated decision to retain the profits of technology rather than distribute them as wages.'[30]

A FEW ACTS OF KINDNESS

Carnegie was astute enough to realize that public sentiment had turned against him: not simply because of Homestead, but as a result of his public U-turn when it came to increasing wages during periods of spectacular profit. Sensing his waning popularity, he increased his philanthropic giving, mentioning to his senior staff that he had noticed that the disbursement of gifts seemed to help console struggling workers. In December 1892 he sent a Christmas greeting to his management team along with some words of advice: 'The mass of Public Sentiment is not with us about Homestead on the direct issue of re-adjustment of the [wage] scale – people did not understand it, but I observed that Opinion was greatly impressed by the few acts of kindness . . . especially of investing savings of men at high rate of interest – this one feature attracted the most favorable notice. Library came in also.' He added: 'The partner who can devise a new way by which the Firm can benefit the workmen – improve their surroundings, and make it better for their wives and children, will deserve the medal next year . . . In wages paid, we must be governed by the Market of course, but in things showing thought for the comfort and pleasures of the workmen and their families, we can be our own masters.'[31]

Carnegie's first 'Wealth' essay was published in 1889, a few years before the carnage at Homestead. There's a hint of convenience to the timing of the publication. Was Carnegie simply trying to boost his public image in the face of growing public discontent over political concessions granted by Washington power-holders to industrialists such as Carnegie?

Grover Cleveland's successful bid for the presidency in 1884 seemed, at first glance, a reversal of that trend – a triumph for working men and women. He was a Democrat. Prior to his election, he was widely believed to represent the interests of labourers, while the Republican candidate James Blaine seemed like a man of the moneyed class. But Cleveland wasted little time in surrounding himself with wealthy advisors, and he was careful to assure industrialists that he was sensitive to their needs, telling them 'no harm shall come to any business interest as the result of administrative policy as long as I am president'. He kept his word. Despite a huge federal surplus in 1887, Cleveland axed a bill that sought to offer $100,000 in relief funds for Texan farmers. The bill was aimed at buying seed during a particularly devastating drought. In the same year, Cleveland drew on the federal surplus to pay bondholders off at $28 above the $100 value of each bond. It was a not insignificant gift – an early gesture of corporate welfare – amounting to $45 million.[32]

During the 1888 elections, Cleveland lost out to the Republican candidate, Benjamin Harrison, a prominent attorney who had prosecuted striking workers from the Great Railroad Strike of 1877. Moneyed voters must have felt they were in safe hands with the new president, and in some ways they were: he presided over the introduction of the McKinley tariff, which raised the average duty on foreign imports to almost 50 per cent, a boon to domestic steel manufacturers such as Carnegie. But in other ways Harrison's actions ran counter to the interests of the status quo. He was a progressive reformer. He tried, but failed, to earmark federal funding to institute voting rights for African Americans. He did manage to edge through a piece of legislation with lasting effects: the Sherman Antitrust Act, passed in 1890. The author of the act, Senator John Sherman, rationalized the legislation with the following comment: 'They had monopolies . . . of old, but never before such giants as in our day.

You must heed their appeal or be ready for the socialist, communist, the nihilist . . . Society is now disturbed by forces never felt before.'[33]

Carnegie voiced a similar sentiment in his first 'Wealth' essay. Be prepared to surrender at least some of your wealth, he cautioned his fellow industrialists, or feel the brunt of socialist workers who will wrest it from you. It wasn't simply fear and disdain for socialism that drove his musings on philanthropy. It was the rather paternalistic belief that he had the means, the intelligence, and the skill to invest in community projects far more effectively, as he put it, than 'the community . . . could or would have done for itself'.

Recollections from men and women close to Carnegie's circle suggest that a willingness to sooth his ego, to kindle his confidence in his own intellectual foresight, was essential if you wanted to curry his favour and receive philanthropic support. In the early 1960s, a few months before his death, W. E. B. Du Bois met for an interview with Ralph McGill, a prominent white anti-segregationist news editor. Du Bois recalled his and Booker T. Washington's efforts to work with early benefactors such as Carnegie, an effort that required endless supplication, if not obsequiousness – a skill that Washington was more adept at than Du Bois.

Washington's and Du Bois's starkly different political tactics are well known. Washington was an outspoken supporter of the 'separate but equal' doctrine, a legal regime which sanctioned legal segregation between blacks and whites as long as the social and educational services offered to each group were in principle equal. Du Bois refused to condone segregation. He was a fierce critic of Washington's conciliations towards the nation's elite: not simply political legislators but their moneyed entourages, men like Carnegie whose fortunes helped to anoint Republican kings. In the eyes of Du Bois, Washington was far too willing to promise assurances of black docility in return for financial support from leading industrialists. 'Washington would promise them happy and contented labor for their new enterprises. He reminded them there would be no strikers . . . as I came to see it, Washington bartered away much that was not his to barter.'[34]

Once, when they were on amicable terms, Du Bois accompanied Washington on a visit to Carnegie's office (Carnegie had been an early funder of Washington's educational efforts for black youths). 'Have you read Mr. Carnegie's book?' Washington asked Du Bois on the way over – a reference to the 'Wealth' essay.

'No', Du Bois replied.

'You ought to', Washington said. 'Mr. Carnegie likes it.'

After they reached Carnegie's office, Washington left Du Bois sitting downstairs rather than taking him up to see Carnegie in person. 'I never did know', he tells McGill, 'whether Mr. Carnegie had expressed an opinion about me or whether Washington didn't trust me to be meek. It was probably the latter. I never read the book.'[35]

Carnegie's faith in his unique ability to provide for community members led to a curious paradox. Once he became convinced that parting with his wealth was the most appropriate action, he became equally convinced that he had a moral duty to accumulate as *much* wealth as possible, even if it meant exacting ever more pain from his workers in order to create that wealth. Carnegie had once distinguished himself from other industrialists by adopting a sympathetic stance towards trade unions. Like the socialist firebrand Eugene Debs, he had once thought that, as Debs suggested at the time of the labour strikes of 1877, there was no 'necessary conflict between capital and labour'. Both men soon changed their minds. While Debs embraced unionism and socialism, Carnegie cultivated his own personal creed of philanthropy. It was a Janus-faced ideology; one side of Carnegie was extraordinarily generous, expending time and vast financial sums on goals such as military disarmament and racial equality. On the other side, he adopted ever more draconian policies towards his workers the more convinced he became that his wealth would ultimately benefit the larger community.[36]

As the historian David Nasaw describes, Carnegie's altruism did not emerge from a sense of guilt, or the need to expiate past business sins. Rather, his faith in the righteousness of his own benevolence grew in direct proportion to his belief in the fairness, even the glory, of his own personal business success. He believed it was *dutiful* to keep wages low in order to augment his own fortune so that he had more surplus wealth to spend on worthy causes. He saw his own acquisitiveness as the highest moral virtue.[37]

This belief was rooted in his admiration for the writings of Herbert Spencer. Carnegie was proud of his own scholarly outputs: from an early age he would immerse himself in the verse of Shakespeare and Robert Burns; later in life he repeatedly swore oaths to himself to cease focusing personally on business affairs in order to dedicate himself entirely to writing, reading, and philanthropy. He would break the oath often (like many business leaders today, Carnegie was a man of many retirements, often professing to leave active management of his business empires while quietly continuing to play lead roles). As part of his public image as a man of letters, Carnegie cultivated friendships with leading intellects such as Herbert Spencer and Matthew Arnold.

Through much of the mid to late nineteenth century, Spencer was the foremost intellectual in the world, fostering a formidable mini-industry in tracts, manifestos, and theses inspired by his efforts to apply the latest developments in biology and psychology to all of social life. He was one of the earliest and most influential social Darwinists, propagating the belief that ever greater industrial complexity was a sign of man's evolutionary advancement. To Carnegie, Spencer's theories were a source of intellectual manna and, importantly, a source of moral sanction, providing a way to rationalize acquisitiveness as the font of human greatness. Nasaw makes this point well, emphasizing that Spencer's philosophy helped to assuage Carnegie and his fellow industrialists of any doubt over the morality of rising inequality levels: to them, inequality was an unfortunate consequence of the 'natural' laws of the market which, much like evolutionary forces, were beyond the realm of human governance. Just as people, animals and ecologies evolved in ways that could never entirely be tamed or halted by human machinations, any effort to intervene in the regulation of economic affairs was seen as a perversion of natural prosperity.

Appealing to Spencer's authority, industrialists scorned the notion that governments should be prevailed upon to provide social assistance for society's poorest members. Such interference was seen as contravening what Spencer described as 'beneficent necessity': the notion that human progress did not result from mere accident or chance, but was rooted in overarching evolutionary forces that would propel man towards ever-greater achievement. Casualties such as human suffering or death may be unfortunate, but they are necessary for historical progress, and thus to be endured, if not seen as munificent. In his landmark 1850 book *Social Statics*, Spencer wrote that it 'seems hard that a labourer incapacitated by sickness from competing with his stronger fellows should have to bear the resulting privations. It seems hard that widows and orphans should be left to struggle for life or death. Nevertheless, when regarded not separately, but in connection with the interests of universal humanity, these harsh fatalities are seen to be full of the highest beneficence.'[38]

Carnegie's faith in the Spencerian diktat of non-interference was relaxed only when it came to governmental support for his own industry. For years, he spent time and money lobbying the government for protective steel tariffs on imports from Europe. In 1870, the Republican government imposed a $28-a-ton tariff on imported steel. It was a move that set in motion America's ability to compete against British industry, until then the undisputed kingpins of the global steel industry. Carnegie would later state that the governmental tariff was the defining action that compelled him to enter the steel business in the first place. A Republican for most of his life, Carnegie admired two things most about the GOP: their opposition to slavery (he was a fervent abolitionist) and their support for high duties on foreign steel. During the 1884 elections, Carnegie wrote to his business partners with the news that a coalition of steelmakers had each offered $5,000 to the Republican National Committee. 'We have been asked to give the same amount', he added, 'which I think is only fair.'[39]

Carnegie publicly defended trade tariffs by claiming they directly benefited labour, enabling him to pay his men better wages. But in the years after the 1890 imposition of a nearly 50 per cent duty charge on imported steel, Carnegie did the exact reverse. In a widely acclaimed biography of Carnegie, Nasaw makes this point clearly:

> Contrary to Carnegie's promises in the 1880s, his workingmen did not share in the firm's remarkable prosperity. On the contrary, there was, through the 1890s, an inverse relationship between the firm's revenues and profits and the amount of money distributed to the workforce as wages. According to figures compiled by the geographer and historian Kenneth Warren, while the value of goods shipped from the Carnegie mills increased by some 226 per cent in the seven years following the strike of 1892, the percentage paid out in wages *decreased* by 67 per cent.[40]

More than two decades later, in 1908, Carnegie outraged Republicans by publicly changing tack on tariff. With much fanfare, he wrote a news article calling for the protective tariff to be repealed, justifying his about-face by pointing to the nation's newfound economic dominance. He had made his fortune, and he no longer saw any national or personal need to curtail free trade. 'Today', he wrote, '[US manufacturers] need no protection, unless perhaps in some new specialties unknown to the writer, because steel is now produced cheaper here than anywhere else.'[41]

Carnegie and his fellow industrialists' seesawing when it came to both courting and denouncing governmental support was hardly lost on the US public. Lester Frank Ward, the first president of the American Sociological Association and an intellectual inspiration for later welfare reforms that took hold during the 1930s, gave voice to growing resentment in 'Plutocracy and Paternalism', an influential essay published in 1895. 'Those who denounce state interference', he pointed out, 'are the ones who most frequently and successfully invoke it. The cry of laissez-faire mainly goes up from the ones who, if really "let alone", would instantly lose their wealth-absorbing power . . . Nothing is more obvious today than the signal inability of capital and private enterprise to take care of themselves unaided by the state.'[42]

Protective tariffs and military might are just two of the areas where Carnegie and his peers had cause to thank the government for regularly coming to their aid. Twenty years after Carnegie's first 'Wealth' essay was published, a labour dispute erupted at John D. Rockefeller's Colorado Fuel and Iron Company. Today, Ludlow is a ghost town in Las Animas County, Colorado, a neglected stretch of land ignored by most motorists driving along Interstate 25 on route to the city of Trinidad. A century ago, on 20 April 1914, it was the site of an ambush by the Colorado National Guard, who attacked a miners' colony set up by 1,200 striking miners and their families. The stand-off lasted for fourteen hours. State militia sprayed the colony with machine-gun fire and eventually torched the encampment. Two women and eleven children, trapped in a pit they had dug underneath a tent, were among the dead, asphyxiated and burned by the raging fire.[43]

A few months before the massacre, in December 1913, Rockefeller Jr., who was by then playing a stronger management role in the oil conglomerate that his father built, congratulated the Fuel and Iron Company management for standing firm against the striking workers. He praised them for 'fighting the good fight, which is not only in the interests of your own company but of other companies in Colorado and the business interests of the entire country and labouring classes quite as much'.[44]

It's not surprising that very few American workers were convinced by this vein of management-speak. As historian Andrea Tone describes, public animosity against the Rockefeller family reached a feverish level. Picketers took to protesting outside the company's New York headquarters. Letters were sent in the hundreds. One letter included a newspaper clipping featuring a graphic illustration of a woman who was, as Tone writes, 'impaled on a bayonet, the caption "Crucified! Glorious Motherhood! Innocent Childhood!" written below.' Next to the drawing, 'the sender had left Rockefeller a message: "Hide your miserable head in Shame, Shame, Shame"'. Labour supporters, climbing on soap-box pedestals, suggested that given the circumstances it wouldn't be remiss, in one orator's words, to shoot Rockefeller 'like a dog'.[45]

Their growing dissent unnerved the political elite. From 1913 to 1915, in response to public outrage over labour conditions, the US government convened the Walsh Commission on Industrial Relations to study work conditions in America. The time was ripe for an investigation into corporate and philanthropy power. In his inaugural address, US president Woodrow Wilson lambasted an 'industrial system' that 'holds capital in leading strings, restricts the liberties and limits the opportunities of labor, and exploits without renewing or conserving the natural resources of the country'. In his first message to Congress, in 1913, he added that 'we must abolish anything that bears even the semblance of privilege or any kind of artificial advantage'.[46]

Frank Walsh, a lawyer appointed by Wilson to chair the inquiry, summarized the commission's impetus. 'It has been stated many times', he said, 'that it might be better for people controlling very large industries, instead of devoting the excess profits to the dispensation of money along philanthropic and eleemosynary lines, that they should organize some system by which they could distribute it in wages first, or give to the workers a greater share of the productivity of industry in the first place'.[47]

Leading philanthropists were called before the committee. During his testimony, Rockefeller Sr. commented, 'I should be only happy to surrender my holdings, in part, in any or all, that the labourers might come into the relation to the enterprise.'[48] The offer was quite disingenuous: his workers would never become co-owners of Standard Oil. But in his defence, it's understandable he was feeling rather cagey during his testimony. His oil conglomerate had recently been the subject of one of the most notorious anti-trust suits in American history, launched by the Department of Justice in 1909. Two years later, Standard Oil's managers were found guilty of numerous abusive business practices. The Supreme Court ruled that the company must be dissolved under the Sherman Antitrust Act and split into thirty-four smaller companies known as 'baby Standards'. Exxon and Mobil are two of the most well-known offshoots of this break-up.

Perhaps of all the early industrialists, Rockefeller comes closest to personifying Max Weber's notion of the Protestant 'spirit of capitalism', incarnating the relationship between Puritan asceticism and capitalist excess that Weber elucidates through close analysis of the writings of early reformation leaders such as John Calvin, Martin Luther, and Richard Baxter, a seventeenth-century English church leader. The cultural ethos nurtured by Protestant preaching, Weber suggests, was 'an amazingly good, we may even say a pharisaically good, conscience in the acquisition of money . . . the bourgeois business man, as long as he remained within the bounds of formal correctness, as long as his moral conduct was spotless and the use to which put his money was not objectionable, could follow his pecuniary interests as he would and feel that he was fulfilling his duty in doing so.'[49]

Rockefeller was a firm Baptist, and would often profess 'God gave me this money.' He tithed 10 per cent of his first pay cheque and kept up the practice throughout his life. Biographer Ron Chernow reports that Rockefeller would often reiterate his personal motto at Sunday school classes, something he taught on a regular, volunteer basis: 'I believe it is a religious duty to get all the money you can, fairly and honestly, to keep all you can, and to give away all you can.'[50] In church, Rockefeller's 'eyes darted around the room as he selected needy recipients of his charity. Taking small envelopes from his pocket, he slipped in some money, wrote the congregants' names on top, then unobtrusively pressed these gifts into their palms as they shook hands.' An early supporter of education for African Americans, from 1882 onwards he made substantial donations to the Atlanta Baptist Female Seminary, a school for African American women. At the urging of his son, he created, in 1902, the General Education Board, which sought to improve educational opportunities 'without distinction of race, sex, or creed'. His dismay at poverty and his belief in human equality only renders more troubling his role in exacerbating the social and economic inequalities that he seemed to deplore.[51]

The Justice Department's anti-trust suit against Rockefeller's company was launched after Ida Tarbell's investigation into Rockefeller's company was serialized in the popular *McClure's Magazine* and later collected in her bestselling volume, *The History of the Standard Oil Company*. 'Very often people who admit the facts, who are willing to see that Mr. Rockefeller employed force and fraud to secure his ends, justify him by declaring, "It's business"', Tarbell commented after her book was published. 'If the point is pushed, frequently the defender of the practice falls back on the Christian doctrine of charity, and points out that we are erring mortals and must allow for each other's weaknesses!'[52]

Tarbell followed up her bestseller with an intimate biographical portrait of Rockefeller published in *McClure's*. Other members of the press criticized her for what they saw as an *ad hominem* exploration of Rockefeller's personal belief system. Samuel McClure, publisher of the eponymous magazine, defended Tarbell. Both McClure and Tarbell firmly believed, as the historian Steve Weinberg writes, that 'the works of a man's life stand together. They cannot be separated. It is the intimate and intricate relation of the Rockefeller Business

Code with the Rockefeller Religious Code that makes it imperative the public study the man and his influence.'[53]

Rockefeller's most astute advisors recognized that public opinion was increasingly on the side of critics such as Tarbell and not behind Rockefeller. Rockefeller's philanthropic right-hand man, Frederick Gates, strove to assuage public ire by mobilizing the considerable philanthropic opportunities open to Rockefeller. It was Gates who counselled Rockefeller on how to disburse his fortune in a way that, as Chernow suggests, could accomplish a two-fold goal. First, philanthropy helped to sooth Rockefeller's own conscience, demonstrating that 'rich businessmen could honorably discharge the burden of wealth.' Second, it wasn't lost on either Rockefeller or Gates that the 'judicious disposal of his fortune might also blunt further inquiry into its origins.'[54]

One of Gates's most important publicity strategies was the deliberate effort *not* to court publicity. The Rockefellers rarely extolled their own giving in the same way that Carnegie did. Although Rockefeller greatly admired Carnegie's charity – Chernow notes that Rockefeller sent a congratulatory note after Carnegie opened the Carnegie Library in Pittsburgh, writing 'I would that more men of wealth were doing as you are doing with your money' – the cascade of opinion articles and self-congratulatory essays that Carnegie showered upon publishers in the US and England was not to the Rockefellers' taste. Theirs was a more modest style, a form of canny self-deprecation that was carefully cultivated by Gates, who once explained that the Rockefellers deliberated shied from giving interviews about their donations because speaking openly of their benefactions would 'inevitably lend colour to the suspicion that [Rockefeller's] gifts are not free from the taint of self-seeking.'[55]

Their quiet giving is one of the most marked ways that benefactors such as the Rockefellers differ from today's TED Heads: highly loquacious donors for whom the chance to receive praise for a donation seems as important as the gift itself. It's a new twist on the old philosophical dilemma: if one offers a considerable sum to an organization or a cause and no one writes fawningly about it, did the donation really happen?

Unlike Rockefeller or Carnegie, Henry Ford was not an early believer in the value of philanthropic trusts. The Ford Foundation wasn't set up until 1936, after Ford spent decades building his wealth through business practices and personal politics even more controversial than those of Carnegie and Rockefeller. Both an early supporter of high wages and a fierce opponent of labour unions, Ford was something of a paradox. He stunned fellow industrialists in 1914 by introducing a wage in his industries of five dollars a day, for eight hours' work, at a time when the average wage was two and a half dollars for ten hours' work.

In an interview for *World's Work*, Ford explained that a shorter week and higher wages led to more productive employees. The value of permitting more leisure time was, Ford asserted, a 'cold business fact'. Offering his workers two days off weekly freed them up to spend more time and money on consumer goods. As Ford put it, 'The more well-paid leisure workmen get, the greater become their wants. These wants soon become needs . . . Instead of business being slowed up because the people are 'off work', it will be speeded up, because the people consume more in their leisure than in their working time. This will lead to more work. And this to more profits.'[56]

Ford shared Carnegie's belief that the wealthiest in society were best placed to understand the needs of workers 'far better', in Carnegie's words, than the workers themselves. Ford's staunch opposition to labour unions was rooted in his view that union leaders tended to undermine efforts to increase overall productivity. Their interest in safeguarding jobs blinded them to the need to cut labour costs in order to serve overall economic growth. Personal and collective interests were seen as naturally inseparable by many of the leading early twentieth-century business magnates.[57]

Ford's workmen were placed under strict surveillance. A firm believer in the importance of alcohol abstinence and thrift, Ford saw the increased wage as an opportunity to instil his personal beliefs in the wider community. One corporate press release at the time announced, 'The idea Mr. Ford has in mind is to help the men to a LIFE – not a mere LIVING.' The Ford Motor Company established its own Sociological Department, employing an initial team of fifty and then a total of 160 'investigators' tasked with circulating in the community and paying impromptu visits to the homes of Ford's workers, each of whom needed to be confirmed as sober, thrifty (through making regular bank deposits), and 'clean of person' to qualify for the new five-dollars-a-day remuneration scheme.[58]

Ford's most controversial views stemmed not from his business tactics but from his personal politics. From the early 1920s on, he financed the *Dearborn Independent*, a small weekly newspaper known for virulently anti-Semitic views. A collection of the paper's articles were collected in a four-volume publication titled *The International Jew: The World's Foremost Problem*. In it, Ford's editorial staff suggested that the world's non-Jews must unite in combating the global influence of a group 'permitted to obtain an undue and unsafe amount of power'. One early editorial, written in 1921, offers a snapshot of the sort of rhetoric featured in those pages. One reads that Jews are 'a people that has no civilization to point to, no aspiring religion, no universal speech, no great achievement in any realm but the realm of "get" . . . and these people endeavour to tell the sons of the Saxons what is needed to make the world what it ought to be.'[59]

Ford's views were embraced by Hitler and his burgeoning Nazi party. The historian Neil Baldwin, a former executive director of the National Book Foundation, has written a definitive account of Ford's anti-Semitic publications and their worldwide reception. He points out that if one had happened to arrive in Munich in the winter of 1922 and chose to visit the headquarters of the National Socialist German Workers' Party, one might have noticed a table featuring numerous copies of *Der Internationale Jude*. A German preface to the translated version of *The International Jew* praises Ford's 'great service' in condemning Jews. Baldwin quotes a former leader of Hitler Youth on the importance of Ford's legacy: 'The younger generation looked with envy to the symbols of success and prosperity like Henry Ford. And if Henry Ford said that the Jews were to blame, why, naturally we believed him.' Inside Hitler's private office at the small Munich headquarters, a large portrait of Ford was proudly displayed on the wall.[60]

In some ways, Ford's views weren't at odds with mainstream sentiment in America, but sadly reflected what the essayist and novelist Pankaj Mishra describes as the 'overheated racial climate of the early twentieth century'. At this time, 'Yellow Peril seemed real, the Ku Klux Klan had re-emerged, and Theodore Roosevelt worried loudly about "race-suicide"'. In 1917, justifying his reluctance to involve the United States in the European war, Woodrow Wilson told his secretary of state that 'white civilization and its domination over the world rested largely on our ability to keep this country intact'. Regardless of the fact that Ford's views weren't distinct from the mainstream climate – or indeed, *because* of how closely they resembled and helped to strengthen spurious notions of white superiority, consoling elites who held similar views – Ford's prejudice sheds light on a problem facing organized philanthropy then and today.[61]

For the most part, the philanthropic interests of early foundations, including the Ford Foundation, focused on commendable projects: the funding of public schools, hospitals, and galleries. Carnegie's vision – to provide public access to goods once seen as private luxuries – became entrenched in the ethos of his foundation long after his death. The freedom to fund whatever areas foundation staff wished to invest in was seen as an unquestionable right. 'Not even God himself can stop me from giving my money to the University of Chicago', Rockefeller Sr. once declared. Today, the statement strikes us as endearing; as evidence of the stubborn pride of a feisty humanitarian. Ultimately, of course, he succeeded. Then as now there are very few checks on how and where philanthropists spend their money. It's their money, most people tend to agree, and they can do whatever they like with it.

Philanthropy and management expert Peter Frumkin exemplifies this perspective. Saluting Bill Gates's investment in science grants for minority students, Frumkin suggests that 'rather than second-guess' philanthropic investment, we should embrace it – with no questions asked: 'we all stand to benefit from this very personal form of giving – and from active, committed donors who use their funding to express their own, sometimes quirky, visions of the common good'.[62]

But if 'Ku Klux Klan' is substituted for the 'University of Chicago', then the problems with unfettered philanthropic investment become more apparent. The biases of men such as Ford might seem merely lamentable, a depressing reminder of the acceptability of anti-Semitic and racist views in respectable circles for much of the twentieth century and beyond. But the wealth and influence of philanthropic donors then and now renders the prejudices of leading 'humanitarians' more than simply lamentable. It makes philanthropy a matter of public concern.

What was to stop men such as Ford from financing socially divisive policies, rooted in class and ethnic stereotypes? What checks were in place to prevent philanthropic trusts and their stewards from gaining unwarranted political power? These questions were reiterated time and again during the twentieth century, leading in the 1950s and 1960s to growing criticism of the power of foundations. Concerns stemmed from the left and the right, with observers at either end of the political spectrum capable, as the historian and journalist Mark Dowie puts it, of 'examining the same creature and drawing very different conclusions about its nature'.[63]

Those on the right bemoaned the 'socialist' agenda of the foundations. Their leading representative was J. Howard Pew, whose father Joseph founded the Sun Oil Company. Howard was appointed president in 1912 and by 1941 had nurtured the company into the nation's largest manufacturer of oil tankers. Pew was a vehement critic of New Deal policies, particularly of the effort to lower oil costs through price limits. Invited to liaise with leading conservative economists such as Friedrich Hayek at meetings of the Mont Pelerin Society, Pew quickly become one of the Society's staunchest philanthropic patrons, determined to battle against 'Socialism, Welfare-state–ism, Marxism, Fascism and any other like forms for government intervention . . . antithetical to the teaching of Jesus'.[64]

In 1954, Pew contacted the evangelist preacher Billy Graham to see how they might work together in establishing a 'scripturally sound political economy'. He invested heavily in Graham's work, at first through anonymous donations, then by openly bankrolling a number of Graham's endeavours, including publications such as *Christianity Today*. Noted historian of US history Olivier Zunz suggests that Pew's alliance with Graham was a canny political power play. It was a masterstroke enabling Pew 'to advocate a political agenda as part of God's design for America'.[65]

On the other side of the political spectrum, those on the left complained that foundations were elitist and plutocratic, serving mostly to rehabilitate the image of industrialists who earned their fortunes through predatory, often illegal actions. Large foundations such as the Carnegie, Ford, and today, the Gates Foundation, are often sole sources of income for smaller non-profit organizations. The power invested in foundations has led, as Dowie writes, to numerous complaints over the 'secretive', 'rigid', and 'ideologically motivated' nature of foundation funding processes. Non-profit organizations have few legal means to challenge the rejection of funding proposals, leading to profound feelings of political impotency among fledgling non-profits.[66]

In the late 1970s, Henry Ford II – grandson of the original Henry – became chairman and CEO of the Ford Motor Company. He shared his grandfather's political proclivities: he once rejected a proposal to put a Honda engine in a Ford car on the basis that 'no car with my name on the hood is going to have a Jap engine inside'. He also shared the belief that philanthropy should only be encouraged to the extent that it furthered the interests of corporate profits. In 1977, Ford startled the American public by resigning from the board of the Ford Foundation. In a public letter to the board, he listed his many complaints: 'The Foundation exists and thrives on the fruits of our economic system . . . It is hard to discern recognition of this fact in anything the Foundation does . . . I am just suggesting to the Trustees and the staff that the system that makes the Foundation possible very probably is worth preserving.'[67]

The foundation, in other words, had become too anti-capitalist for his liking. The board's management reacted with a brand of polite nonchalance that must have irritated him. 'He has a right to expect people to read his letter carefully, but I don't think one letter from anyone is going to change the foundation's course', McGeorge Bundy, then president of the Ford Foundation, commented.[68]

During the 1980s, thinkers on the left noticed a new trend, one evident since the 1940s but its magnitude underappreciated until the election of Ronald Reagan. Left-leaning policy-makers began to grasp just how influential a tight network of right-wing think-tanks had become in DC, helping to cement Reagan's victory and guiding his hand in economic decisions. Their criticism had an element of envy, as some on the left bemoaned the lack of similar funding towards 'progressive' think-tanks. Often prioritizing much-needed investment in fledgling, grassroots non-profits based in poor communities, they had failed to develop intellectual networks equivalent to those at the Mont Pelerin Society, the Cato Institute, and the Heritage Foundation.

Whether on the left or the right, the one thing most agreed on was that foundations were too powerful. Dowie makes this point well, pointing out that philanthropists deploy 'wealth in the framing of public policy through non-democratic processes. And that fact bothers American conservatives as deeply as it does liberals.'[69] Government reforms in the 1960s sought to temper concerns. A set of provisions with the Tax Reform Act of 1969 required foundations to divest themselves of almost all shares in their founding corporation; to file a tax return with the IRS; and to distribute a minimum percentage of their assets annually to charity. The act also requires foundations to list every grant made.[70] This 1969 act was the last time that philanthropic foundations faced any serious legislative restrictions in US history. Since then, foundations have grappled with a far different challenge to those of the 1950s and 1960s.[71]

For much of the twentieth century, foundations were seen as excessively powerful. Whether on the left or the right, critics feared that philanthropy worked *too* well. The new objection raised an entirely opposite concern. Observers felt that philanthropy was, on the whole, remarkably *ineffective*. From the 1980s onwards, a new generation of management scholars accustomed to scrutinizing corporate bottom lines turned their gaze to the non-profit sector, and they found the field wanting. The problem with traditional foundations, they proclaimed, was their failure to meet or even clearly state objectives, to adopt clear performance measures, or to reduce operating overheads.

The ideas of these management scholars have been instrumental in the rise of trends such as social innovation and social entrepreneurship, as well as a bewildering array of new terms for describing the 'business' of giving: venture philanthropy, catalytic philanthropy, strategic philanthropy, philanthrocapitalism, philanthropreneurism. What exactly are these things? Definitions vary, inspiring heated debate among the new philanthropists themselves. One thing is certain: you're sure to find an aficionado of each trend at the annual Skoll World Forum.

CHAPTER TWO

TED Heads

There's an anecdote about Bill Gates's enrolment at Harvard: he once told a friend he went to Harvard to learn from people smarter than him . . . and left disappointed.

Each March, 900 attendees descend on the Skoll World Forum with similar hopes: to be galvanized by inspiring people; in this case, by 'social entrepreneurs' in the fields of business, microfinance, and charity.[1] Hosted annually at the University of Oxford's Saïd Business School, the 2012 Skoll World Forum featured talks and performances from George Soros, Arianna Huffington, and Annie Lennox. Queen Noor of Jordan offered a closing plenary talk in 2011. Nobel laureate Al Gore, a Skoll regular, gave the closing speech in 2008.

The conference is the brainchild of Jeff Skoll, an eBay billionaire who has become a leading spokesperson for the new blend of business and philanthropy that seeks to make capitalism more socially sustainable. Since 2003, the Skoll World Forum has become a flagship event on the social entrepreneur's annual calendar – as hotly anticipated by some as it is unknown to those struggling to understand what a social entrepreneur *is*, let alone realize there's a conference complete with its own fringe festival, the 'Oxford Jam' – an opportunity, the 2011 Skoll conference programme promises, for late-night networking and cabaret performances.

Alongside Skoll and the World Economic Forum, there are smaller events such as Hedgestock – a 2006 gathering in Knebworth, Hertfordshire, where 4,000 hedge fund managers paid £500 per head to network in open pastures flanked by market stalls selling tailor-made golf clubs and holiday homes in Europe. The recent financial crisis hit some attendees harder than others. DKR Capital, which had business reps milling around at Hedgestock advertising 'Peace, Love, and Higher Returns', saw its assets fall to $40 million in 2011 from a peak of $4.3 billion in January 2008. The 2006 event ended up being a one-off, a casualty of the pending financial catastrophe that was unfolding unnoticed by many of the milling Hedgestockers. A flurry of similar conferences soon filled its place.[2]

'So, there's a list, okay?' Google co-founder Eric Schmidt told the journalist Chrystia Freeland. 'There's Davos. There's the Oscars. There's the Cannes Film Festival. There's Sun Valley. There's the TED conference . . . they're not nearly as much fun as they were when I was reading about them in the paper. Because the pictures were much better than the reality. But because I see myself as a global citizen, I go anyway.'[3]

An important stop on the elite conference circuit is the Milken Global Conference, an offshoot of the Milken Institute, founded by Michael Milken one year after he pleaded guilty to multiple felony charges for violating US securities law. In the TED Head world, as one former initiate put it, even 'Wall Street's criminals, like Michael Milken and Ivan Boesky, become larger than life. In a society that celebrates the idea of making money, it was easy to infer that the interests of the financial sector were the interests of the country.'[4]

The entrance fees are not cheap. TED conferences can cost upwards of $6,000 per ticket. And even if you have the dough, you're not guaranteed a seat at the table. Skoll is an invitation-only event – 'though we encourage applications', the website notes.

I worked as a researcher at the Saïd Business School from 2008 and 2010, and managed to finagle a free ticket to the 2009 Skoll World Forum, something that did not endear me to older, more established members of staff who found themselves *non grata* when big-ticket events like Skoll or TED came to town. 'Where did you get *that?*', a senior faculty member snapped at me one afternoon, nodding at my orange Skoll pass. 'You know, some of us have worked here for years. You'd think we'd be allowed in.'

The fact that events such as TED or Skoll, touted as promoting global democracy and increased prosperity for the poor, are far too exorbitantly priced for most of the world's poor – or even most jobbing management scholars at some of the world's oldest universities – is not something that troubles organizers. If anything, the exclusivity of the events is their strongest appeal. 'We don't have castles and noble titles, so how else do you indicate you're part of the elite?' Andrew Zolli, the executive director of PopTech, an annual ideas fest in Camden, Maine, commented to *New York* magazine.[5]

Zolli neatly captures the ambitions of Generation TED Head, many of whom share a sort of doe-eyed blitheness about the magnitude of their objectives. Singular solutions for eradicating something like 'world poverty' might daunt those who have worked in global development. But many TED Heads have never set foot in the field of development. 'There will be someone in our century who wins the Nobel Peace Prize for solving the problems of poverty', Zolli earnestly told *Entrepreneur.com*. 'And in the process that person will become a billionaire.'

By building an international architecture of celebrities and policy-makers championing the emergence of 'social entrepreneurship', the Skoll Foundation's influence extends beyond considerable monetary outputs. The foundation, and Jeff Skoll himself, have grown rich in what Pierre Bourdieu termed 'symbolic capital', the cultural and social resources available to an individual on the basis of honour, prestige, or public recognition.

In a short period, the rise of social entrepreneurship has shifted mindsets in both the non-profit sector and the for-profit world of commerce, leading a new generation of business leaders and philanthrocapitalists to proclaim that 'charity is dead', as the UK-based journalist Zoe Williams found during an interview with Victor d'Allant, executive director of Social Edge, the online forum of the Skoll Foundation. 'It's all about social entrepreneurship versus charity', d'Allant told Williams. 'Nobody wants to do charity anymore. Charity doesn't work.'[6]

As Williams asks: If charity is indeed dead, who or what killed it? Philanthrocapitalism? Or venture philanthropy? Or social enterprise? Or social innovation? What do these terms mean?

Simply defined, social entrepreneurship is the idea that innovative business models can tackle social problems and foster collective public benefits. The term was popularized in the 1980s by Bill Drayton, the founder of Ashoka, a non-profit organization set up in Washington, DC in the eighties to fund 'changemakers' – civically minded individuals working creatively for social gain. The concept was later embraced by enthusiasts such as Klaus Schwab, founder of the World Economic Forum. In 1998, he set up the Schwab Foundation for Social Entrepreneurship to promote social entrepreneurship and innovation. By the time Schwab started extolling the virtues of social entrepreneurship, the field had undergone a subtle, important shift. Drayton's Ashoka is a non-profit organization, but many social enterprises today are for-profit. The consequences of this shift have left many early enthusiasts querying whether their objectives are compromised the more the field is commercialized.

If the definition above seems a little general and broad, that's because the phenomenon *is* general and broad: there's no particular aspect of the concept that distinguishes it from earlier efforts to use innovative ideas or methods to create social change. Take a description from John Elkington and Pamela Hartigan, two well-regarded proponents of the concept. In a recent book, they suggest 'there is no standard-issue entrepreneur, but there is a consensus on what entrepreneurs do. Through the practical exploitation of new ideas, they establish new ventures to deliver goods and services not currently supplied by existing markets.'[7] What sets the 'social' entrepreneur apart from more traditional ones is an emphasis on *motivation*. According to Elkington and Hartigan, the new breed of socially aware entrepreneur is motivated by a deep sense of injustice at market imbalances that prevent the disadvantaged from accessing market goods. 'Time and again', they write, 'these entrepreneurs have had a life-transforming experience, some sort of an epiphany, that launched them on their current mission.' They note that: 'Among those who have reported some form of conversion experience are people as diverse as Bob Geldof, Bono, Fazle Abed of BRAC, Bunker Roy of Barefoot College, Roy Prosterman of the Rural Development Institute, and, in the corporate mainstream, Wal-Mart CEO Lee Scott (whose transformative experience came in the wake of Hurricane Katrina).'[8]

Unfortunately, specific definitions of what that 'mission' may be and how it is accomplished are often quite vague. Lee Scott is mentioned only once in the book. What steps he took to act on his 'conversion' experience after Hurricane Katrina are not described. Although he did spearhead a much-trumpeted 'sustainability campaign' during his tenure, a 2013 report published by the Institute for Local Self-Reliance found that Walmart remains a major financial contributor to initiatives focused on *blocking* laws to mitigate environmental catastrophe, and that Walmart's use of renewable energy sources is meagre compared to other large corporations. Scott often suggested that competition from rivals hindered Walmart's ability to raise its notoriously low wages. In his last year as CEO, he received a package in excess of $30 million, and he's reported to own $220 million worth of Walmart stock. Why Elkington and Hartigan uphold him as a 'social entrepreneur' isn't clear.

Let's look at the others mentioned above. Bono and Bob Geldof's widely reported global aid efforts have invited praise and derision in equal measure. Geldof's 2014 re-release of his perennial Christmas single, 'Do They Know It's Christmas?' seemed a particularly inflammatory move, with legions of Africans reacting with either bemusement or outrage. Al Jazeera published some of their responses. Abdullahi Halakhe, a policy analyst based in Kenya, pointed out that 'the Christian population in Nigeria alone is almost three times the number of Christians in England and Wales. How couldn't they know it's Christmas?' He added: 'the idea that Africa needs to be saved in 2014 by washed-up C-list pop artists is a perverse example of a messiah complex'.[9]

BRAC is a successful microfinance organization, one of the few main players in the field that has resisted shifting to a for-profit model once the commercial opportunities have become clearer – I discuss microfinance in more depth below. Barefoot College is a forty-year-old NGO that provides access to services in underserved Indian populations. Roy Prosterman's Rural Development Institute works to secure land rights for marginalized populations. While there's much to commend in these organizations, they're not particularly new. Two of them are over forty years old, and all build upon infrastructures established through earlier development efforts implemented through the twentieth century. In the case of Barefoot College, founder Sanjit 'Bunker' Roy has often stressed that Mahatma Gandhi's spirit of selfless service is the inspiration for his own non-profit work.

And yet, despite the generality of the term, the many historical parallels, and the discomfort over whether Bunker Roy's vision sits comfortably next to Lee Scott's, proponents of social entrepreneurship continue to proclaim, without pointing to much evidence, that social entrepreneurship heralds a revolutionary break from past business practices. Jeff Skoll has suggested that 'at the world's great foundations, universities, and charitable institutions, social entrepreneurship has rapidly become the most influential idea of our time'.[10] Ashoka founder Bill Drayton has suggested that the 'defining quality of leading social entrepreneurs is that they cannot come to rest until they have changed the pattern in their field all across society. Their life vision is the new pattern. Scholars and artists take delight in seeing and expressing an insight; professionals in serving a client . . . It is only the entrepreneurs who can't stop until they have changed the whole society.'[11] Skoll's and Drayton's comments are outlandish in equal measure. To suggest that it's 'only the entrepreneurs who can't stop until they have changed the whole society' makes a mockery of the historical legacy of the labourers who lost their lives at Homestead and Ludlow fighting for better working conditions. They, too, wanted to change society. They didn't stop until they were shot dead by the hired guns of leading philanthropists.

Even efforts to define social entrepreneurship in a more specific manner end up highlighting both the vagueness and the ordinariness of the term. Take this example from Sally Osberg, CEO of the Skoll Foundation, and Roger Martin, former Dean of the Rotman School of Management at the University of Toronto. Asserting that 'a clearer definition of social entrepreneurship will aid the development of the field', they offer the following description. It's a little verbose but worth repeating in full:

> The social entrepreneur should be understood as someone who targets an unfortunate but stable equilibrium that causes the neglect, marginalization, or suffering of a segment of humanity; who brings to bear on this situation his or her inspiration, direct action, creativity, courage, and fortitude; and who aims for and ultimately affects the establishment of a new stable equilibrium that secures permanent benefit for the targeted group and society at large.[12]

It looks quite impressive at first glance. But what's the passage actually saying? Examined closely, not that much. The social entrepreneur is someone who targets an 'unfortunate but stable equilibrium'. This could refer to pretty much anything. Like the fact that most pharmaceutical companies prioritize research and development on diseases that affect the world's richest individuals, rather than diseases that are particularly burdensome in poor countries. An unfortunate problem but certainly not something that social entrepreneurs were the first to identify.

Then there's the midsection: a social entrepreneur is one 'who brings to bear on this situation his or her inspiration, direct action, creativity, courage, and fortitude'. This, too, could refer to a whole range of human endeavours, from activism, to establishing a small business, to lobbying for less patent privileges for large pharmaceutical manufacturers. Again, not particularly new. And lastly: 'who aims for and ultimately affects the establishment of a new stable equilibrium that secures permanent benefit for the targeted group and society at large'. In other words, someone who manages to establish a new form of service provision, whether for-profit, non-profit, or a hybrid of both, from which social benefits follow.

Or do they? How does one measure whether a 'new equilibrium' provides social benefits for a targeted group? Or, even harder to measure, for 'society at large' – whatever society at large means in practice. Corporate benchmarks such as increased revenue, more generous dividends, or higher share valuations simply don't translate as neatly into measuring social outcomes as social entrepreneurs often presume. Most social entrepreneurs want to prove that their business practices or their activism yield positive social results – something that's dubbed, in the TED Head world, 'social return on investment' (SROI). Like generations before them, they quickly confront one of the oldest challenges of the social sciences: proving causality. It is very hard to know whether one particular grant or initiative directly produced measurable improvements in health, education, or social well-being when multiple factors – for example, a growing national GDP, fluctuating commodity prices, or changes in interest rates – might have contributed to an end result. Given this challenge, many philanthropic institutions and social enterprises turn to proxy measures in order to gauge their effectiveness. One such measure is leverage: the ability to attract other philanthropic funders, governments, or market players to your cause.

It's not a new emphasis. Early philanthropic advisors such as Frederick Gates were outspoken about the need to harness partners in government and the private sector when choosing where to invest philanthropic dollars. But in recent years the term has taken on increased import. Today, 'leverage' is used as a proxy for showcasing how effective grants are. If a foundation succeeds in rallying outside actors to its cause through matched funds or other signs of support, it is seen as more successful.

Of course, many entrepreneurs are smart enough to see the limitations of this. Solving the world's problems is not exactly the senior prom. How many dance partners a foundation or social enterprise manages to secure might give a sense of their popularity but it doesn't prove that leverage produces actual *results*. Worse, it is difficult to measure counterfactuals, such as the *cost* of smaller organizations abandoning personal strategies in order to fall in line with more powerful voices.

Ruth McCambridge, editor-in-chief of the influential *Nonprofit Quarterly* magazine, has emphasized this concern, querying whether the rise of increasingly powerful 'mega-philanthropies' with increased leverage over smaller organizations may be creating a situation where 'well-funded organizations with great marketing capacity and social capital to spare have been perhaps overcapitalized – arguably well past the real value of what they add'. She worries that 'once tens of millions of dollars have been invested in one organization, what will the willingness be to reverse that course, even if it is clearly falling short or failing or causing unanticipated harm to communities or community infrastructures?'[13]

McCambridge has also queried the remarkable flexibility and interchangeability of terms such as 'entrepreneurship' and 'innovation' which often pepper grant proposals or marketing pamphlets. As she puts it: 'You do not necessarily need a new idea to be an entrepreneur . . . The most common definition of an entrepreneur is "one who organizes, manages, and assumes the risks of a business or enterprise" . . . entrepreneurs open up pizza places and spas, and build carpeting emporiums – none of which is especially innovative.'[14]

One rhetorical advantage of the ambiguity of the term 'social entrepreneur' is that it is so remarkably elastic that very few individuals working in global health, development, or social services could escape the charge of being one.

On its website, Ashoka lists the following people as historical examples of 'leading social entrepreneurs': Florence Nightingale, Susan B. Anthony, Vinoba Bhave, John Muir, Jean Monnet, and Maria Montessori. All remarkable individuals, surely. But their grouping is somewhat arbitrary, if not absurd. Susan B. Anthony, one of the leading women's rights advocates of the nineteenth century, had close ties to socialist leaders such as Eugene Debs; Bhave, a disciple of Gandhi, pioneered the Bhoodan land-gift movement – he travelled throughout India persuading wealthy landowners to gift their land to the poor; Monnet was a diplomat and leading architect of the European Common Market, a precursor to the EU; Montessori, the famed educator, is often upheld by the US right as a sort of foe to influential, left-leaning educationalists such as John Dewey – but in reality she emphasized the importance of the state's role in education, and sympathized with the views of leading socialists in her day, suggesting that 'socialists and communists . . . started a movement in order to obtain better conditions of life for the working man'.[15]

In the case of Florence Nightingale, the epithet of 'social entrepreneur' seems incongruous to those who emphasize that Nightingale often fought against the commercial tendencies of her time, battling fiercely to make public health a collective right rather than a luxury of the few who could afford it.

In recent years, partly to mitigate unease over the commercialism conveyed by social entrepreneurship, the phrase 'social innovation' has grown in popularity. Geoff Mulgan, former CEO of the London-based Young Foundation, defines social innovation as 'new ideas that meet unmet need'. He points to the legacy of Michael Young, a prominent British sociologist and activist who founded institutions such as the Open University and Which?, a consumer rights watchdog. Young's work is rightly held in much esteem by admirers from across the political spectrum. The question is: what distinguishes Young's work from other efforts to improve the livelihoods and rights of marginalized populations? Policy initiatives such as child benefit programmes and maternity and paternity leave; justice movements such as the fight for labour rights and the Civil Rights movement – each of these was guided by the aim to meet unmet need. Do they all qualify as social innovations?

According to Mulgan, they do. He suggests that social innovation can be understood as processes of change 'sometimes resulting from the work of heroic individuals (such as Robert Owen or Muhammad Yunus); sometimes as resulting from much broader movements of change (such as feminism and environmentalism), or from market dynamics and organizational incentives'. This is so broad that a neighbourhood eight-year-old selling, say, kiwi juice rather than lemonade might be called a social innovator. What, then, is unique about social innovation?[16]

One thing touted as new is the effort to increase capital flows to social enterprises and non-profits through so-called 'social capital banks'. In many ways, social capital banks *could* help to answer an urgent requirement in the non-profit world: the ongoing need for more capital to expand operations or scale to other regions: basically, to reach more users in need. The non-profit sector has always faced difficulty securing funding for new ventures. A basic criterion for a commercial bank lending to a new enterprise is the profitability of the venture. By definition, many non-profits are not commercially viable or profitable: they are reliant on charity or state-support. They're not good financial bets. Commercial lenders also understand that offering financing to non-profits can lead to reputational suicide – being seen to repossess a slew of homeless shelters or women's refuges can tarnish a bank's image.

This problem led to the creation of projects such as the UK's Big Society Capital bank, established by the Conservative-led coalition government in 2012, nearly a decade after the previous Labour government first raised the idea. Aimed at providing financing for social enterprises, the £600-million bank is funded through funds siphoned from dormant bank accounts at commercial lenders such as Lloyds. The funds remain the property of customers and can be reclaimed at any time – but most tend to languish unclaimed. And yet, from the outset, it's been unclear whether the Big Society bank will charge interest rates and expect commercial returns typical of standard banks. If so, sceptics suggest, the bank is no different from any high street lender.

At a press conference in 2012, David Cameron praised the initiative, suggesting that Big Society Capital is about 'supplying capital to help society expand'. Cameron's message is part of his much pilloried 'Big Society' initiative: the effort to encourage individual and community solutions to social programmes once supported by the state. After winning the UK national election in 2010, the Coalition government traversed the UK publicizing the initiative through the use of colourful posters and banners carrying two slogans written in bold letters: 'Big Society' and 'Big Government'. The government apparently felt the British electorate needed some visual help grasping the vital importance of their message. On their publicity banners, the letter 'o' in the phrase 'Big Society' was illustrated with a cartoon smiley face, while the 'o' in 'Big Government' was embellished with a frowney face.

The initiative was greeted with derision by those who pointed out that Cameron's government slashed spending for the non-profit sector, hamstringing the very community programmes and social services he claimed to support. In 2010, the government announced austerity cuts totalling £83 billion, including a cut of £8 billion from the government's affordable housing programme. While the prior Labour government had built 22,000 new homes in 2009, the programme was halted when the Tory-led Coalition came to power.

'The Tory government's austerity measures', Oxford health economist David Stuckler and Stanford epidemiologist Sanjay Basu write, 'tipped about 10,000 UK families into homelessness.'[17] Since the Conservatives were elected in 2010, more than 2,000 charities in England have faced major cuts or seen their funding withdrawn altogether by local councils. To the staff of charities facing crippling demand, forced to make redundancies, unable to give individuals the support once provided in the past, Cameron's proclamation that the Big Society is about 'liberation – the biggest, most dramatic redistribution of power from elites in Whitehall to the man and woman on the street'[18] – is more than derisible. It hits like them a boot in the gut.

One frustrated non-profit employee, a woman named Celosia Mendes, published a *Guardian* editorial in 2010 describing her bewilderment at Cameron's exhortation for more volunteers to fill the gaps left by a receding state. She wrote as a staff member of Volunteer Centre Hackney, a non-profit that enlists and supports volunteers in one of London's most deprived areas. Mendes ran Props, a volunteering programme for ex-offenders. Demand was so high that many prisoners wrote to Props before their release asking for suggestions about how to volunteer. After two years, the programme was axed, a casualty of cuts to the NHS primary care trust which had co-sponsored the initiative. 'When our very existence is threatened', Mendes asked, 'how on earth can we be expected to nurture or promote the "big society"?'[19]

Another weakness of Cameron's notion is that it ignores the respect and dignity that people place on governmental support in comparison to charity handouts. This sense of dignity is particularly salient in the UK, where, as the sociologist Darren Thiel has found, the introduction of national insurance programmes in the twentieth century solidified a sense of social contract between citizens and the government: individuals serve their country through regular payments to the benefits system, and therefore feel they've earned compensation and reimbursement in times of economic hardship.

This expectation is particularly acute among those in the armed services, who often resent the premium placed on charitable support at a time when state support is being slashed. Drawing on Frank Ledwidge's study of Britain's recent war in Afghanistan, the journalist and novelist James Meek reports the case of 'Peter', a reservist severely injured in a bomb attack in 2006. He fought for compensation after the Ministry of Defence told him he was not entitled to any. He eventually received a reasonable payment, but many others do not. 'Help for Heroes and charities like it', Peter commented, are simply 'fig leaves for a government that wants to pass on the costs to an unaccountable charitable sector.'[20]

In 2012, Cameron announced a cut of 5 per cent to the top marginal tax rate, leading to an additional saving of £14,000 per week for approximately 40,000 millionaires. Tax cuts for the wealthy are part of the Big Society's legacy. This, fundamentally, is philanthrocapitalism in action: introducing policies that help concentrate wealth in the upper echelons of society in the hope that the wealthy will donate to the financially strapped rest.[21]

Phil Buchanan, president of the US-based Center for Effective Philanthropy (CEP), remarked to me that there's something curious about cherry-picking historical figures who achieved social goals and 'posthumously labelling all of these people . . . philanthrocapitalists'. He suggested that such historical revisionism ends up 'caricaturing the non-profit sector in ways that are not helpful', adding that the management guru Peter Drucker is routinely upheld as a philanthrocapitalist when in reality 'Drucker wrote an article in *Harvard Business Review* in 1989 called "What Business Can Learn from Non-Profits"'.

Long accustomed to working with meagre funds, non-profit organizations have throughout history found innovative ways to help low-income populations. While examples of mismanagement in any sector are not hard to find, dysfunction in the non-profit world has rarely approached the level of mismanagement resulting in catastrophes on the scale of Worldcom, Enron, or the 2008 subprime mortgage crisis. At a time when reckless lending in the private sector has rarely been more apparent, charities are being asked to increasingly emulate for-profit operating strategies, exhorted to emulate the private sector when logic suggests that the reverse should be the case.

Proponents insist that what separates philanthrocapitalism and social entrepreneurship from early forms of enterprise is an emphasis on social value. I'll quote once more from Martin and Osberg on this point: 'Ventures created by social entrepreneurs can certainly generate income, and they can be organized as either not-for-profits or for-profits. What distinguishes social entrepreneurship is the primacy of social benefit.'[22] This is an important point. Social entrepreneurs, more so than traditional entrepreneurs, are adamant that their services and products generate social value as a fundamental, defining goal – over and above an emphasis on financial returns. A number of phrases are used to underscore this preoccupation with social value, from 'shared value' to 'blended value' to 'triple bottom line' (referring to a company's social, financial, and environmental impact). On the one hand, it might seem like a good thing for companies to worry about their environmental and social impact. On the other hand, evidence to support Martin and Osberg's suggestion – that creating social value is the *primary* objective and end result of social entrepreneurship – is rather limited. When you scrutinize some of the flagship ventures to date in this field, from support for small-medium enterprises, to the microfinancing craze, to the rise of 'impact investing', you quickly see that hype has outpaced outcomes – at least for the global poor.

Take microfinance. It's the brainchild of Muhammad Yunus, a Bangladeshi entrepreneur who founded the Grameen Bank (or 'village bank') in the early 1980s. Yunus's much-celebrated concept – he and the Grameen Bank were jointly awarded the Nobel Peace Prize in 2006 – turns on the realization that lack of access to bank credit is a major liability for those living in poverty. That realization was not necessarily new: the poor have long found creative ways to pool money and secure loans when they're either living in an area with a dearth of sophisticated banking infrastructures, or when they're excluded from formal channels. In western Africa, for example, 'susu' collectors (meaning 'small small') would pool monetary contributions in a fund that could be accessed by other tribe members for a small fee, a practice observed by anthropologists as early as the 1950s.[23] In wealthy nations, the challenge of securing credit from main street lenders led to vibrant networks of informal lending schemes that flourish to this day. Often schemes are ethnically organized, with members of an ethnic community banding together to negotiate mortgages or provide financing for both illegal and legitimate small businesses.[24]

But Yunus's work pioneered the development of formal microlending operations on a large scale. He was the first to establish a non-profit organization dedicated to securing small loans for poor Bangladeshis, a practice that soon spread to other nations as microcredit was embraced by the UN, USAID, the World Bank, and investors in the west. Dozens of lenders mushroomed in Grameen's wake. Today, tens of millions of borrowers worldwide have received loans from microcredit institutions. The UN declared 2005 the International Year of Microcredit. Enthusiasts suggest that Grameen and its successors have 'demonstrated that it was possible to mitigate poverty on a massive scale'.[25]

But has it?

Dozens of studies have explored the effect of microfinance on poverty levels. Taken together, the studies indicate that even for the more successful programmes there's 'an absence of a clear statistical link between microfinance and poverty alleviation'.[26] And that's in the case of the *success* stories. In cases documented in Bolivia, Morocco, Nicaragua, Pakistan, and Bosnia, microfinance had been shown to mire borrowers in crippling debt, worsening poverty

rather than improving it. Yunus founded Grameen Bank as a reputable alternative to local Bangladeshi loan sharks who would offer
credit at usurious rates. And yet many of today's legal microfinance
institutions have rates that are just as gruelling as the harshest
back-alley lender, with some, such as Mexico's Compartamos, charging interest that exceeds 100 per cent. The high rates have led to calls
for regulatory caps on the interest rates, something resisted by news
outlets such as the *Economist*, which ran a proselytizing article in
2010 insisting we should 'leave well alone' as 'capping microfinance
interests rates will hurt the poor'.[27]

One of the largest studies to date, carried out by the World Bank and
published in 2014, *did* appear to show a positive impact. Lasting for
more than twenty years, the study followed more than 3,000 households in eighty-seven villages across Bangladesh. The researchers
discovered that a 10 per cent increase in men's borrowing directly
raised household spending by 0.04 per cent, while borrowing by
women increased household spending by one and a half times as much.
It also demonstrated that a 10 per cent jump in women's borrowing
raised the female labour supply by 0.46 per cent, boys' school enrolment by 0.07 per cent, and girls' school enrolment by 0.08 per cent. The
results *were* statistically significant, but they were also very modest.[28]

David Roodman, a development expert who supports the concept
of microfinance, pointed out that the results are quite limited when
it comes to their real-world application. This happens often with
statistical findings. They might well be significant – as in, definitively
attributable to the intervention under study rather than a result of
chance. But their effects are so miniscule that they have very little
bearing on actual life. For example, you could have a cancer therapy
that is statistically found to extend life expectancy by an average of
one week. That finding might be statistically significant, but it would
not be worth putting yourself through the gruelling side-effects that
might accompany the therapy. The same thing applies here. After
tracking the impact of microfinance loans over a twenty-year period,

the investigators found an almost negligible increase in schooling and a minor jump in household spending. This is not exactly groundbreaking stuff. I mentioned earlier that Bill Clinton has praised microcredit loans for helping to 'lift more than 100 million people out of poverty across the world'. I think he may be confusing access with benefit. At least 100 million people *have* received microfinance loans to date. But whether that's helped or hindered their livelihoods is a source of ongoing debate.

Berhanu Nega, a former mayor of Addis Ababa, Ethiopia, who currently teaches economics at Bucknell University in the United States, has written critically about the persistent belief that microloans are a transformative development tool. I spoke with him in November 2014. He pointed out that there is both ideological and financial investment among microcredit supporters in the value of the concept, and this prior investment may hinder them from recognizing the trend's limitations:

> These are people who are, in one form or another, benefiting from these institutions . . . they want to believe – and some of them I think do believe – that what they are doing is good despite the fact that the data does not show that – especially at the level of larger societal issues such as poverty alleviation. You might be able to deliver $100, $200 loans to farmers in different places for temporary easing of their burdens but that cannot be a solution to long-term development. That has been very, very obvious.

One group *has* profited handsomely from microfinance, and that's the investors, most of them based in wealthy nations. During 2009, the $30 billion industry saw a year-end return of 4.47 per cent, in comparison to a 22 per cent loss by the Standard & Poor's 500-stock index. Two years later, two microfinance advocates, Jed Emerson and Antony Bugg-Levine, emphasized that 'impact investors in microfinance bonds received a consistent 6 per cent return . . . not a bad financial return at all'. In other words, microfinance *is* working. Just not for the poor.[29]

Another example of a trend widely hailed for alleviating poverty is impact investing. This is the idea that individuals can earn market-rate financial returns for investing in projects geared at providing environmental and social benefits. In 2010, wild estimates of the financial potential for investors started to appear – a report from JPMorgan, the Rockefeller Foundation, and the Global Impact Investing Network predicted that the profits could range from $183 billion to $667 billion. Investors flocked to the field. Since then, the field has faced a reality check. There are very few companies that are proven to offer simultaneously both financial and social returns on investment. Many offer a handsome *financial* return, but do not demonstrate direct social benefits. And vice versa: socially promising ventures abound, but the potential for profit is too paltry to excite investors.

The experience of the Acumen Fund, a non-profit group that funds market-based solutions to development challenges, illustrates this problem. After considering 5,000 potential companies over ten years, it invested in just sixty-five of them. Advocates of impact investing admit that investors are wary of putting their money on the line when the financial pay-off is uncertain. Because of the reluctance, one report suggests, 'Truly realizing the impact in impact investing will require more, not less, philanthropy.'[30]

This last comment points to something curious about the recent hype for 'market-based' initiatives in global health and development. Often, these initiatives are *not* actually market-based at all. That's to say, they are not initiated or sustained by market investment on an open exchange, but nurtured and bulwarked by enormous injections of state and philanthropic funding. In 2003, for example, the UK's Department for International Development (DFID) provided just under £1 million in a donation to Vodafone to establish M-PESA, a system allowing villagers in Kenya to pay bills via text messages on their mobile phones. By 2007, Vodafone and Saraficom, a Kenyan company partly owned by Vodafone, had M-PESA up and running. Within two years, more than 20 per cent of Kenya's population was registered for the service, and the M-PESA scheme accounted for a significant portion of Safaricom's £150 million annual profits. By 2008 Safaricom wasn't simply Kenya's largest company – it had grown to be the largest and most profitable company in all of East Africa.[31] In 2007, Vodafone partnered with Citibank to extend the M-PESA scheme worldwide. In 2010, the Gates Foundation offered a non-repayable grant of $4.8 million to Vodacom, a Vodafone subsidiary, to enable the company to roll out M-PESA in Tanzania. The following year, it offered Vodacom an additional $2.9 million grant.[32]

By December 2011, Vodafone, the second-largest mobile operator in the world, had a market capitalization of £89.4 billion. In 2010, the London-based company came under criticism for tax avoidance schemes that enabled it to save approximately £6 billion in revenue by routing the acquisition of a German corporation through a Luxembourg subsidiary. In 2014, for the third straight year in a row, the company's annual report indicated that it had paid no UK corporation tax at all. This tax saving came during a year when the company posted a post-tax profit of £59.4 billion. Despite Vodafone's ample resources and history of tax avoidance, the UK government was kind enough to offer the company a no-strings grant to help get its mobile operations in East Africa off the ground. Which was lucky for Vodafone, because a company rep has gone on record stating that without the £1 million from DFID, he could never have persuaded Vodafone executives to invest in the venture.[33]

Most popular press articles on M-PESA celebrate the entrepreneurial acumen of Vodafone and Safaricom. They don't mention DFID. A recent article in *Wired*, for example, hails M-PESA as a 'non-governmental, cashless system', calling it a 'rare example of Africa successfully leapfrogging the developed world's legacy infrastructure and moving straight into a mobile system'.[34]

Despite the fact that private companies are often remarkably risk-averse, begging governments for a leg-up on innovation ladders, there's a widespread belief among the public and economists that private actors are inherently more innovative and entrepreneurial than governments. Two economists determined to dispel this myth are Mariana Mazzucato and William Lazonick. Mazzucato has pointed out that the algorithm that led to Google's success was funded by a US National Science Foundation grant, and that the UK's Medical Research Council financed the early discovery of molecular antibodies instrumental to the develop of biotechnology, something that attracted venture capital only after government-funded research showed signs of promise.

Governmental willingness to invest in the most uncertain phase of a fledgling sector's development underscores the fact that states do not simply regulate markets, they *are* the market: an indispensable pit stop on the road to commercializing a new venture. And yet, even among those who recognize the strong role played by states in creating new markets in developing regions, very few mainstream economists, Mazzucato and Lazonick suggest, appreciate the role of the 'state as a leading actor even in the most developed regions of the world, such as Silicon Valley'.[35]

Many economists also fail to appreciate that there is a growing disconnect between the economic actors driving innovation, including governments, and those reaping the financial rewards of governmental investment. 'While risk-taking has become more collective – leading to much discussion about *open* innovation and *innovation* ecosystems', Lazonick and Mazzucato write, 'the reward system has become dominated by individuals who, inserting themselves strategically between the business organization and the product market ... lay claim to a disproportionate share of the rewards of the innovation process.'[36]

Microfinance is a good example. During the 1980s and 1990s, the field received approximately $20 billion in subsidies from philanthropic foundations and governmental aid. A report from the consultancy firm Monitor has stressed that before the field was financially promising, 'subsidies in the form of grants, soft loans, and guarantees from philanthropists and aid donors' were key to the field's growth.[37] A curious sort of cognitive dissonance is at play here. Microfinance advocates often berate governments for placing regulatory caps on interest rates – and yet all admit that without government support the field would have withered long ago. As Lester Frank Ward presciently observed, those who decry state interference are typically the same people whose capital and investment choices depend on state support.[38]

It is now over a century since Ward wrote those words. What's new today is that as well as benefiting from the government's largesse, for-profit organizations are increasingly privy to generous gifts from private philanthropists such as the Gates Foundation. The Gates Foundation frequently offers grants to for-profit companies such as, to name just three recent beneficiaries, Vodacom, Ogilvy, and ABC News (which is owned by Disney and which pays many of its news staff seven- and eight-figure salaries). Charity law in the US does not prohibit direct grants from a private philanthropist to for-profit companies, but a number of provisions must be met in order for a foundation to receive tax relief for the donation. A foundation such as the Gates Foundation must, for example, demonstrate that a grant is used solely for charitable purposes. In the case of Vodacom, I have not seen evidence that this criterion was met. While most people would agree that better mobile access and services in developing regions is a positive development, many would also suggest that Vodafone should incur its own business costs, seeing as the company and its shareholders have full entitlement to all profits, minus taxes. When, that is, taxes are actually paid.

It takes a moment to realize the full significance of what's happening here. Progressives and conservatives alike often complain of the spectre of 'double taxation' – the levying of a tax by more than one jurisdiction on the same declared income. What's happening in the world of large mega-philanthropies and their corporate beneficiaries is the spectre of double *exemption*. Despite being headquartered in Britain, Vodafone avoided paying UK corporation tax for *three straight years* – and that during a period of drastic government spending cuts. Then the Gates Foundation reduces Vodafone's expenses even further by offering the company's subsidiary non-repayable grants worth over $6 million. Finally – and here's the double exemption part – the Gates Foundation's founders receive a tax break for their contribution to Vodacom, so US taxpayers lose out as well as UK ones.

On its website, the Gates Foundation emphasizes that the Gates's tax savings are minor in comparison to their disbursements, and that's true. The website notes that from 1994 to 2006, Bill and Melinda donated more than $26 billion, resulting in savings of 8.3 per cent, or just over $2 billion. And yet, is a gift from the Gates Foundation to a highly profitable company really the best use of money that, if it had been taxed as income rather than placed in a trust, could have benefited federal or state relief programmes?

The cognitive dissonance I've described above – the continued insistence that new entrepreneurial movements are playing a revolutionary role in global poverty reduction despite the lack of clear evidence – is the truly distinctive aspect of social entrepreneurship. Unlike ideas of corporate social responsibility which were popular in the 1980s and 1990s – and which often had an aura of expiation about them, implying that socially oriented philanthropy was needed to make amends for corporate abuses – the new social investors believe that business success *is* evidence of social value. There is no longer any whiff of atonement or reparation for past corporate practices. The only sin is insufficient commercial expansion to untouched realms.

What's remarkable about this belief is its resilience at a time when the recent subprime mortgage crisis seemed poised to douse the enthusiasm of social entrepreneurship champions – a resilience that surprised even staffers at places like the World Economic Forum. In March 2009 I sat in the WEF's Geneva office with a WEF policy advisor. 'When this crisis hit last autumn', she said, 'I [thought] that's going to impact us a lot because no one is going to want to send a CEO for five days or four days in this time of crisis.' She was relieved when the 2009 forum had a 'record attendance . . . I was really happy because the forum wants to be a neutral platform where discussions are held at a high level . . . in times of crisis, we want to be even more useful. And this is exactly what we proved with Davos this year.'

The value of pro-market solutions particularly during times of economic catastrophe has been one of the most common themes to emerge out of the 2008 collapse, a crisis which initially led to questions over whether the private sector was, as Georgia Keohane writes, 'the best exemplar of corporate governance, accountability, or long-term investment savvy'.[39]

At the 2009 Skoll World Forum, just months after the collapse of Lehman Brothers and Bear Stearns, there was very little acknowledgement of the role that business played in destabilizing markets. Rather, there was a remarkably self-congratulatory, proselytizing tenor to proceedings, a sense that the 'new' socially oriented entrepreneurship offered salvation in dark times. Soraya Salti, a representative of INJAZ al-Arab, an organization that draws on Arab business leaders to help build entrepreneurialism among Arab youth, praised attendees with the following passage from Kahlil Gibran: 'You work so that you may keep pace with the earth and the soul of the earth. For to be idle is to become a stranger unto the seasons and to step out of life's procession that marches in majesty and proud submission towards the infinite . . . when you work you fulfil a part of earth's furthest dream assigned to you when that dream was born.'

She concluded by hailing Jeff Skoll as a 'modern-day prophet'. Taking the stage to a standing ovation, Skoll offered an evangelistic call to action: 'You are a keystone species in the social change architecture. Your role is strengthened by the economic crisis. We leave Oxford with a renewed sense of what is possible. Last year we said social entrepreneurs had arrived; now I say they are to take [the] lead and show the way to the rest of the world. A crisis is a terrible thing to waste.'[40]

CHAPTER THREE

Mandeville's Bastards

In the late 1990s and 2000s, Mark Kramer, a lawyer and founder of Kramer Capital Management, collaborated with Michael Porter, an influential management scholar based at Harvard, in setting up two organizations: the Center for Effective Philanthropy (CEP), established in 1999, and the Foundation Strategy Group (FSG), created in 2000.

Earlier, in 1983, Porter had co-founded the Monitor Group, a consulting firm that came under scrutiny in 2011 for its past contracts with Muammar Gaddafi's regime in Libya. Monitor faced criticism for failing to register its lobbying activities under the Foreign Agents Registration Act, and for conducting some of the academic research for Saif Gaddafi's doctoral dissertation at the London School of Economics. The Monitor Group declared bankruptcy a year later, and was purchased by Deloitte. Porter currently directs the Institute for Strategy and Competitiveness at Harvard.

Porter and Kramer initially served on the board of the Center for Effective Philanthropy. They left after protracted battles with CEP board members who were uncomfortable with the fact that both were profiting from philanthropic consulting work at FSG while advising CEP, which strives to offer impartial data useful to clients and the philanthropic sector as a whole. 'They had both established the Foundation Strategy Group which was initially a for-profit', Phil

Buchanan, the current president of CEP, told me. 'Mark Kramer was running FSG and the board chair of CEP'. After discussions with his management team, CEP decided they 'did not want to be running the non-profit business development arm of a for-profit consulting firm.'

Buchanan's concern strikes at one of the thorniest, long-standing, and divisive tensions in the realms of philanthropy and enterprise: the question of whether a self-interested action can ever be truly philanthropic. It's a problem that has, for centuries, played a role in shifting foreign policy (Britain's move away from mercantilism was prompted by the view that private trade helps to foster cooperation among nations, promoting the public good through individual economic enrichment), and helped to establish entire academic disciplines (the term 'altruism' was first coined by Auguste Comte, one of the fathers of sociology): where does the line between self-interest and altruism lie? Are selfishness and selflessness inevitably incommensurable sentiments, or are they more reconcilable than is commonly thought?

The most influential Enlightenment-era writer to broach this question was Bernard Mandeville. He was born in Rotterdam in 1670, the son of a well-respected physician. After training as doctor, Mandeville moved to England to learn the language. An essayist in his spare time, he penned a series of sardonic missives that enraged London's intelligentsia and drew the ire of the Middlesex Grand Jury which accused Mandeville of blasphemy, declaring his writing a public nuisance. Later on, that same writing earned Mandeville a legacy as one of the greatest – perhaps *the* greatest – precursors of laissez-faire ideology, hailed as an inspiration for Adam Smith's political economy, and revered by twentieth-century economists such as Friedrich Hayek.[1]

Mandeville's most famous work is *The Fable of the Bees*, a lengthy satirical poem published anonymously in 1705 with the title 'The Grumbling Hive: or Knaves Turn'd Honest'. In this poem, Mandeville offers a microscopic glimpse of an ideology that, once fully developed, would later inspire generations of thinkers such as Hayek who staunchly opposed the notion that planned economies could ever achieve social progress through deliberate design.

Mandeville adopts the metaphor of a beehive. Within the hive, he writes, there thrived a mass of industrious and ingenious bees, many of whom were knaves – they were deceitful, vain, fickle, foolish, envious, avaricious – and yet their wants helped to make the 'whole mass a Paradise'. Their fraud, their greed, their desires all fuelled a dynamic industry, creating such comforts that 'the Poor / Liv'd Better than the Rich before'. Progress, in other words, was rooted in *vice*, and not virtue. For Mandeville, virtue was more often the culprit of stagnation – even social decline. When some of the industrious bees complained of the deviousness of the knaves, and sought to impose virtue, industrial efforts withered, and the comforts fuelled through vice gave way to a more desolate, bleaker life, marked by men toiling arduously for bare necessities alone. Mandeville includes a short verse that almost reads like a biblical commandment for today's laissez-faire thinkers scornful of state-guided economic development: 'Fools only strive / To make a Great an Honest Hive.'[2]

Twenty years later, Mandeville came out with a third edition of the poem, and included two influential appendices: 'An Essay on Charity and Charity-Schools', and 'A Search into the Nature of Society'. It was these additions – and in particular his comments about charity – that earned Mandeville public notoriety and disgrace. His views on charity were immediately denounced as a vindictive attack on institutions widely regarded as the most sanctified realms of Christian virtue: the church and its clergy, universities such as Cambridge and Oxford, and, his most inflammatory target, the vibrant network of 'charity schools' celebrated for offering poor children an escape from drudgery and vice.

Mandeville's arrival in London had coincided with a flourishing of catechetical charity schools which had fast become the preferred receptacle for the philanthropy of conscientious early eighteenth-century Londoners. These institutions were mushrooming before Mandeville's eyes: by 1711, the schools had grown from a mere handful in the 1690s to over a hundred, educating more than 2,500 boys and 1,490 girls in reading, writing, and arithmetic, as well as instruction in the doctrines of the church. Mandeville's criticisms of the schools were far from subtle. Declaring that 'Pride and Vanity have built more Hospitals than all the Virtues together', he queried whether education could ever lead to the development of virtue. His argument was at once simple and, especially for the city's elite, highly insulting. He pointed out that the wealthy and the better educated tended to be far craftier and more self-serving than the poor – so why assume that virtue is something that increases with education? As far he could tell, greater learning tends to reduce it.[3]

These criticisms flowed from Mandeville's underpinning argument about the nature of reason – an argument that at first enraged his audience before winning over successive generations of establishment thinkers in a complete ideological coup d'état. His ideas spurred a reversal of opinion so absolute that many of his most ardent twentieth- and twenty-first-century admirers would later misperceive the main kernel of his thought. In short, he suggested that reason was *not*, as was widely believed at the time, the main guiding force behind human action. Rather, it was a *post facto* rationalizing force, used in retrospect to justify decisions made from baser, more animalistic and self-serving instincts. As his biographer Frederick Kaye writes, Mandeville suspected that 'all our acts – even those apparently most altruistic and unselfish – are, traced to their source, due to some variety or interplay of selfish emotion.'[4] And then Mandeville really astonished people: he insisted it was selfishness that helped economies to soar to heights unimagined in the past. As Kaye puts it, 'he felt it a pretty good world, too, in which . . . human self-seeking, properly controlled, could be made to produce a prosperous and happy state of affairs.'[5]

Mandeville's insistence that self-seeking must be *properly controlled* in order for private vice to reap 'publick benefits' is curiously ignored by his followers today. Although he is upheld as the preeminent founding spokesman for laissez-faire policies, in reality, as the economist Albert Hirschman emphasizes, 'Mandeville actually invoked throughout *The Fable of the Bees* the "Skilful Management of the Dextrous Politician" as a necessary condition and agent for the turning of "private vices" into "publick benefit".'[6]

This stipulation is apparent from Mandeville's earliest writings on the usefulness of vice, like this verse from *The Grumbling Hive:*

> *So Vice is beneficial found*
> *When it's by Justice lopt and bound.*

Throughout much of the eighteenth and nineteenth centuries, Mandeville's ideas about the economic value of self-interest were championed while his caveats about the need for government intervention were neglected. Free economic trade was upheld as an antidote to the proliferation of political conflicts stemming from the narrow pursuit of national objectives by European nation states. That vision held until the mid to late nineteenth century, when Marx's theories of the destructive nature of capitalist growth began resonating with working men and women – as well as working children (until the twentieth century, a child in the United States and Europe was more likely to be a family's second main wage earner than a wife; the first workers employed at Samuel Slater's spinning mill set up in 1790 in Rhode Island were nine children between the ages of seven and twelve).[7]

What's absent in the peppy optimism of today's TED Heads ('A crisis is a terrible thing to waste!') is recognition of the historical struggles over private profits and public gain that have shaped labour relations at least since Mandeville's day. When they acknowledge that history, which isn't often, today's philanthrocapitalists praise a bastardized version of early political economy, one that ignores the emphasis that Mandeville and later Adam Smith placed on the need for government regulation. Mandeville would not have found that surprising. He would have seen such selectiveness as the typical sort of *ex post facto* rationalization that often masquerades as common sense or obvious virtue but which blankets an underlying logic: the instinct to advance one's own interest. Not only would he have found it unsurprising, he likely would have pointed to such rationalizations as the reason why claims about the benefits of self-regulation shouldn't be left in the hands of those who voice them.

As we've seen, the question of whether private gain serves the public welfare has a long and conflicted history. Recently, with considerable bravado, a high-profile team of management scholars claimed to have cracked the problem. The solution, they proclaimed, is the notion of 'shared value.' The term was coined by Kramer and Porter, who since the 1990s have been at the forefront of an outspoken group of management scholars upbraiding the US philanthropic sector for its perceived failures. Often these scholars have raised highly important criticisms, emphasizing that organizations that enjoy generous tax breaks have an obligation to serve the public welfare. But the solutions they champion – like diktats to increase the role of business in problem-solving, relax regulation, and reduce corporation tax – may be entrenching the very economic inequalities which they purport to lament.

An influential article in this field was a 1997 piece in the *Harvard Business Review* by Christine Letts, William Ryan, and Allen Grossman. Calling for more 'venture philanthropy' (the term itself was first used as early as the 1960s), the article pointed out that venture capitalists and philanthropists often share similar challenges. Both groups must select the most worthy recipients of money from an abundance of applicants searching for funds, and both groups must find a way to be accountable to the third party whose funds they are investing. In finance, the third party is the investors. Venture capitalists need aggressive, hands-on strategies for making sure risky funding bets pay off. In philanthropy, the third party is society itself. If philanthropic investments are not creating social value, then why should the taxpayer subsidize them through the tax breaks philanthropists enjoy?[8]

Kramer and Porter joined the chorus, pointing out that on average, foundations donate only about 5.5 per cent of their endowment assets to various causes, a striking difference over operating charities. 'Much of the $330 billion currently held by foundations', they asserted, 'represents a future benefit to society, one that will be realized only when the money is finally given away . . . We as a nation pay up front for deferred benefits.' To ensure foundations create value for US taxpayers, Kramer and Porter advised some policy shifts: foundations must work harder at 1) selecting the best grantees; 2) 'signalling' other funders – as in, educating and attracting other funders to their own causes through matching grants; and 3) improving the performance of grant recipients by moving from the role of simple capital provider to a 'fully engaged partner'.[9]

They then turned their gaze from philanthropic foundations to a new focus: corporate donors. It's *here* that a new, pugnacious, explicitly commercial form of philanthropy emerged. It's this spirit of *explicit* material reward that distinguishes the new philanthropy from earlier models and practices throughout the nineteenth and twentieth centuries. Earlier philanthropic foundations *were* businesslike. They were obsessed with measuring and showcasing results. But while Rockefeller and Carnegie vowed to run their philanthropic trusts in an efficient, businesslike way, in line with the same operating principles that fuelled their business practices, they stopped short of openly admitting that their giving was aimed at directly increasing their corporate profits. To have done so might have sabotaged their efforts to establish their trusts in the first place. It would have offered robust proof to people like George Wickersham, the

former US Attorney General who condemned Rockefeller Sr.'s philanthropic gambits as a 'scheme for perpetuating vast wealth'.[10]

Sensitive to such charges, few donors were willing to crow openly
about the profits they could make personally through charitable
giving. That's no longer the case. In their 2002 article 'The Competitive
Advantage of Corporate Philanthropy', Kramer and Porter asserted
that to be genuinely 'philanthropic', corporations should deliberately
pursue philanthropic strategies that align with their own financial
goals. This, they suggest, would ensure that companies obtain a
'competitive edge' through giving, helping them to earn greater
financial returns as a direct result of their charitable endeavours.[11]

In a number of articles, Kramer and Porter uphold Nestlé, the
Swiss-based food conglomerate, as one of the best exemplars of
their 'shared value' approach, suggesting that since the 1960s, Nestlé
has contributed to increased living standards in India's Northern
region of Moga through enrolling local dairy farmers in supplying
milk for the company. They credit the company for strengthening
its own supply chain in a cost-effective way while simultaneously
empowering local distributors. 'Nestlé's experience in setting up
collection points, training farmers, and introducing better technology in Moga has been repeated in Brazil, Thailand, and a dozen
other countries . . . in each case, As Nestlé has prospered, so has the
community.'[12]

This admiration for Nestlé is not universally held. The company
has faced considerable criticism for allegedly encouraging intimi-
dating and lethal union-busting tactics in Colombia, and for
aggressive patenting tactics that restrict access to affordable medical
procedures and food substances. A unit of Nestlé, Prometheus,
recently lost a high-profile patent case that reached the US Supreme
Court. Prometheus Laboratories had endeavoured to patent a diagnostic method which monitored changes in a patient's body in order
to establish optimal dosage levels. The Mayo Clinic launched a
lawsuit against the company, suggesting that it was trying to patent a

natural process of medical observation. The Supreme Court sided with Mayo, stating in a twenty-four-page opinion that 'the patent claims at issue here effectively claim the underlying laws of nature themselves. The claims are consequently invalid.' More recently, Nestlé has been fighting for a patent for an extract from the fennel flower, which has long been used as a natural remedy in communities throughout the Middle East and Asia. In an effort to counter Nestlé's claim, the social justice organization SumofUs created a petition which has now gone viral online, with nearly 800,000 signatures. That Porter and Kramer uphold Nestlé as an exemplary company suggests they're either ignorant of such opposition or see its threat to the company's marketing efforts as negligible.

Another example is General Electric, which recently launched Ecoimagination, an initiative committing the company to spend $10 billion on developing a line of environmentally friendlier products by 2020. Porter and Kramer praise the company for 'making a lot of money ($18 billion in 2009) out of ecologically friendly products'. And yet, as Steve Denning writes in *Forbes*, $18 billion in sales is a mere 11.5 per cent of GE's total sales, 'Thus 88.5% of GE's sales are still "business as usual" i.e. not ecologically friendly.'[13] The company has also consistently sought to minimize its own decades-long role in dumping toxic PCBs into the Hudson River, lobbying extensively for legislation that stalled clean-up efforts.

Management theorists Mark Aakhus and Michael Bzdak point out that GE is ranked by watchdog groups such as Corpwatch as one of the world's top ten 'greenwashers', a term for when a company spends more time and money on green marketing tactics than working to change deeply entrenched and often harmful business practices. Aakhus and Bzdak have queried whether the notion of 'shared value' is really a new departure from long-standing business practices, or whether it mostly parrots the familiar rhetoric that what's good for business is good for society.[14]

*   *   *

Whether you think their concept is derisible or inspiring, one thing is clear: Kramer and Porter's ideas are embraced by Generation TED Head, leading to significant changes in how philanthropists approach their giving and creating new constraints for non-profits that are increasingly dependent on philanthropic donations at a time when state funds are dwindling.

Garry Jenkins, a legal scholar and expert on the philanthropy sector based at the Ohio State University, has studied how a deluge of new trends and buzzwords – strategic philanthropy, catalytic philanthropy, philanthrocapitalism – are affecting the sector. He found that in recent years there's been a sharp spike in 'limited-purpose' grants, where a grantee must spend dollars on a specific priority area identified by foundation managers, over 'general support' grants. This trend often leaves recipients feeling increasingly hemmed in by donor expectations, prioritizing short-term benchmarks at the expense of long-term organizational planning.

Foundations are also embracing 'invitation-only' policies, refusing to consider unsolicited applications from charities or academic groups. The need to 'prove' impact has seen foundations increasingly turning to a trusted pool of applicants, something that saves valuable time for foundation staff, but also slams the door on smaller non-profits that haven't got a foothold with a foundation. Fifteen years ago, closed or semi-closed policies were exceptionally rare. Today, they're far more common. Jenkins compared giving policies at the largest corporate and independent US foundations between 1994 and 2008. He found that only 6 per cent of all large foundations had invitation-only grant policies in 1994. In 2008, the percentage was 29 per cent. In other words, a substantially larger number of foundations had adopted a 'don't call us, we'll find you' approach, something that underscores the worry that foundation leaders are becoming increasingly paternalistic, implying they know more about service delivery than those working in the field.[15]

A key objective of the new philanthropy is to focus on a few key priority areas and to rally others to one's vision. As a recent book on philanthropy notes, successful 'philanthropreneurs' are those who 'commit to a cause'. By picking a strategic focus and not veering from it, funders are purportedly 'able to achieve more than donors who scatter their funding and attention across many disparate causes'.[16]

Just two decades ago, many foundation leaders believed that 'letting a thousand flowers bloom' was a sound funding strategy. More recently, the Center for Effective Philanthropy carried out a survey indicating that no CEO of a philanthropic foundation held the same view today. All had been persuaded to focus only on select areas. As one CEO put it, 'You have to begin with the end in mind.' As Stanley Katz points out, that goal suggests that it's possible to know, at the outset of a development or funding programme, the best method for achieving an outcome. Determining an end goal is comparatively easy. The difficulty is determining what methods will produce it. To believe that's an easy process is, as Katz argues, to overestimate the effectiveness of contemporary social science.[17]

New demands on how grantees must spend their money leave recipients feeling increasingly vulnerable, increasingly beholden to shifts in foundation policy that force them to fall in step, even when the scientific or social benefits of doing so are not clear. There's also the concern that close ties between donors and their favourite grantees may leave recipients cash-starved when unexpected catastrophe hits a foundation. This happened in the case of the Children's Investment Fund Foundation (CIFF), established by Chris Hohn and his wife Jamie Cooper Hohn in 2003.

Hohn is the UK's largest philanthropist, having donated over £1 billion to charitable causes to date. He established his hedge fund, The Children's Investment Fund Management (known by the acronym TCI) in 2003 and structured it so that a proportion of profits were automatically directed to CIFF, a charity run by his wife with a focus on improving children's education and health in developing countries. CIFF was hailed as pioneering example of the 'new' breed of charity, emphasizing the importance of return on investment and demonstrable impact. In 2013 the couple divorced. Hohn chose a year later to reduce proceeds from TCI to the charity he co-founded. The *Telegraph* reported that 'instead of donating profits to the foundation, his company paid out more than £26 million in a bumper pay deal for around twenty members of staff, with Mr Hohn understood to have taken the lion's share'.[18]

The problem when a society becomes dependent on the 'crumbs that fall from the rich man's table' is that those dining at the table have no legal obligation to continue flinging morsels to their feet. Hohn's decision to withhold contributions to his charity came after a bumper year for TCI; the hedge fund generated a 47 per cent return, adding billions to its bottom line. Some of the profit came after TCI sold part of its stake in the UK's Royal Mail just three months after the government chose to sell two-thirds of the company to private investors. In October 2013, a number of City analysts warned that the £2.6 to £3.3 billion valuation was dangerously low, underestimating Royal Mail's property assets in prime places such as London and depriving UK taxpayers of revenue. After shares floated, TCI emerged as Royal Mail's largest private shareholder with a 5.8 per cent stake. Within weeks, TCI's profit on paper had grown to more than £57 million. TCI sold a portion of its stake in January 2014; shares were trading by that stage *80 per cent higher* than their original float price. UK taxpayers lost billions through the botched public offering.[19]

TCI is known for taking an aggressive stance as a minority shareholder in a range of companies in Europe and internationally (German politicians once called Hohn a 'locust'). In 2012, TCI launched a series of lawsuits against Coal India, in which 90 per cent of the shares are held by the Indian government. TCI bought a 1.1 per cent stake in the company in 2010 when the government floated 10 per cent of its shares. Almost immediately, TCI began objecting to Coal India's prices on coal, suggesting they were below international market value and therefore deprived minority shareholders of an adequate return. Coal India, one of the largest coal companies in the world, defends its pricing structure based on sector-wide need: the company insists that providing a robust supply of coal to steels mills, power companies, and other businesses is crucial to overall national economic stability and growth. TCI insisted that Coal India's price limits undermined its own profits, telling media in June 2012 that it wanted 'hundreds of millions in compensation'. It launched arbitration proceedings against India's government under the Cyprus-India bilateral protection treaty. Coal India reacted with outrage, with its management reportedly explaining to TCI staff during an earnings call in August 2013 that as the company was 90 per cent owned by the Indian government, it had a 'duty to serve the interests of the nation as a whole', rather than cater to the interests of a company which held just over 1 per cent of shares.[20]

TCI quietly sold its stake and dropped its suit in 2014 after a backlash from health and poverty activists, who had argued that TCI's battle against the Indian government was simply the latest in a long list of examples where corporations have exploited trade treaties to bully and sue national governments who try to protect the interests of their own populaces.[21] Perhaps the greatest irony of TCI's failed suit against the Indian government is that CIFF, the charity Hohn stepped away from after his divorce, focuses much of its efforts on fighting child mortality in India.

In April 2012, I spoke with Steven Hyman, a former provost at Harvard who now directs the Stanley Center for Psychiatric Research at MIT-Harvard's joint Broad Institute. Holding his hands up to mimic a puppeteer, he said that many senior scientists resent being jerked back and forth whenever a powerful donor like the Gates Foundation decides to prioritize a new area. To curb this problem, he suggested that philanthropic foundations should develop 'intellectual hedges'. By this he means funding strategies that deliberately emphasize risky or less obviously promising areas of research, in part to avoid being curtailed or blinded by the limits of one's own knowledge in the present. As he put it:

> I would say that if you recognize that you are disproportionately large, you should have an intellectual hedge. I would advise taking some proportion of the money and trying to use it in an orthogonal way. If your goal is a short-term victory over HIV by creating a vaccine, maybe you hedge by taking some of the money and allowing the very best scientists working very long-term, in human immunology or in human virology, to develop alternative strategies with no sense of an immediate pay-off.

Hyman suggests that such hedges are increasingly rare in funding environments that celebrate entrepreneurialism without realizing that entrepreneurs are subjected to different pressures than non-profit organizations.

Entrepreneurs face market pressures that force their businesses to either evolve or go under. Philanthropists don't face the same pressure, and this is both an advantage and a danger for them. To their advantage, foundations can prioritize politically sensitive areas that governments won't touch – a good example is the Gates Foundation's willingness to support contraception use in developing regions, where the US government has at best shied from funding family-planning initiatives, and at worst penalized foreign NGOs that provide such support, occasionally contributing to their demise.[22] Often, charities and foundations are the sole form of support for the world's most vulnerable populations – abused spouses, homeless children, addiction sufferers – all groups typically low on purchasing power. At the same time, the lack of market pressure can be a liability for philanthropies and non-profits. Unpopular governments face the wrath of voters. Publicly listed companies face stock devaluations. Philanthropic foundations face far fewer external checks on their operations.

'Entrepreneurs are successful precisely because of their laser-like focus and ruthlessness', Hyman suggests. 'And they're disciplined by the market. But in [the philanthropic] sector, you actually lack that external discipline. So I think you would create internal hedges with some percentage of the funds. I haven't seen that happen.'

Perhaps the most far-reaching and sobering change fostered by the new, avowedly hands-on philanthropy is that donors' bullish insistence on 'working with' grantees seems to have curtailed, if not entirely abolished, recognition of the fact that independence from a donor's self-interest is what makes a gift an actual gift.

The need to safeguard grantee independence has long been a valued principle in non-profit and academic settings. The reasons for this are obvious – or at least they should be. If a research team is forced to prioritize research or policy decisions stipulated by a donor who monitors and punishes any divergences from the donor's demands, there are no limits to a donor using philanthropy as a veneer for increasing personal or corporate profitability, something that's often detrimental to science and the public welfare.

This problem can be seen most clearly when it comes to corporate philanthropic donors who often bankroll much of the academic and clinical research in the life and medical sciences. Two examples reveal how the University of Toronto, one of Canada's most prestigious universities, threatened or dismissed academics following complaints from corporate philanthropic funders.

During the 1990s, Nancy Olivieri, a haematologist, was involved with a University of Toronto–based clinical trial to test deferiprone, a drug used in the treatment of thalassaemia major, a blood disease affecting 200,000 children a year. Treatment requires multiple blood transfusions, which can lead to cirrhosis of the liver and death as a result of haemosiderosis, a form of iron overload in the body. Deferiprone is a chelation agent used to treat haemosiderosis. During the course of a clinical trial funded by a company called Apotex to test deferiprone, Olivieri found signs of potentially lethal toxicity. Apotex threatened her with legal action when she asked to inform participants on the trial of the drug's risks.[23]

The University of Toronto, which was negotiating at time with Apotex for a multimillion-dollar donation for a new building – the largest ever corporate gift to the university at the time – refused to support Olivieri's request. Breaching her agreement with Apotex, Olivieri published her findings in the *New England Journal of Medicine*. She was dismissed from her position as director of the Hospital for Sick Children Program of Hemoglobinopathies, but later reinstated.[24]

In 2000, David Healy, an Irish psychiatrist currently working as a professor of psychological medicine in Wales, was offered a position of clinical director at the University of Toronto's Centre for Addiction and Mental Health, a leading international centre for the study of mental health. In November 2000, Healy gave a talk at the University of Toronto titled 'Psychopharmacology and the Government of Self'. During the talk, Healy discussed the limitations of clinical trials in medical research. He emphasized a widely known problem: the inability of most clinical trials to reveal rare side effects that often become visible only after a medical trial is completed and a drug is distributed clinically to hundreds of thousands or millions of users.[25]

Healy pointed to the example of selective serotonin reuptake inhibitors (SSRI) antidepressants, a class of drug that includes Eli Lilly's Prozac, one of the bestselling pharmaceutical drugs ever produced. In 2001, revenues from Prozac amounted to $2.5 billion, a full quarter of Eli Lilly's annual revenues. Touching on a controversy that had been raging since Martin Teicher, a Harvard psychiatrist, published a 1990 study in the *American Journal of Psychiatry* which outlined cases where patients experienced suicidal thoughts while on Prozac, Healy suggested that 'Prozac and other SSRIs can lead to suicide'. Eli Lilly is a major philanthropic donor to the University of Toronto, providing 52 per cent of the budget for the Mood and Anxiety Disorder Clinic that Healy was asked to head up. A few weeks after his talk, Healy's job offer was retracted.

After his dismissal, a number of news articles reported that Eli Lilly had suppressed evidence from clinical trials where patients suffered adverse reactions to Prozac. At the behest of the US Food and Drug Administration, GlaxoSmithKline, the manufacturer of Paxil, another bestselling SSRI, sent a letter to US physicians reporting that clinical trials testing Paxil had indicated a statistically significant, six-fold suicidal risk over placebo. This evidence vindicated Healy's concerns.[26] He was later awarded an undisclosed settlement by the University of Toronto, and was offered a visiting professorship at the university.

Both the Healy and Olivieri cases are seen as instrumental in reshaping policies across North America on the corporate funding of medical research. In a bid to make funding more visible, recent provisions included in the United States' 2010 Patient Protection and Affordable Care Act require pharmaceutical manufacturers to file annual reports with the government about their financial ties to individual doctors and institutions.

Conflicts of interest are, of course, not restricted to universities. They're equally visible in politics, both at the personal level, where campaign contributions are seen as buying influence, and in foreign policy, where 'tied aid' development schemes require recipient nations to spend aid dollars on products manufactured in donor countries. Tied aid is criticized as a form of protectionism, reducing the ability of recipient governments to find the best deals. When recipients are forced to buy products from a donor nation, project costs can be raised by up to 30 per cent. Tied aid schemes obviously undermine free competition, restricting the ability to find cheaper alternatives on an open market. A similar problem – the entrenchment of cronyism rather than its abolishment – may be growing more acute in the North American non-profit sector, where, rather than fostering competition, the new philanthropists are stifling it.[27]

As Jenkins's research shows, a close-knit group of donors are increasingly controlling who can apply for funds, which sorts of grants will be considered, and which strategies should be pursued by grantees. The voice of grant recipients, those with the most in-depth knowledge of the social programmes they are seeking funds for, are increasingly eclipsed in funding climates where, as Eduardo Galeano once quipped of economic development projects in Latin America, 'numbers live better than people'.[28]

Of course, given who holds the purse strings, the relationship between philanthropic donors and recipients has always been marked by disproportionate control from donors. As the saying goes, he who pays the piper calls the tune. How the new philanthropy stands out is by *celebrating* this control – and insisting that it must be strengthened further. The unequal relationship between donors and recipients has been exacerbated by donors who are, as Jenkins writes, 'becoming more paternalistic, leaning toward foundation-centred problem-solving models that disempower grantees and the communities they serve'.[29]

Philanthropists often seem genuinely baffled by a grantee's desire for a level of independence from donors. In 2012, Jim Balsillie, a co-founder of the Canada-based company Research in Motion (RIM), attempted to broker a $60 million donation to Toronto's York University to host the Centre for International Governance (CIGI), a think-tank set up by Balsillie. Thirty million was to come from Balsillie himself, and $30 million from the government of Ontario. As part of the deal, Balsillie, who has no experience in international law, wanted input into faculty hires at York's Department of Law, veto rights over job offers, and a say over curriculum development.

The conditions earned nearly universal condemnation from York's faculty. Two hundred faculty members signed a letter stating that the deal gave CIGI an 'unprecedented voice in matters of academic governance'. York University's Osgoode Law faculty, consistently ranked in the top two law departments in the country, rejected the CIGI plan with by a vote of thirty-four to seven with eight abstentions. In April 2012, York chose to turn down the donation from Balsillie.[30]

Balsillie and staff at CIGI seemed astonished by the decision. Fred Kuntz, CIGI's vice president of public affairs, blamed the failure of the deal on a 'union agenda'. Balsillie suggested in an op-ed in the *Globe and Mail,* one of Canada's leading national newspapers, that the university's decision reflected 'old-think, coupled with an unrealistic sense of entitlement to public moneys'.

'Old-think' isn't, of course, an actual word, perhaps supporting the view that individuals without any legal qualifications should not oversee curriculum development at leading law institutions.

Rightly or wrongly, strict donor oversight is celebrated as an example of the new philanthropists' passion for bringing a hands-on approach to their giving. A widely lauded example of such involvement was Gates's 2008 decision to transition from a day-to-day position at Microsoft to head the Gates Foundation. Many people would agree that increased philanthropic investment from leading entrepreneurs, both in terms of time or money, is welcome. The question is whether the practices associated with the new philanthropy – tighter control of grantee decision-making; a demand for swifter indicators of project success – might be stifling ingenuity and progress rather than engendering it.

TAXES ARE FOR LITTLE PEOPLE

During the mid-twentieth century, America's richest and poorest citizens grew more financially equal. The income share of the wealthiest 1 per cent of Americans fell from nearly 16 per cent in 1940 to 7 per cent in the 1970s. Taxes were high throughout those years – the top marginal rate was about 70 per cent. But high taxes did not thwart economic growth. Between 1947 and 1977, the economy grew, on average, 3.7 per cent each year.[31]

Since the 1970s, we've seen the reverse situation: the income share of the 1 per cent has been steadily increasing. In 2010 alone, 93 per cent of additional income created in the previous year went to the top 1 per cent of taxpayers – those with at least $352,000 in income. When looking at overall total wealth rather than incomes, the numbers are even more startling. The top 1 per cent now controls over 40 per cent of the nation's wealth. Faced with growing wealth divides, 'do we believe', as sociologist Jacob Hacker asks in conversation with Judith Warner, that 'the rich should be trusted to tithe, or should we have a society with a basic taxing-and-spending structure that ensures a modicum of economic security for all people?'[32]

Proponents of philanthrocapitalism favour a tithing option. Some suggest that they pay more than enough in 'self-tax' – willing donations to philanthropy – and that these gestures replace the need to pay any income tax at all. Speaking with the journalist Chrystia Freeland, Foster Fries, a Wyoming fund investor and deep-pocketed Republican supporter, made this point clear: 'People don't realize how wealthy people self-tax', he suggested. 'You look at Bill Gates, just gave $750 million, I think, to fight AIDS . . . It's that top 1 per cent that probably contributes more to making the world a better place than the 99 per cent. I've never seen any poor people do what Bill Gates has done. I've never seen poor people hire many people.'[33]

Wealthy individuals who disagree with Fries's views on taxation often find themselves unwelcome at TED events. In 2012, a millionaire entrepreneur and tech investor named Nick Hanauer – he made a windfall as an early Amazon investor – gave a TED presentation that expressed a starkly different view from Fries. His TED talk called for more progressive tax measures. He also lambasted the notion that entrepreneurs are society's primary 'wealth creators'. In his words, 'Anyone who's ever run a business knows that hiring more people is a capitalist's course of last resort, something we do only when increasing customer demand requires it. In this sense, calling ourselves job creators isn't just inaccurate, it's disingenuous.'

TED, which operates with the tagline 'ideas worth spreading', refused to air the video of his talk online. Asked why, TED curator Chris Anderson said the talk was 'too political' to be posted during an election year, and that 'a lot of business managers and entrepreneurs would feel insulted' by some of Hanauer's arguments.[34]

What's particularly objectionable about Anderson's suggestion that calling for more taxation 'insults' business managers and therefore should be silenced, or Fries's suggestion that wealthy individuals pay enough in 'self-tax', is the fact that a significant proportion of philanthropic donations from the rich don't contribute to the needs of the poor. Study after study has proven than only a small percentage of charitable donations from wealthy donors reach poor individuals. Most of it tends to go to alma maters or cultural institutions frequented by the wealthy. The rich also give *less* of their incomes, proportionately, than the poor do. For decades, poor Americans have donated a higher degree of their incomes than wealthier individuals. A 2001 study from the think-tank Independent Sector, which represents a coalition of non-profit and philanthropic foundations, found that households earning less than $25,000 a year gave away an average of 4.2 per cent of their incomes, while those earning more than $75,000 gave away 2.7 per cent.[35]

Before Fries's day, political leaders once sought to challenge the notion that 'self-taxation' or a patchwork of charitable foundations were sufficient for securing the basic forms of social security that characterize a prosperous society: things such as affordable healthcare, public education, and unemployment relief.

When Franklin D. Roosevelt first entered office in 1933, one of his objectives was to wrest the provision of charity from a loose network of non-profits and government agencies offering social assistance in a piecemeal fashion. His predecessor Herbert Hoover, on the other hand, was a firm believer in the power of private philanthropy. Even as the economic woes of the early 1930s grew more severe, Hoover was anxious to avoid direct governmental financial support for poor-relief efforts. His reticence was not simply laissez-faire tightfistedness as some historians have implied. Hoover *did* increase corporate taxes, and raised the top rate on personal income tax from 25 per cent to 63 per cent. But he was also the poster child for the ideals, as he put it, of 'rugged individualism' and voluntarism. Like Alexis de Tocqueville, he thought that a defining feature of American culture was the charitable impulse that seemed to characterize many American communities; their dedication to what Olivier Zunz has called 'mass philanthropy'. His reason for refusing to provide direct federal relief was simple – he didn't want charity efforts to 'dry up'.[36]

Hoover's treasury secretary was the wealthy industrialist Andrew Mellon, a firm advocate of the Carnegie approach to wealth: increase concentration at the top and hope wealth reaches the masses through charitable bequests. Before the crash of 1929, Mellon had been the architect of sweeping income tax cuts in the 1920s. At his urging, the tax rate fell from 77 to 24 per cent. His main pet peeve was tax-free government bonds. Slash income taxes, he proclaimed, and the rich will stop squirreling their money into tax-free bonds – they will invest instead in stock, generating more revenue than high taxes on personal income could ever bring.

For a brief, sparkling period, government surpluses swelled. Then speculative fever reached its doomed heights, and the coffers of government, reliant on the revenues from an overheated market, were fast depleted. Even as the market's crash crippled the government, Mellon managed to cling fiercely to his personal creed. Historian Jackson Lears suggests that 'he simply could not get the hang of the public-private divide'.[37]

Unfortunately, the charities that Mellon and Hoover assumed would sustain the country's most vulnerable citizens ended up dying out on their own, starved of funding. Between 1929 and 1932, one-third of the private charities in the US vanished. Roosevelt foresaw their demise, predicting early in the 1930s that private charity efforts would wither. Government aid, he argued, must be extended 'not as a matter of charity but as a matter of social duty'.[38]

The policies of the Hoover-Mellon alliance have been much commented in recent years, as both Democrats and Republicans advance fiscal policies reminiscent of Mellon's time in the US treasury. The economist Paul Krugman puts it bluntly: 'Mellon-style liquidationism is now the official doctrine of the G.O.P.'[39] But the recent focus on economic similarities has overshadowed attention to something less perceptible: shared ideological commitment. Like Carnegie before him and Fries today, Mellon was a firm believer in the credo that wealth concentration will inevitably foster collective benefits. The idea that we should augment the wealth of the richest 1 per cent so they have more to spend on charity is trickle-down theory in its baldest form. Bishop and Green have made this clear: 'Today', they write approvingly in *Philanthrocapitalism*, 'Carnegie would be called a believer in trickle-down economics. As he argued, it is "much better this great irregularity than universal squalor".'[40]

Their praise for Carnegie's ideas about wealth is not surprising in itself. Carnegie's writing has many fans, including Bill Gates, who reportedly consulted the *Gospel of Wealth* when establishing his own foundation. But what *is* surprising about Bishop and Green's praise for Carnegie is their *openly* approving use of the phrase 'trickle-down economics'. And not in an ironic manner.

The economist J. Kenneth Galbraith used to scornfully liken trickle-down policies to what he described as the 'horse and sparrow' theory of economic growth: the idea that 'if you feed the horses enough oats, something will pass through to the road for the sparrows'.[41] Jabs from left-leaning economists such as Galbraith have long struck a sensitive chord with those on the right. Long deployed by most commentators in a pejorative manner, no political party has ever *openly* advocated trickle-down economics – not even those assumed to have most embraced its spirit: the Republicans under Reagan or the Conservatives under Thatcher. While Thatcher once famously proclaimed 'it is our job to glory in inequality and see that talents and abilities are given vent and expression for the benefit of all' – even she stopped short of using the phrase.

It's true that many on the right explicitly align themselves with supply-side economics, a tradition in macroeconomics that suggests low taxes and reduced regulation will foster more production, consumption and economic growth. But 'trickle-down' economics has never been explicit, publicly vocalized party policy, perhaps because many on the right are canny enough to realize that making it an official doctrine would expose political incumbents to accusations of failure whenever the reality of how rarely wealth actually *does* trickle to the poorest members of society becomes obvious. The phrase has long been something of an assault weapon – it's a popular way for those on the left to deride the economic assumptions of the 1 per cent.

Until now.

Philanthrocapitalism is the proud embodiment of a once phantom theory. Its supporters, with their crowing claims of the public benefits of naked self-interest, are like the exhibitionists of laissez-faire economic theory, breezily standing in a roomful of dumbfounded observers ('What? You want me to put clothes on? There's no need to!'). Proponents unabashedly claim that trickle-down policies are our best answer for combating growing economic and social inequalities. Don't take my word for it. See for yourself at the next Skoll conference – if you can get in.

CHAPTER FOUR

Pintsized Profit-makers

The United States has a long history of using government contracts to secure private windfalls. One of the most well-known examples hails from the 1860s and 1870s, a period of massive rail expansion, when isolated towns throughout the Midwest urged officials to secure them a place on rail routes. Governmental subsidies were central to the transport boom. It was a time when shrewd investors and developers harnessed their financial and engineering acumen to win financial grants from local, state, and national governments. Securing a rail contract, the historian Kevin Phillips writes, was not 'unlike getting royal approval . . . it could be epic – the stuff of Drake, La Salle, or Lewis and Clark – or several hundred miles of swindling and larceny (the origin of the term: "railroaded")'. Phillips quotes a wartime profiteer named Jim Fisk who crowed at the time, 'You can sell anything to the government at almost any price you've got the guts to ask.'[1]

Fisk's sentiment has held throughout the following decades. It's a maxim that applies to numerous for-profit operators who got into the game after social services once provided by the state were contracted out to private companies on the assumption that increased competition would lower costs – from prisons, to care homes, to militarized law enforcement. Often, the switch to for-profit operators has not been as cost-effective as was hoped, leading even advocates of the privatization turn to question whether tax dollars are spent efficiently when the private sector is enrolled in service provision.

Today, for example, there's widespread doubt over the value of handing the US prison industry over to private contractors, a practice that was first banned in the early twentieth century and then rejuvenated during the 1980s when the government embraced private operators in a gambit to lower the costs of overcrowded prisons. Against the assumption that private competition reduces costs, the *Economist* has pointed out that most for-profit prisons cost *more* on a per-prisoner basis than public institutions do. The problem with for-profit prisons, the article concludes, is their very efficiency: when it comes to increasing inmate numbers 'private firms may well turn out to be even more efficient and effective than unions in lobbying for policies that would increase prison populations.'[2] Years ago the philosopher Michel Foucault offered a similar observation, albeit from a different ideological standpoint: 'the prison, apparently "failing", does not miss its target; on the contrary, it reaches it', he wrote in *Discipline and Punish*. 'So successful has the prison been that, after a century and a half of "failures", the prison still exists, producing the same results, and there is the greatest reluctance to dispense with it.'[3]

The 'kids for cash' scandal is perhaps the most egregious example of the negative repercussions of privatized detention centres. Two judges in Luzerne Country, Pennsylvania, received millions in kickbacks from Robert Mericle, a local owner of two for-profit juvenile detention facilities, for sentencing thousands of children to jail for minor offences. Children as young as eleven were shackled and detained. Their infractions were negligible: a thirteen-year-old was jailed for throwing a piece of steak at his mother's boyfriend; an eleven-year-old did time for calling the police after his mother locked him out of the house.[4]

But a quieter scandal has flourished almost undetected. As the 'kids for cash' scandal reminds us, making money off of the backs of children is hardly a new phenomenon. But what *is* new today is the *legal* exploitation of public education in order to earn profits out of government cash. If the expansion of the railroad was the nineteenth century's great government-funded windfall, and if the military and prison complex dominated the twentieth century, the recent embrace of for-profit primary and secondary schools may be this century's 'Henry George moment': a time when a few lone voices of dissent are out-shouted by the cacophony of private speculators proclaiming that their 'efficient' use of government contracts is for the nation's good.

George, although little known today, was in his own lifetime one of the most popular economic thinkers of the late nineteenth century. At his death in 1897, more than 100,000 mourners attended his funeral, the largest group of mourners to gather in New York City since the funeral of Abraham Lincoln more than two decades earlier. George was an avid believer in the benefits of commerce and free trade. And yet he felt that growing wealth concentration was a risk to the fair distribution of economic profits. Even in the midst of the unprecedented growth of the American economy in the years after the Civil War, 'some get an infinitely better and easier living', he observed, 'but others find it hard to get a living at all'.[5]

In his 1868 essay, 'What the Railroad Will Bring Us', George predicted that rail expansion would largely enrich a handful of developers fortunate enough to secure government contracts at the expense of the rest of the population. He proposed the idea of a 'single land tax' on any community resources rooted in nature, including the physical land increasingly dominated by long swaths of rail track; he thought this would help to tame *rentier* profits: the tendency for owners to benefit from increases in the value of a commodity regardless of any specific investment by the owner.

His stance, detailed in his masterpiece *Progress and Poverty*, won him legions of influential followers: As the economist Michael Hudson writes, Thorstein Veblen did his best to impress the importance of George's work on his fellow economists. But by Veblen's time, the discipline of 'economics was in the throes of a counter-revolution sponsored by large landholders, bankers, and monopolists . . . The new post-classical mainstream accepted existing property rights and privileges as a "given."'[6] Will later historians and economists look back at public education and see its privatization as a 'given'? If so, how did this come to pass?

Diane Ravitch, a historian and former US assistant secretary of education during the administration of George Bush Sr., has suggested that US public education is being undermined by a select group of philanthropists she calls 'the Billionaire Boys Club'. Never before, she suggests, has a single group of philanthropists had such a strong voice in reshaping national education policy. And the most influential of them all is Bill Gates.

Investing philanthropic dollars in primary and secondary education has been a goal of Bill and Melinda Gates since their earliest years as young philanthropists. On 1 January 1994, Bill married Melinda French, a former business, computer science, and engineering major at Duke University who had joined Microsoft seven years earlier. Twelve months after the wedding, Gates established a fund called the William H. Gates Foundation, financed through a gift of $94 million.

Initially run by Gates's father, William, a Seattle-based lawyer, this early foundation had two main priorities: community development in the Pacific-Northwest and improving global health. In 1997, Gates expanded into education. Through a gift of $200 million, he established a second fund, the Gates Library Foundation. The Library Foundation built on an earlier programme initiated at Microsoft – donating personal computer software to libraries. The donation of Microsoft equipment raised eyebrows among some critics. The late historian Theodore Roszak suggested that 'this doesn't even count as philanthropy. It's just seeding the market. You're simply lubricating future sales.'[7]

Until he married Melinda, Gates had been a small player in philanthropy, criticized by the general public and fellow billionaires for his perceived stinginess. In 1997, the US broadcasting mogul Ted Turner publicly chided Gates for not donating enough of his personal fortune to charity – just as today Gates and Buffett chastise fellow billionaires for their reluctance to sign the Giving Pledge, a commitment to donating at least half of one's wealth during one's lifetime.

Things changed dramatically in 2000, when the Gates Library Foundation merged with the William H. Gates Foundation and was renamed the Bill and Melinda Gates Foundation. The amount of money Gates pledged to the new foundation made the endowments of his early foundations seem like small change. He committed $16 billion in 2000, making it one of the largest foundations in the world – double the size of many of the largest foundations trailing in the Gates Foundation's wake.

A 2000 *New York Times* article by Jean Strouse described the magnitude of Gates's giving. 'Even the greatest philanthropists of the past did not give away as much in real dollars over their entire lifetimes as Gates has at the age of forty-four', Strouse reports. The article compared the sums pledged by Gates to earlier philanthropic donations. Carnegie donated about $350 million, worth about $3 billion in today's dollars. Rockefeller Sr. distributed $540 million, equivalent to $6 billion today – a figure less than a third of what Gates had committed in 2000. 'As a percentage of the gross national product', Strouse writes, 'Gates's gifts do not yet match those of his predecessors, but he is just getting started.'[8]

Less than fifteen years after Turner exhorted Gates to donate more of his personal fortune to charity, the *New York Times* ran an op-ed in which Gates was described as 'the real secretary of education'. How has Gates, at one time a negligible actor in US philanthropy, managed to wield such influence over US education?

His shift from perceived miser to one of philanthropy's most generous donors is not unusual: Henry Ford followed a similar path from the 1920s onwards. What's unusual today is the speed at which Gates's investments have taken effect. In just over two decades, policies championed by the Gates Foundation, from the introduction of private charter schools to radicalizing remuneration schemes for teachers, have transformed US education at a breakneck pace, leaving a record of controversial projects in the foundation's wake.

MEASURING SUCCESS

For centuries, education has been a pet project for philanthropists. Carnegie established over 2,500 free public libraries in the early years of the twentieth century. Julius Rosenwald, a former president at Sears Roebuck, spent much of his fortune building thousands of schools for African Americans in the years prior to 1954, when the landmark Supreme Court case *Brown v. Board of Education* declared state laws allowing separate white and black public schools unconstitutional.

The penchant for business magnates to invest in primary and secondary schooling goes back at least as far as Tudor England, when many successful business merchants founded and financed schools. Then, as now, philanthropists have taken a hands-on approach to education outcomes, demanding measurable results in exchange for their money.

In *Hard Times*, Charles Dickens satirized Victorian education philanthropists through the figure of Thomas Gradgrind, the Coketown headmaster who forces his educational charges – addressed as 'Girl number twenty' or 'Boy number five' rather than by name – to learn nothing but rote facts, berating them if they offered their own opinions about the data they're absorbing. In a notorious passage Gradgrind explains his education philosophy: 'Facts alone are wanted in life. Plant nothing else, and root out everything else. You can only form the minds of reasoning animals upon Facts: nothing else will ever be of any service to them.'

Something similar – no longer fiction this time – may be happening in the twenty-first century, in the wake of the 2002 US federal law

No Child Left Behind (NCLB). The law is based on the premise that establishing measurable goals can improve individual outcomes in education. The NCLB expanded the federal role in public education through annual testing, annual academic progress, and report cards, administered through statewide standardized tests. Every state must assess its students in maths and reading skills at select grade levels in order to receive federal school funding. Schools must demonstrate that students meet Adequate Yearly Progress (AYP) standards on annual tests. If they don't, schools face escalating corrective measures, from the replacement of entire staff to school closure.

While the act was popular at the time of its passing, receiving bipartisan support from Republicans and Democrats, the problems it generated have become more evident each year. Schools complained they received no additional funds to meet heightened proficiency requirements. The NCLB has led to incentive schemes that tend to *compound* school failure through stripping funds from low-performing schools rather than increasing resources in a way that could help test scores improve.

Test results have been repeatedly 'gamed' in infamous cheating scandals. A 2011 investigation into Atlanta test scores revealed widespread cheating by students, teachers, and administrators on standardized tests in Georgia's elementary and middle public schools. Some schools organized 'erasure parties' where teachers gathered together to correct results. In other cases, teachers obtained advance copies of tests and answer keys and gave students the answers in classrooms. The Atlanta Public School system has approximately 100 schools. Cheating was discovered in forty-four of the fifty-six city schools investigated.[9]

The Atlanta scandal followed reports of cheating in Washington, DC, Baltimore, and Philadelphia. Researchers have found that cheating scandals have tended to peak during periods when high-stakes testing such as NCLB forces schools to report improved performances measures regardless of whether resources for education delivery improve or decline, or whether wider economic trends, such as increased poverty, affect the demographic of students.

NCLB didn't inaugurate a new era of cheating – it simply exacerbated a prior trend. In the late 1980s, a number of US states began offering schools financial awards in reward for improved test scores. Scores improved rapidly. Some observers suspected results were too good to be true. They were.

A doctor practising in West Virginia, John Cannell, grew curious when his adolescent patients, many of whom were illiterate, received high scores on standardized tests. Many of his patients complained of feeling lost at school despite their impressive test results. His interest was kindled further when, in 1985, he read media reports announcing that all fifty-five West Virginia counties had tested above the national average, begging the question, 'how could all the counties in West Virginia, perhaps the poorest and most illiterate state in the union, be above the national average? Moreover, if West Virginia was above average, what state was below?'[10]

He began investigating standardized testing and found that all fifty states were testing above the national average in elementary achievement – a statistical impossibility. Cannell privately published his study, calling it the 'Lake Woebegone' report after the writer Garrison Keillor's Minnesota town where 'all the women are strong, all the men are good-looking, and all the children are above average'. Cannell's report led to front-page articles in national media. In 1990, Morley Safer of *60 Minutes* travelled to Cannell's house to film a special report, *Teacher is a Cheater*. To Cannell's surprise, nothing happened. The *60 Minutes* report provoked little public reaction or outrage.

Just over a decade later, NCLB was signed into law. Reports of cheating soared in its wake. A 2011 investigative series in *USA Today* documented 1,610 cases of standardized test-score manipulation in six states and Washington, DC between 2009 and 2010.

One elementary school in Gainesville, Florida jumped from 5 per cent maths proficiency to 91 per cent proficiency over the course of three years. As the education journalist Dana Goldstein writes, school administrators have little incentive for investigating or exposing dubious test improvements when doing so could jeopardize funding streams. Under NCLB, if a school administrator exposes cheating, the 'reward' for their honesty is the possibility of school closure and public shaming. Time after time, school administrators have chosen to countenance and encourage cheating rather than to curb it.

Even in school districts where outright test manipulation has not been detected, parents and educators fear that NCLB's emphasis on reading and mathematics proficiency has led to a 'drill and kill' approach to education delivery. Subjects such as geography, history, art, and physical education have been slashed from curriculums as schools routinely dropped subjects because they are not tested under NCLB.

After ten years of NCLB, many students who appear to outperform national standards in school tests in reading and maths still need remediation when they enter college. Arne Duncan, the secretary of education under Barack Obama, has suggested that NCLB is 'far too punitive, far too prescriptive'. The 2002 law has 'led to a narrowing of the curriculum. None of those things are good for children, for education or, ultimately, for our country.'[11]

I spoke with Dora Taylor, a parent and education activist based in Seattle who lamented the 'boot camp' atmosphere created through increased emphasis on high-stakes testing: 'They are just getting children to memorize and regurgitate back to the teacher. That's not the kind of person I want to see growing up in our society.'[12]

Among policy-makers and education experts, NCLB has very few supporters, but Bill Gates is one of the few. In a 2012 interview with the *Chronicle of Higher Education*, Gates referred to NCLB as a 'gold standard' that should be replicated at the level of higher education in order to ensure more consistency in college and university teaching and outcomes. The Gates Foundation has a policy of publishing an annual letter written by Gates on the foundation's progress and goals. In 2009, Gates suggested that, 'while not perfect, [NCLB] has forced us to look at each school's results and realize how poorly we are doing overall. It surprises me that more parents are not upset about the education their own kids are receiving.' And yet, as he would soon discover – they are.[13]

SHADOW MINISTRIES OF EDUCATION

At first, the Gates Foundation's spending on education was modest. It focused on reinventing a number of 'small schools' in order to create new prototypes that could inspire school districts to adopt the foundation's reforms. But the foundation's management grew frustrated with the lack of immediate results. 'We needed to figure out what things we could do that would flip the system', Patty Stonesifer, former CEO of the Gates Foundation, said.[14]

The Gates Foundation is now the largest philanthropic supporter of US primary and secondary education, followed by the Walton Family Foundation. The third major philanthropic player in US education is the Eli and Edythe Broad Foundation, founded in 1999 by Eli Broad, a home-building and insurance tycoon.

Their shared cause is a popular one. US philanthropic donors spend almost $4 billion on education reform each year. Only religious organizations receive more charity dollars in America than schools. Still, $4 billion is a small sum compared to the over $500 billion that it takes to run the US primary-secondary system. How can it be that a handful of donors has wielded such increased leverage over political decision-making?

The answer, as Ravitch argues, lies in a complex mixture of factors: vulnerable schools willing to reshape their policies in exchange for much-needed cash injections; bipartisan political support for recent market-based school reforms; and savvy publicity campaigns heavily funded by philanthropic organizations intent on building a grassroots base in local communities. The offer of a multimillion-dollar grant from a private foundation is often difficult to refuse, even when a school board or superintendent must reorganize their priorities as a condition of the donation.

There are some notable differences between the big three foundations above, something emphasized to me by Stefanie Sanford, a former Director of Policy and Advocacy for the US Program at the Gates Foundation. 'We have very different investment approaches', Sanford said. 'If you look at Walton, they have focused more politically. Broad does a lot of name-branded things, like their Superintendents Academy. The lion's share of our work is around teacher development, teacher improvement.'[15]

And yet, time and again, the three organizations have collaborated on the same core policies, from introducing more charter schools to emphasizing standardized testing. I'll examine these in turn.

TRUSTING IN CHARTER SCHOOLS

The concept of charter schools was first proposed in 1988 in an academic paper by Ray Budde, a professor of education administration. Budde suggested that charters could be run by collectives of teachers who could apply to run schools within districts. Each charter would set a term, and be rigorously vetted to see if it had met its goals within the specified time limit. If not, its charter would not be renewed. Also in 1988, Albert Shanker, then president of the American Federation of Teachers, floated a similar idea, suggesting that public school teachers could approach their colleagues in order to try to create small schools within larger institutions. Five years later, in 1993, Shanker renounced his support for the idea, frustrated by the fact that for-profit corporations had started to exploit charters as a promising business opportunity.[16]

Nearly twenty years later, there are more than 6,000 charter schools in the US, with the number expanding at a rate of 7.6 per cent per year since 2006. Many of them are proving to be a financial bonanza for a new crop of for-profit operations that receive state funding to educate children. Ravitch captures the wide appeal of charters succinctly: they were welcomed by free-market enthusiasts who hoped that charters would stimulate competition and raise standards; by educators on the left and the right who felt that charters would provide much-needed specialized care for vulnerable students; by entrepreneurs who sensed a business opportunity; and by various ethnic groups who sensed they might provide space for the teaching of distinctive cultural heritages. Ravitch herself was once a strong advocate, asking why parents shouldn't choose a school as easily as they choose their jobs or their shoes or their car.

The answer is – they don't. Just as the poor don't have an easy time switching cars or jobs. Turn schools into a commodity, and they become just that – a luxury of the few rather than a right of the many. Wealth buys flexibility. At the lower end of the spectrum, where consumers have little purchasing power, flexibility ebbs and choices grow scarcer.

Studies to date indicate that most charters perform either no better, or worse, than traditional public schools. Approximately four out of five – or over 80 per cent – of charter schools achieve no better test results than traditional public schools, and some are considerably worse. A meta-analysis (a study that pools existent data in order to compare multiple studies) conducted at the Center on Reinventing Public Education in Seattle found that charters were better at teaching reading and mathematics at the primary level, while high school charters fared worse in maths and reading outcomes than traditional schools. A 2012 study at the University of Minnesota found that charters in the cities of Minneapolis-St Paul ranked 7.5 per cent lower for maths and 4.4 per cent lower for reading than elementary public schools.

Two specific factors help to account for the success of the charters that *do* earn outstanding results: increased resources and the freedom to send low-performing students back to traditional secondary and elementary schools. A 2008 study by Mark Schneider and Jack Buckley found that Washington, DC charter schools enrol a far smaller number of children with special needs than traditional schools. Twenty-eight of the thirty-seven charters they looked at had a smaller proportion of English-language learners than DC public schools. Buckley, a former Deputy Commissioner at the National Center for Education Statistics, and Schneider, a visiting scholar at the American Enterprise Institute, are hardly anti-choice sceptics. Prior to 2008 they published a supportive study on charter schools, revealing that a substantially higher number of parents reported feeling positive about charter school teachers, principals, and facilities than about traditional schools.

But after examining data on DC schools going back a decade, they found that charter school students are not outperforming students in traditional public schools. Rather, the quality of charter school education often varies widely from school to school. They also found that parent enthusiasm for charter schools often starts out strong but fades over time.[17]

High-performing charters often spend far more money per child than traditional schools – often thanks to philanthropic support. Bill Gates has been an outspoken supporter of the charter school movement. In 2010, he travelled to a number of film festivals to help publicize *Waiting for 'Superman'*, a pro–charter school documentary. At the Sundance festival, Gates told media, 'Many of these high schools are terrible, and this film, *Waiting for "Superman"* by Davis Guggenheim, which I have a very minor part in, tells this story in a brilliant way.'[18]

Guggenheim's documentary follows the efforts of working- and middle-class parents struggling to secure a place for their children at well-performing charter schools. In cases where a charter school is oversubscribed, placements are generally allocated through a lottery system. These lotteries tend to be dramatic affairs, taking place in annual shows of pageantry in school auditoriums dotted across the nation.

'Tonight, if you win this lottery, treat that as if your life depends on it – because it does', announced the director of MATCH charter school in Boston during one recent lottery. A tiny number of children hear their names called at such events. Most do not. One parent remarked to media at MATCH's 2010 lottery, 'Why are we put in the situation of the education of your child depending on the flip of a coin?'[19]

Since hitting theatres, Guggenheim's film has faced criticism for what some say is a one-sided portrayal of US public education. Throughout the film, Guggenheim continually emphasizes the dire state of US public schools, declaring that students are lagging far behind their counterparts in other nations in literacy and numeracy. These claims are at once inflated and too vague: they both exaggerate the decrepitude of US public education, and fail to emphasize the fact that poor student performance is linked to external factors such as poverty.[20]

Gates and Guggenheim share the belief that teaching performance is crucial to a student's success or failure. 'Repeat after me', Guggenheim urges in a recent op-ed article, '*We can't have great schools without great teachers.*'

'Every teacher I followed', he goes on, '[knows that] it's not about the latest debate: The curricula. Or class size. It's not about the reform du jour. It's simple. It's all about great teachers!'[21] He is right about the value of great teachers. A number of studies have shown that the quality of a teacher is highly influential on student achievement, accounting for about 10–20 per cent of outcomes. What Guggenheim doesn't mention is that factors *outside* a school matter a great deal more than teachers. Published in 1966, a government study known as the Coleman Report first provided evidence that external factors such as a parent's income and their own educational background, neighbourhood environment, and access to healthcare tend to account for two-thirds of a student's performance in school. Studies conducted since have consistently confirmed this ratio. Recent research by Dan Goldhaber, an economist based at the

University of Washington, backs up the Coleman Report, showing that approximately 60 per cent of student achievement can be explained by factors outside of school.[22]

Gates has suggested that class sizes should be *increased* in order to allow effective teachers to reach more students. 'We know that of all the variables under a school's control, the single most decisive factor in student achievement is excellent teaching', Gates writes in an article for the *Washington Post*. 'One approach is to get more students in front of top teachers by identifying the top 25 per cent of teachers and asking them to take on four or five more students. Part of the savings could then be used to give the top teachers a raise.'[23]

Gates himself attended Lakeside, a private school in the Seattle area where students average about sixteen per class. Many charter schools emphasize the small size of their own classes as an enticement to parents. The Harlem Children's Zone charter schools, one of the models lauded in the *Superman* documentary, boast small class sizes, largely thanks to private philanthropic donations that enable the charter schools to spend about $16,000 per student in the classroom each year, plus thousands of dollars in out-of-class spending on field trips and social services – an admirable programme but not one easily replicable across the nation.[24]

New York doyen Michael Bloomberg has repeatedly stressed that class size does not matter. The average number of students per classroom in New York public schools ballooned during his tenure as mayor. In a speech given at MIT in 2011, Bloomberg said that in his ideal world, he would fire half the city's teachers and pay those left standing twice as much to teach classes double the current size.

Gates's, Bloomberg's and Guggenheim's assertions about class size appear to be based on scant evidence. Countless variables, from growing child poverty to changes in curriculum, can affect achievement, something that makes it hard for researchers to isolate the effect of class size. As in most areas of social policy, the evidence is unclear and often mixed. While existent studies are by no means conclusive, the majority of them indicate a *positive* correlation between small classes and increased achievement, particularly for younger students.[25]

Actions tend to speak louder than words. Bloomberg's daughters attended Spence, where there are ten to fifteen girls per classroom. Writing in the *New York Times*, the columnist Michael Powell lists the institutions where many of New York's elite educate their children: Trinity, Dalton, Riverdale, Horace Mann. All charge $35,000 or more per year, and classes rarely exceed twelve in the lower grades.[26]

The journalist Joanne Barkan had suggested that the 'mantra-like' claim that US students are trailing their international peers lacks evidence. As she writes, two of the three major international tests on students – the Progress in International Reading Literacy Study and the Trends in International Math and Science Study – break down student outcomes according to different poverty levels. The 2006 results indicated that students in US schools where the poverty rate was less than 10 per cent came out first in science, first in reading, and third in math. As the poverty rate grew, student outcomes, not surprisingly, began to sink compared to other nations. Public schools in affluent areas routinely produce some of the world's highest performing high school students on numeracy and literacy tests. The problem, Barkan suggests, is not public schools. It is poverty.

In recent years, a profound change has taken place in policy debates on US education. A once 'noisy and impassioned national conversation about how best to combat poverty', education writer Paul Tough suggests, 'has faded almost to silence'. Tough is an education specialist who has written positively of charters such as the Harlem Children's Zone. He believes charters are an excellent fit for many children, partly because they often invest more per pupil than typical public schools. But charters alone can't solve deepening poverty levels. In the 1960s, poverty was a key focus of public intellectuals and policy-makers, drawing 'smart, ambitious young people in Washington' to work at Lyndon Johnson's Office of Economic Opportunity. Today, things are different. Barack Obama, who spent a large part of his early career battling poverty as a community organizer in Chicago, has, while in office, 'spent less time talking publicly about poverty than any of his recent Democratic predecessors'.[27]

Strangely, the greater the debilitating toll poverty takes on the lives of America's schoolchildren, the more taboo discussions of poverty have become. Pointing out the link between poverty and education is deemed an 'excuse' seized on by teachers to exonerate their poor performance. Poverty becomes, literally, inexcusable – not because reformers want it eradicated, but because of the opposite: they refuse to see it addressed. The topic of poverty is quietly ignored, just as politics or religion are ignored in polite company.

Why is this? One answer is simple, if cynical. As a recent article in the *New York Times* suggests, if the wealthy financiers were to admit that a 'substantial part of the problem was poverty and not bad teachers, the question would be why people like them are allowed to make so much when others have so little'.[28]

Another reason has less to do with avoiding culpability than with seizing opportunity. Many financiers have grasped something even less mentionable in polite company than poverty. That is the fact that poor kids *are* themselves the opportunity. Easy cash is being generated off of the backs of children subjected to weeks of standardized testing, forced to transfer institutions in the wake of school closures, or lured to 'online' schools through canny advertising gimmicks. A closer look at the online school movement illustrates how tax dollars and philanthropic donations are being used to fuel huge windfalls in the private sector.

One of the largest cash cows in the K–12 education market is the growth of online schools. These are primary and secondary schools that have no bricks-and-mortar classrooms, and minimal physical interaction between teachers and students, but offer accredited courses in the same way as traditional institutions. Most schooling is offered via distance learning, administered over the internet. Today, there are over a dozen major for-profit companies running online public elementary and secondary high schools in the US, serving hundreds of thousands of cyberpupils. Often these schools produce dismal student outcomes. At Agora Charter School in Wayne, Pennsylvania, for example, 60 per cent of students are behind grade level in math, a third of them do not graduate on time, and hundreds of pupils withdraw within months of enrolling. Despite the high withdrawal rate, Agora made about $72 million in income in 2011. Agora is managed by K12, a company founded by William Bennett, a former education secretary who suggested that setting up more online schools could help socially shy or bullied children to learn in the privacy of their homes. With investments from Michael Milken, K12 was soon pitching itself to state funders as a cost-effective alternative to public education, reaping vast profits in the process.[29]

Today, K12 receives about $5,500 to $6,000 per student from state and local governments. Many online schools run aggressive recruiting campaigns, spending taxpayer money on vans, billboards, and radio ads geared at enticing more students – a practice condemned by critics such as Jack Wagner, Pennsylvania's state auditor general, who has suggested that it is 'unfair for the taxpayer to be paying for additional expenses, such as advertising'. Tax dollars also help to subsidize K12's government lobbying efforts, including campaigns to introduce legislation easing restriction against for-profit education at the state level.[30]

Teachers at online schools – some of whom manage more than 250 students – have told media that they're often pressured to pass students who do little work. Students who repeatedly fail to hand in assignments are kept indefinitely on rosters, allowing K12 to continue collecting state funds for their enrolment. Virtual schools are rife with 'ghost' pupils, students who are enrolled on the books but whose presence often can't be verified during state investigations into attendance records.

Just as investigative reports into the thriving for-profit prison industry in the US have shed light on the financial incentives leading prison operators to deliberately keep incarceration rates high, for-profit online schools have an interest in padding official enrolment numbers – regardless of whether pupils show up or not. The ever-fluctuating cycle of high enrolment and quick drop-out patterns is known as the 'churn rate'. The more kids churned through the system, the higher the profits.[31]

One of the most remarkable examples of for-profit schools receiving ongoing taxpayer support despite a history of failure hails from Ohio, where over half the charter schools in the state are run by management companies operating on for-profit basis. The largest virtual provider, the Electronic Classroom for Tomorrow (ECOT), received approximately $64 million in state funding, a considerable proportion of which goes towards the salary of ECOT's founder and CEO William Lager, a former office supply executive with no experience in education. He earns about $3 million per year. The average teacher salary at ECOT is $34,000.

ECOT's graduation rates rarely exceed 40 per cent per year. In 2001, barely half of ECOT's third-grade students received a score of proficient or better on state reading tests, and only 49 per cent scored proficient in math, compared with state averages of 80 per cent and 82 per cent. In 2001, a year after ECOT was established, an investigation by Ohio state auditors found that while the state had paid ECOT to educate more than 2,000 students during one month, only seven children had logged on to ECOT's computer system. Stephanie Mencimer from *Mother Jones* reports that state auditors were unable to determine 'whether the rest of its student body even existed'.[32]

For companies such as K12 and ECOT, the primary vehicle for influencing state policy is the American Legislative Exchange Council (ALEC), an organization that has introduced dozens of model bills on digital education adopted by state legislatures across the US in recent years. ALEC is a registered charity managed by a rotating board of individual state legislators who pay $50 a year to belong to the organization. The majority of the organization's funding comes from its 200-plus private-sector members, whose annual dues of $7,000 to $25,000 accounted for most of ALEC's $7 million budget in 2010.

Many corporations contribute far more. Although ALEC keeps its record of donations secret, a leaked 2010 tax return obtained by the *New York Times* indicated that AT&T, Pfizer, and Reynolds American each contributed $130,000 to $398,000. Microsoft is a member of ALEC's Telecommunications and Information Technology Task Force. The Gates Foundation has contributed over $350,000 to ALEC for initiatives to support 'teacher effectiveness'.

ALEC's main role is to act as a forum for legislators and private-sector members to collaborate in writing draft legislation which the corporations would like to become law. Nearly 2,000 state legislators belong to ALEC. They are provided with talking points and directives on how to vote on hundreds of bills focused on public education, labour laws, and immigration policy. ALEC members deny they are a lobbying organization – they insist their organization is non-partisan. But a quick scan of the nearly 1,000 model bills it drafts each year suggests mostly conservative causes, such as legal protections for corporations against product liability or fraud litigations, and efforts to repeal minimum wage laws.[33]

Members of ALEC's education committee include Foundation for Excellence in Education, an advocacy organization founded in 2008 by former Florida governor Jeb Bush. In October 2011, his organization funded the expenses of Stephen Bowen, Maine's education commissioner at the time, to travel to a California-based summit on virtual education. Shortly after his trip to California, Bowen began pushing aggressively for reforms that would enable firms such as K12 and Connections Education (a subsidiary of Pearson, a titan of the education publishing industry) to open full-time virtual charter schools in Maine.[34] In December 2014, in a surprise announcement, Bush announced he was stepping down from the foundation he founded six years earlier. It was a decision made two weeks after declaring he was strongly considering a run for president in 2016.

Since 2008, the Gates Foundation has been a top donor to Bush's foundation, offering it over $5 million in grants. Through its support of virtual schooling, the Gates Foundation has helped position online technology giants such as Pearson and Microsoft to profit from the for-profit schooling bonanza. In July 2012, as journalist Stephanie Simon reported, a group of 100 financiers met at New York's University Club for an event billed as 'private equity investing in for-profit education companies'. Rob Lyttle from Parthenon Group, a Boston consulting firm, extolled the potential of the for-profit education publishing industry. 'You start to see entire ecosystems of investment opportunity lining up', Lyttle told the group. 'It could get really, really big.'[35]

It already is. In some states, such as Michigan, about 80 per cent of charter schools are run by for-profit Education Management Organizations (EMOs). Rupert Murdoch, one of the largest investors in online education, has predicted that the digital education market could grow to $500 billion in upcoming years. He recently bought Wireless Generation, a US educational technology firm, for $360 million, telling investors he hoped to see a time when News Corp's media content was transmitted directly to pupils' terminals.

Teaming up with Murdoch's News Corp, the Gates Foundation supplied the bulk of funding for a $100 million electronic database, launched in 2013, that stored the personal information of millions of secondary and primary students, including their names, addresses, test scores, personal learning difficulties, and in some cases, social security numbers, career goals, and extracurricular activities. The database was run by inBloom Inc., an organization that provided the data to for-profit groups contracted to supply educational materials to schools. Parents were not consulted about inBloom's release of their children's names and addresses to third-party contractors. Many expressed fury over the project, penning letters of protest to school boards across the country. One by one, states such as Georgia and New York began pulling their support for the initiative. In 2014, inBloom announced that the operation was closing. The $100 million initiative ended in failure.[36]

SMALL IS GOOD . . . OR NOT?

In 2005, Gates gave a public speech pronouncing traditional high schools 'obsolete'. The solution, he argued, lay in community-based 'small schools' that would replace the impersonal bureaucracy of traditional schools with more targeted attention to individual learners.

From 2000 to 2008, the Gates Foundation invested $2 billion in small schools, helping to establish 2,602 schools across the US, affecting a total of nearly 800,000 students. Almost as abruptly as the money was injected, it was withdrawn, leading a number of schools to close. In 2008, Bill and Melinda invited a number of prominent figures in the field of education to their home in Seattle. They made a surprise announcement: their small schools investments had failed to produce the results they had hoped for. Consequently, the foundation would now increase its focus on other initiatives: better data collection on teacher effectiveness, the introduction of performance-based teacher pay, and strengthening national standardized testing for students.[37]

In an interview with the *Wall Street Journal*, Gates explained that the small schools had failed to improve college acceptance rates to a degree that he had hoped for. 'The overall impact of the intervention, particularly the measure we care most about – whether you go to college – it didn't move the needle much . . . We didn't see a path to having a big impact, so we did a *mea culpa* on that.'[38]

A number of media reports suggested that Gates had simply 'misread the numbers' on the effectiveness of small schools. Wharton School statistician Howard Wainer suggested that Gates's early belief – that small schools are overrepresented among the nation's high achievers – might have stemmed from his misreading of a statistical anomaly: small schools are overrepresented among the highest *and* the lowest achievers. The reason? The smaller the school, the more likely its test results can be skewed by a few outstanding students or a few very poor students at either end of the spectrum.[39]

Advocates of small schools insist that the reality is more complex. Small schools *can* and do achieve excellent results, they claim. As they see it, the failure of the Gates Foundation's policies stemmed from how they were administered, not from some intrinsic deficiency in the small-school model itself. 'In district after district, the foundation's arbitrary goals and timelines began to clash with those of local reformers and educators', writes Michael Klonsky, a well-known educator and activist whose early writing on small schools helped invigorate the small schools and charter movements. 'In some districts, such as Cleveland and San Francisco, the threat of a Gates invasion led to the departure of veteran superintendents.'[40]

In Colorado, the Gates Foundation tried to develop three so-called Learning Communities within Denver's Manual High School. Perhaps because of the need to uphold a successful, replicable model that could be rolled out on a national scale, the foundation insisted on its own tight timeline for changes to take root. Teachers and parents' groups – given little notice of the changes or a say in how to implement them – fought the reforms.

The funding was eventually pulled, and Manual High was shut down. Its former students were shipped throughout the city. Three years after its closing, researchers at the University of Colorado found that only 52 per cent of students who were juniors when Manual was closed went on to graduate. The school previously had a 68 per cent graduation rate. Historically, about 6 per cent of Manual students dropped out. After it was closed, the chance that a displaced student would drop out entirely rose to 17 per cent.[41]

'There was actually some pretty good evidence that small schools could be a good strategy', Julie Woestehoff, the executive director of

Parents United for Responsible Education, suggested to me. 'The failure of the Gates small-school investments had more to do with their ignoring the culture of a school, or refusing to give an opportunity for the community and teachers in the school to be part of the change.'

Was funding pulled at Manual and elsewhere because small schools simply weren't as promising as the foundation had hoped, as Bill and Melinda suggested to their guests in 2008? Or did the foundation's own poor management of its grants thwart the very objectives it sought? A final nagging question: was the decision to pull funding a contributing factor to poor outcomes at the schools? By emphasizing some policies over others, those policies inevitably receive more money, media attention, and political support than others. The policies the Gateses champion often succeed or fail *because* they are pouring extra money into them or withdrawing funding prematurely, not necessarily because they have intrinsic merits or deficiencies. When the foundation pulls the plug on a programme, kids lose out. In the case of small schools, some school districts had less than three years to show significant improvement before the foundation started signalling a change in direction, slashing funding at the very time when many schools felt they needed more resources to stay the course.

'In the area of education', William Schambra, of the Hudson Institute's Bradley Center for Philanthropy and Civic Renewal, based in DC, said to me, 'I'm a down-the-line conservative. I'm a believer in school choice and I'm a believer in charters. I'm a believer in anything that can break the monopoly of public sector unions in the field of education.'

The problem with the Gates Foundation's increased role in public education, he went on, is that large-scale efforts to reengineer education systems end up circumscribing rather than expanding choice at the community level. The Gates Foundation's top-down approach thwarts community groups from having a voice in local decision-making. 'Last week I was in Milwaukee', Schambra said. 'They spent

$15 million of Gates money in Milwaukee . . . For Gates, it's fine to say, well, that was an interesting experiment and it didn't work out and walk away from it. But for Milwaukee, that's real money, and those are real children that we're talking about . . . For the folks in Seattle it's an "oopsie", but for the folks in Milwaukee it's a major disruption.'

Similar frustration has flared up over the Common Core initiative, involving the implementation of national reading and maths standards for primary and secondary school children. The Gates Foundation played a central role in bringing the standards to fruition. Spending over $233 million to back the standards, the foundation dispersed money liberally to both conservative and progressive interest groups. The two major teachers' unions, the National Education Association and the American Federation of Teachers, each received large donations, as did the US Chamber of Commerce. Gates himself suggested that a benefit of the standards is that they open avenues towards increasing digital learning. In 2014, Microsoft announced it was partnering with Pearson to load Pearson's Common Core classroom material onto Microsoft's Surface tablet. Previously, the iPad was the classroom frontrunner; the Pearson partnership helps to make Microsoft more competitive.

Republicans, despite initially backing the guidelines, became frustrated by the imposition of a federal initiative at the state level. Common Core was dubbed Obamacore, and numerous Tea Party satellites rallied in opposition to the new guidelines, decrying the loss of local autonomy. The pedagogical approach of the standards has also been much mocked: in addition to (some say in lieu of) imparting traditional skills such as division, multiplication, subtraction, and addition, students are asked to show an understanding of how numbers correspond with each other. Some parents report blood-curdling efforts trying to help six-year-olds with homework that directs children to demonstrate an understanding of four different ways to add numbers together. Facing the growing uproar from parents, a number of states passed laws pulling their constituencies out of the Common Core standards.[42]

At least one foundation that used philanthropic grants to profit from Common Core has faced a serious legal penalty. In 2013, New York Attorney General Eric Schneiderman announced that his office had obtained a $7.7 million settlement with Pearson Charitable Foundation after the non-profit was found to have misused its charitable funds in a manner intended to generate revenue for its corporate parent organization. 'The law on this is clear: Non-profit foundations cannot misuse charitable assets to benefit their affiliated for-profit corporations', Schneiderman stated in a press release announcing the settlement. In a longer report, Schneiderman determined that Pearson executives intended to use its charitable arm to win endorsements and grants from a 'prominent foundation' in the hopes that the sanction of the 'prominent foundation' would 'enhance Pearson's reputation with policy-makers and the education community'. While unnamed, the *New York Times* and other outlets reported that the foundation was believed to be the Gates Foundation.[43]

In 2007, the Gates Foundation appointed Vicki Phillips to the role of director of education. A former secretary of education for the state of Pennsylvania, one of Phillips's first moves was to ask Thomas Kane, an economist based at Harvard University, to head up the foundation's data and research group.

Kane had earlier published an academic study with a stark conclusion: his research suggested that teachers ranked in the top 25 per cent four years in a row in the cohort he examined were gifted 'enough to close the black-white test score gap'. Kane and his co-authors offered a severe policy recommendation: any teacher who ranked in the bottom quarter after their first two years of teaching should be fired.[44]

Kane and Phillips teamed up to develop the Gates Foundation's next major education strategy: reshaping America's teaching system by developing better tools to track teacher performance and make it easier to fire poor performers. In 2007, just before the first Democratic presidential candidates' debates, the Gates and Broad foundations announced that they would be teaming up on a $60 million campaign aimed at convincing both candidates to adopt three key reforms if elected: introducing more consistent curriculum standards across the nation, lengthening the school year and day, and introducing pay-for-performance targets for teachers.

As Joanne Barkan reports, it was the most expensive single-issue campaign initative in a presidential race to date. And one of the most effective. After Obama was elected, he appointed Arne Duncan to lead the Department of Education. Duncan's core policies were identical to the reforms championed by Gates and Broad: the creation of more charter schools and the introduction of performance pay.

Although Duncan has criticized No Child Left Behind for being too restrictive, within a short period he introduced policies that have entrenched the standardized testing regimes fostered through NCLB. His administration's first major initiative was Race to the Top (RTTT), a stimulus package that earmarked $4.3 billion in federal money for state education. The stimulus package came with a catch. States needed to compete for RTTT money by introducing statewide proposals for education reform. To be eligible, states needed to ensure certain criteria were met, such as introducing and passing state legislation that would allow the use of student test scores to determine a teacher's effectiveness.

Cash-starved states jumped through the hoop: they swiftly repealed legislative limits on the number of charters permitted. A number of select states quickly found themselves favoured by an unexpected bonus: the prospect of extra money from the Gates Foundation to help make their application particularly competitive. The foundation looked at each state's reform policies and chose fifteen favourites, offering them up to $250,000 to pay for consultants to help write their application. Those that *weren't* selected were not impressed. As Barkan writes, they cried foul play, pointing out that the foundation's money gave some states an unfair advantage over others.

The foundation changed tack, stating that any state was eligible as long as it met the foundation's eight reform criteria. These criteria, circulated on a checklist, included statements such as 'Does your state have policies that prohibit the linkage and/or usage of student achievement data in teacher evaluations?', and 'Does the state grant teacher tenure in fewer than three years (Answer must be 'no' or the state should be able to demonstrate a plan to set a higher bar for tenure).' The Gates Foundation's spending on education may be a small drop compared to federal spending. But well-timed strategies such as this make it possible for an exclusive group of benefactors to influence exactly where and how federal dollars are spent.

Few disagree that teachers should be evaluated and held accountable for their own performance. The question is how to best evaluate them. The Gates Foundation has been adamant in the past that one of the best ways to measure teachers is through student test scores. It has spent hundreds of millions funding grassroots organizations that lobby states to use 'value-added modelling' (VAM) in order to determine a teacher's value. VAM is a statistical measure that aims to identify a teacher's contribution to student learning through isolating a teacher's *individual* effect on a student's test results. This is very hard to do as it's difficult to know whether external factors, such as poverty or malnutrition, are affecting a child's school performance. But VAM testing enthusiasts are confident that they have developed reliable statistical tools to quantify a teacher's individual abilities in the classroom.

In recent years, the Gates Foundation has funded the $45 million Measures of Effective Teaching (MET) study, which tracks 3,000 teachers in cities across the country.

In 2010, preliminary results from the MET study were released. The results were hailed by media as providing the 'strongest evidence to date of the validity of "value-added" analysis.[45] But this finding was contested. Jesse Rothstein, a professor of public economics at the University of California, Berkeley, and former chief economist at the US Department of Labor, published a re-analysis of the MET results. He found that 'many teachers whose value-added for one test is low are in fact quite effective when judged by the others', and that 'interpreted correctly . . . the results of the MET study undermine rather than validate value-added-based approaches to teacher evaluation'.[46]

A separate 2010 study commissioned by the US Department of Education found that value-added estimates often lead to a considerably high level of random error, misclassifying teachers *up to 26 per cent of the time* – a rather worrying figure for teachers faced with the prospect of their jobs depending on their VAM results.[47]

The dire repercussions of high-stakes teacher testing became clear in August 2010, when the *LA Times* published a 'value-added' analysis of the names and test results of every teacher in the Los Angeles Unified School District. Rigoberto Ruelas, a teacher described as devoted to his students by his family and peers, regularly tutoring students before and after school, received a score of 'less effective than average'. Less than a month later, Ruelas's body was found in Angeles National Forest. His death was ruled a suicide. Family members said that Ruelas's low VAM score had severely upset him. Days after his death, a group of students, teachers, and parents from Miramonte Elementary School marched to the *LA Times* building demanding that Ruelas's name be stricken from the paper's database. For the family of Ruelas, learning that value-added models often misclassify *over a quarter* of individual teachers can only have fuelled their anger.

Was Ruelas's death a casualty of faulty statistics? How many more teachers may see their reputations or their sense of dignity threatened by an obsession with faulty metrics?

Following the lead set by the *LA Times*, similar disclosures of teacher test scores have taken place in other states. In New York, after the city's value-added numbers were published, the *New York Post* ran an article and an accompanying photo of a Queens teacher, labelling him 'the city's worst'. Was the teacher a poor performer, or was he simply one of the 26 per cent of teachers misclassified by VAM scores?

To his credit, Gates has objected to the public shaming of teachers. In the wake of a New York State Court of Appeals decision permitting individual teacher assessments to be published in public databases, he wrote a *New York Times* editorial calling the court's ruling a 'big mistake'. He added: 'unfortunately some education advocates in New York, Los Angeles, and other cities are claiming that a good personnel system can be based on ranking teachers according to their "value-added rating" . . . at Microsoft, we created a rigorous personnel system, but we would never have thought about using employee evaluations to embarrass people, much less publish them in a newspaper.'[48]

Gates's editorial is damningly critical of VAM. Oddly, however, he does not acknowledge that during the 2000s, his foundation was by far one of the largest philanthropic supporters of research championing VAM techniques. As David Labaree points out, 'The Bill and Melinda Gates Foundation has plunged $355 million into the effort to measure teacher effectiveness. Grounded in the value-added approach, this effort is using analysis of videos of teaching in individual classrooms to establish which teacher behaviours are most strongly associated with the highest value-added scores for students.'[49]

Gates also doesn't mention that his foundation is a major supporter of Stand for Children, which received $5.2 million in Gates Foundation grants between 2005 and 2010, or the NewSchools Venture Fund, which has received over $30 million in funding. Both advocacy groups are at the forefront of a national movement dedicated to passing state legislation requiring teachers to be evaluated through value-added measures. At a speech at the Toronto International Film Festival in 2010, Gates stressed that his foundation was 'investing in building these evaluation systems'.[50]

Gates's reference to Microsoft's personnel system raises an important question. By the admission of both Gates himself and Jeff Raikes, the Gates Foundation's former CEO, the foundation often emulates strategies developed at Microsoft. But is adopting Microsoft HR strategies advisable for improving teacher effectiveness in American public schools?

In 2012, *Vanity Fair* published an article on 'Microsoft's Lost Decade' – an investigative piece by the journalist Kurt Eichenwald on how the technology company lost its financial edge over companies such as Apple. Once boasting a market capitalization of $510 billion in December 2000, by June 2012 the company had slid to a market cap of $249 billion. Apple, meanwhile, has grown from a valuation of $4.8 billion to $541 billion over the same period. Halfway through the article, in paragraphs that are eerily familiar to those following current debates on teacher evaluations, Eichenwald describes the lynchpin of Microsoft's personnel system: stack ranking.

> Every current and former Microsoft employee I interviewed – *every one* – cited stack ranking as the most destructive process inside of Microsoft, something that drove out untold numbers of employees. The system – also referred to as 'the performance model', 'the bell curve', or just 'the employee review' – has, with certain variations over the years, worked like this: every unit was forced to declare a certain percentage of employees as top performers, then good performers, then average, then below average, then poor . . . For that reason, executives said, a lot of Microsoft superstars did everything they could to avoid working alongside other top-notch developers, out of fear that they would be hurt in the rankings. And the reviews had real-world consequences: those at the top received bonuses and promotions; those at the bottom usually received no cash or were shown the door.[51]

Sound familiar? The system bears a strong resemblance to the Gates Foundation's Thomas Kane's suggestion for teachers: any teachers ranking in the bottom quarter of a pre-established cohort after their first two years teaching should be let go.

Most teachers, parents, and policy-makers agree that teacher performance needs to be monitored, with persistently poor performers subject to penalty or dismissal. But are policies grounded in Microsoft-style hiring and firing practices – practices widely denigrated by many CEOs outside Microsoft – the best model for school districts to emulate?

Barkan has described the proactive steps that school districts in Toledo (since 1981), Cincinnati (since 1985), and Montgomery County (since 2001) – to name just a few districts – have taken towards identifying teacher effectiveness. They each implemented 'Peer Assistance and Review' (PAR) systems, consisting of two features: a panel made up of seven to twelve teachers and administrators, and a corps of Consulting Teachers (CTs). CTs observe teachers at work, receiving extra pay during their term. The advantages, Barkan suggests, have been considerable: more thorough assessments of teachers, speedier removal of ineffective teachers, and a chance for the best teachers to share advice in a constructive environment. Despite this, Maryland, one of the winners of Duncan's RTTT competition, moved to implement a teacher-evaluation programme that threatened to destroy Montgomery County's proven PAR system.[52] Why? Because, in line with the terms of RTTT, Maryland implemented a system where a great percentage of a teacher's performance is judged through value-added techniques.[53] Eventually, Montgomery County chose to decline to participate in the Race to the Top initiative.

In 2012, Jeff Raikes, CEO of the Gates Foundation from 2008 until 2014, reiterated Gates's concern over teacher shaming, telling media there is a 'perception that what we believe in is a complete focus on standardized-test–based accountability, and that couldn't be further from the truth . . . we need to dial up our message on that.'[54] Two years later, the Gates Foundation issued a press release from the foundation's director of education, Vicki Phillips, reporting that it now *supports* calls for a two-year moratorium on linking perceptions of teacher performance to standardized test scores. Phillips wrote: '[we] agree with those who've decided that assessment results should not be taken into account in high-stakes decisions on teacher evaluation or student promotion for the next two years.'[55]

Let's step back a minute and remember that performance-based teacher pay (with performances linked to rises or falls in student test scores) and the introduction of *more* standardized testing were initiatives that the Gateses vowed to support when they invited 100 education figures to Seattle in 2008 following the withdrawal of their investment in small schools. Seven years later they're once again distancing themselves from initiatives they themselves brought to fruition.

It *is* admirable that the Gateses are willing to change their minds when the evidence suggests they should. They don't seem afraid to admit their mistakes, and that is a rare and commendable trait. The opposite reaction – a stubborn refusal to admit that well-intentioned ideas can reap unplanned negative consequences – would be far more troubling. And yet, the education reforms driven by the Gates Foundation are now entrenched. For many teachers and students, their recent handwringing over the perils of high-stakes testing has come a little too late.

A curious aspect of the Gates Foundation's role in public education is that, partly thanks to the positive press attention that the foundation both courts and receives, the foundation is widely hailed as an organization driven by results. It is perceived as an organization that identifies areas of need and works tirelessly to achieve these ends through targeted grants. There's no shortage of media or academic articles that help to reify this belief. A 2015 article in *Maclean's* suggested, for example, that Bill Gates's 'tight focus on concrete measures and defined results' distinguishes his work from earlier, government-sponsored aid and welfare programmes.[56]

The most influential academic to emphasize this perception of the foundation is Peter Singer, a controversial Australian philosopher who has praised Gates and Warren Buffett for being the 'most effective altruists in history.' During a TED talk in 2013, Singer pointed to a screenshot and said, 'This is the website of the Bill and Melinda Gates Foundation, and if you look at the words on the top right-hand side, it says, "All lives have equal value". That's the understanding, the rational understanding of our situation in the world that has led to these people being the most effective altruists in history, Bill and Melinda Gates, and Warren Buffett.'[57]

When it comes to public education in the US, there's little indication yet that many of the initiatives the foundation has spearheaded have in fact been positive for students. Despite a history of policy reversals and failed efforts, the foundation continues to be upheld as an exemplary and uniquely results-oriented organization. And there's nothing stopping the foundation from itself promoting that perception of its work, a problem that irks teachers. One former teacher, Anthony Cody, summarized this concern clearly in an interview with Valerie Strauss of the *Washington Post*:

> I have found it remarkable that an education reform project built around the concept of "accountability" has no mechanism, no means by which we, the public, can hold its sponsors accountable. We have "bad teachers" who must be held accountable. Schools and students that must be held accountable. But Bill Gates himself? Who holds him and his employees accountable for the devastating effects their reforms have had?[58]

The answer is: no one. As Cody points out, while teachers are increasingly threatened with job loss for their own perceived failures, there is no similar penalty for the Gates Foundation. In fact, the opposite is true: the more that the organization fails to reach its own stated goals, the more opportunities it has to try and mitigate its own past weaknesses. Quite ironically, the answer to ineffective philanthropy is more of it; the failure of philanthropy is its own success.[59] The perceived necessity – even the indispensability – of a donor like the Gates Foundation grows in proportion to its own inability to achieve the unachievable: mitigating the very inequalities that its own presence might be inadvertently compounding. As Foucault once remarked of the prison system, while the inability to reduce incarceration rates may be seen on one level as a 'failure,' it is clear that that seeming failure is what bulwarks the continued sustenance and power of those tasked with implementing and managing the prison system. The same thing happens with philanthropy: it's a model of giving that is not imperilled by its own ineffectiveness. Rather, it thrives upon it.

CHAPTER FIVE

God's Work

For nearly two decades, the Gates Foundation has dedicated itself to battling some of the world's deadliest diseases: over $1.5 billion spent to date on polio; over $2 billion invested in fighting malaria and tuberculosis; more than $2 billion spent fighting HIV/AIDS. The foundation's annual spending on global health is comparable to the World Health Organization – and the foundation wields power accordingly, stipulating how and where other global health organizations should spend their money.

It wasn't the first philanthropic organization to play a defining role in global heath. Huge advances in fighting infectious diseases, improving cancer treatments, and, today, making headway in the fight against HIV/AIDS would not have been possible without the support of organizations such as the Rockefeller Foundation and the Wellcome Trust – Britain's largest charity, established in 1936 to administer the fortune of Henry Wellcome, a pharmaceutical tycoon.

For much of the twentieth century, the Rockefeller Foundation commanded the same authority now enjoyed by the Gates Foundation. It was a pioneer in the field of global health, provoking both adulation and – as the foundation's ties to controversial US foreign policies grew more apparent – vehement public criticism in poor nations frustrated by US economic expansion. From 1913 to 1951, the Rockefeller Foundation's health division operated in more than eighty countries. Its influence was not simply greater than other non-profits or government actors working in international health – it was, for a long spell, the *sole* major funder in this field.

The League of Nations Health Organization (LNHO) was founded in 1922. But unlike its successor, the World Health Organization, the LNHO was weak in both political clout and financial backing. For much of its existence, the LNHO was reliant on the Rockefeller Foundation for almost half of its budget. Indeed, as the historian Anne-Emanuelle Birn points out, the LNHO was partly modelled on the Rockefeller Foundation's structure, sharing its values, expertise, and know-how in disease control.[1]

The WHO, first established in 1948, extended the functions of the LNHO. Until then, the Rockefeller Foundation was the *de facto* world authority in how best to manage the global disease burden, applying domestic US expertise in the treatment of scourges as varied as hookworm and polio across the globe. Foundation staff members were rarely far from controversy.

Take the example of Hideyo Noguchi, the Japanese-born scientist who would later die in Accra from yellow fever. Noguchi made his name with a series of experiments involving lutein, an inactive solution of *Treponema pallidum*, a bacterium that Noguchi had helped identify as the causative agent of syphilis. Historian of science Susan Lederer offers a compelling description of the medical optimism fuelled by Noguchi's lutein tests – and the public outrage they generated. Noguchi was hopeful that tests using lutein in humans would serve as a powerful diagnostic tool, revealing the presence of syphilis at the congenital stage. Working with over a dozen physicians across the New York metropolitan area, Noguchi performed lutein tests on hundreds of subjects, including healthy children between the ages of two and eighteen – a 'normal' control group intended to serve as a counterpart to participants diagnosed with syphilis and parasyphilis. Part of his sample included healthy orphans enrolled without the consent of their legal guardians – a decision inviting outrage from anti-vivisectionist groups who opposed human exploitation. The Manhattan Assistant District Attorney James Reynolds investigated the case. He admitted that experimenting on orphans without consent was technically illegal, but declined to prosecute, suggesting that new legislation was needed to clarify the state's role in regulating new forms of medical experimentation untested by courts in the past.[2]

Vignettes from the early twentieth century – an ambitious scientist condemned for experimenting with vulnerable populations, or an enormous vaccination effort against yellow fever quietly disbanded – are stories repeated through the Rockefeller Foundation's history. Another example is the Khanna study, an initiative aimed at reducing fertility rates in India. Today, the Khanna project is widely seen, as historian Matthew Connolly puts it, as an example of 'American social science at its most hubristic'.[3]

Developed as a collaborative effort between the Harvard School of Public Health, India's Ministry of Health, and a small Christian medical school funded by the Rockefeller Foundation, the study's aim was to discover whether contraceptive tablets could dramatically reduce fertility rates. The study was massive in size: 8,000 people in seven villages in the Punjab were placed under surveillance and subjected to monthly household visits from Harvard epidemiologists who showed little sensitivity in asking questions that few US housewives would likely have countenanced had a team of Indian researchers arrived on their doorstop in the early 1950s. How often did a woman have sex with her husband? Had she suffered any miscarriages? Was she trying to become pregnant? What was her menstrual cycle like?

Often, husbands and wives gave incompatible answers – on say, the frequency of sexual intercourse – hinting at understandable personal tensions over the intrusiveness of the questions. Rather than exploring *why* they might give inconsistent responses, the villagers were treated like lab specimens, subjected to monthly questioning but otherwise ignored, lest an intervention on the part of researchers – such as holding a medical clinic or distributing medicines other than contraceptives – compromised the study's findings. After five years, Connolly reports, the birth rate of those provided with contraceptives was *higher* than that of the control group. After a further follow-up study, the rate was still higher.

It turns out the villagers had accepted the pills out of politeness, and like anyone not wanting to offend a gift-giver, they rarely admitted to not taking them. The villagers spent months treating the Harvard researchers with polite tolerance. Even though many in the village were under the impression that the study was an exercise in mapping household locations in order to build better road systems – and feared that their own homes were slated for demolition – they kindly accepted the presence of the researchers, and good-naturedly kept accepting more contraceptive pills.

When it became clear that the study's objective was to assist with *reducing* conception, the villagers were mystified. Some were incensed by the effort to limit their future progeny. Those that could *not* conceive were hurt and resentful that a team of well-funded scientists refused to help with their own reproductive efforts. None of them could understand why a team based at the prestigious Harvard University could be too dim to grasp the importance of having healthy offspring to care for their economic needs.[4]

The Khanna study took place in the early 1950s. Its failure – the fact that its results confirmed the exact opposite of what researchers hoped – led the Rockefeller Foundation to distance itself from its methodology, but not from its objectives. In years ahead, the foundation funded numerous anti-fertility programmes in India and elsewhere, earning the growing animosity of physicians and poverty activists who felt that the foundation's efforts to control population growth ignored the realities of the persistent poverty that makes large families so indispensable to Indian villagers. Far from being a threat to a family's sustenance, a large family was seen by villagers as their only chance of survival.

Today, the Gates Foundation is pouring money into experimental medical trials that are facing criticisms similar to those directed at the Khanna study. Like earlier philanthropic foundations, the Gates Foundation has the financial and political clout to intervene in foreign nations with relative impunity, and to remain unfazed when the experiments it funds go awry. James Orbinski, a former president of Médecins Sans Frontières now teaching at the University of Toronto, suggested to me that concerns over the Gates Foundation's role in global health 'really come down to issues of political philosophy. How do we see foundations? Is philanthropy a substitute of public policy? What we've seen with Gates is that, by virtue of the sheer volume of its financial research, it has, knowingly or unknowingly, intentionally or unintentionally, had the effect of reshaping the global health research and agenda setting landscape.'

GATES GOES GLOBAL

The foundation has spent over $15.3 billion on global health programmes to date, and the money has done considerable good. In the late 1990s, for example, worldwide donors cumulatively spent a rather paltry sum on malaria research each year – approximately $84 million. Since the Gates Foundation began prioritizing malaria research, the amount spent yearly has more than tripled. The foundation has also boosted global spending on tuberculosis, and recently ramped up efforts to improve sanitation, injecting much-needed funds into finding sustainable solutions to human waste disposal, something garnering colourful media coverage. 'Bill Gates: Reinvent the Toilet, Save the World', one recent newspaper headline ran.

And yet, while the Gates Foundation's spending on health is sizeable, it's not *that* much. It pales in comparison to what rich nations spend collectively on global health initiatives each year. Take the President's Emergency Plan for AIDS Relief (PEPFAR), a US initiative launched in 2003 during George W. Bush's presidency to help strengthen the global treatment of HIV/AIDS. From 2004 to 2008, PEPFAR alone spent over \$18.1 billion on global HIV/AIDS programmes – more than the Gates Foundation's total spend on global health to date.

In recent years, the Gates Foundation has spent more annually on global health than individual nations such as Canada and Germany, but *less* than the UK and US. In 2012, Canada contributed approximately \$379 million to overseas health programmes. Germany spent \$307 million on health aid. The UK contributed \$1.3 billion – a rise of 2.3 per cent over the earlier year. The Gates Foundation, in comparison, spent \$899 million on global health in 2012. US spending amounted to more than the Gates Foundation, Canada, Germany, and the UK combined – its outlay on global health aid in 2012 was \$7 billion.[5]

Given that the Gates Foundation spends less annually on global health than many rich nations, why is Bill Gates a regular presence at summits such as the G20 in 2011? And why has the WHO management taken to consulting the Gates Foundation on major policy decisions?

It's partly a matter of political pressure. As Peter Piot, a well-known global health expert has pointed out, the Gates Foundation often has a galvanizing effect, shaming 'many "donor" governments into contributing more'.[6] The foundation's strong public profile, and significant marketing and publicity expenditures, helps to ensure significant media coverage of the areas it prioritizes. If governments fail to align themselves with the foundation, they risk appearing callous or uncaring, negligent of their own constituencies or the welfare of other nations.

Take the example of polio, a disease that, in the face of some reservation in the global health community, Gates has vowed to eradicate, exhorting rich and poor nations to join his cause. The fight is not a new one. The effort to eradicate the disease is over twenty years old; initially spearheaded by Rotary International, WHO, and UNICEF, it has achieved great milestones. Once endemic in fifty nations, the disease affects only about 2,000 sufferers today. Just over 200 new cases were diagnosed in 2012. Currently, polio is endemic in just three countries: Afghanistan, Pakistan, and Nigeria. Perversely, the smaller the number of sufferers, the more and more expensive and, many argue, counter-productive the final push for eradication becomes.

Donald Henderson, a former WHO epidemiologist who led the WHO's successful campaign against smallpox during the 1960s, has suggested that polio eradication may be a misplaced pursuit: it strips money from other areas of need, forcing nations to prioritize polio immunization at the expense of vaccination coverage for other diseases. Arthur Caplan, an eminent bioethicist who himself suffered from polio as a child, has also criticized Gates's obsession with polio eradication, pointing out that 'government budgets and resources in poor nations are diverted from other far more pressing local problems to try and capture the last marginal cases'.[7]

This point has been voiced again and again by physicians and health workers in countries where the final push against polio may be fomenting unexpected health risks, such as exposing children to multiple polio vaccinations in areas where record-keeping is poor.

In India, for example, after a campaign largely financed by the government – which spent $2.5 billion on eradication, overseeing a gargantuan effort involving 2.3 million vaccinations – the nation has succeeded, for now, in stamping out polio in the country. By January 2012, a full year had passed since the last polio case reported, and India was deemed officially polio-free. That was the good news. The bad news was that cases of non-polio Acute Flaccid Paralysis (AFP) exploded, increasing in proportion to the number of polio vaccines received in each area. Oral polio vaccines can be a direct cause of paralysis. But so can bacteria and non-polio viruses, making it difficult to know whether increased vaccinations are directly linked to the recent surge of paralysis in India.

Uncertainty over the specific culprit of the escalating rates of non-polio paralysis simply fuelled community concern over the vaccine's safety.[8]

Political tensions have also plagued global efforts to eradicate polio. One area where the Gates Foundation has focused its polio efforts is Pakistan, one of the three countries where the disease is still endemic. The foundation has ramped up incentives in the field, paying individual health workers $2 or $3 stipends to disperse vaccines to children throughout the deepest recesses of Pakistan, where the virus is proving particularly truculent.

But these efforts were undermined in 2011 when the CIA staged a fake vaccination drive, replete with agents masquerading as health workers, in order to obtain DNA samples from Osama bin Laden's family members. The ruse proved crucial to rooting out bin Laden's whereabouts in the days leading to his assassination. The plot also jeopardized legitimate vaccination efforts in the country, leading to a bloody backlash that continues to this day, as the Taliban and other extremist groups target polio health workers in retribution for the CIA's subterfuge.

The CIA campaign was widely condemned in the United States and globally by health experts and humanitarian organizations. Renowned global health experts Orin Levine and Laurie Garrett denounced the scheme, suggesting in the *Washington Post* that 'the CIA's plot – recruiting a Pakistani doctor to distribute hepatitis vaccines in Abbottabad this spring – destroyed credibility that wasn't its to erode . . . intelligence officials imprudently burned bridges that took years for health workers to build'.[9]

Since the CIA campaign, dozens of polio vaccinators have been killed in Taliban-led attacks on anti-polio campaigners. Bill Gates has condemned the murders. 'It's not going to stop us succeeding', Gates said in an interview with the *Telegraph* in 2013. 'It does force us to sit down with the Pakistan government to renew their commitments, see what they're going to do in security and make changes to protect the women who are doing God's work and getting out to these children and delivering the vaccine.'[10]

He is right to praise the courage and resilience of health workers. But his choice of wording – chastising the Pakistani government rather than acknowledging the CIA's role in imperilling the safety of health workers – is rankling for observers who see the Gates Foundation as an extension of US foreign policy rather than a neutral presence in global health. And to invoke 'God's work' in the context of deeply entrenched sectarian violence seems particularly regrettable.

Another frustration with the fight against polio is that the campaign has long been rooted in the goals of rich nations – not the objectives of poor ones. Henderson, now a distinguished scholar at the University of Pittsburgh Medical Center for Biosecurity, has made this point clear. When an alliance of international actors, including UNICEF, Rotary International, and the WHO, teamed up in the late 1980s to launch a polio campaign, eliminating the disease was seen as a priority for western nations, *not* developing ones. Then and today, polio kills far fewer people in developing regions than scourges such as malaria, TB, or HIV. When the effort to eradicate polio was first floated at policy meetings in the 1980s, developing nations feared a diversion of resources towards an area where the money was *least* warranted.

'I was there at the discussions in 1988' (the year that 166 member states of the WHO adopted a landmark resolution for the worldwide eradication of polio), Henderson told me by phone from Pittsburgh.[11]

The question was, why should the developing countries be supportive of this programme, when in fact, as was pointed out, this is not a major problem to them. Industrialized countries were concerned about it . . . many of the diseases that plagued the developing countries had been pretty well managed, or were at a very low level. But polio was there. So the rationale offered was, yes, this is a problem for the industrialized countries and by supporting the polio programme they expected that the industrialized countries would pay for all the costs of the programme in the developing countries.

Developing nations, meanwhile, pledged to provide vehicles and personnel in order to aid vaccination efforts. In the case of smallpox eradication, developing countries tended to spend approximately *twice* as much as rich countries on in-country efforts to eliminate the disease. Henderson's worry is that polio efforts will be equally burdensome on cash-strapped developing nations, draining funds better spent on strengthening immunization programmes against multiple diseases – not just polio.

'A basic question', Henderson suggested, 'is whether it is warranted to budget another $6 billion in international contributions to the polio programme for 2013–2018. A figure for national costs has never been provided. For smallpox eradication, the consensus was that for every dollar invested by donors, [developing] countries had to come up with $2. I can't believe that polio costs will be less.'

'When you're doing polio, you're not doing other things', Henderson added. 'At least through 2011, in several countries – Nigeria, India, and Pakistan – they were giving polio vaccines but they were not, for example, giving the DPT [diphtheria-tetanus-pertussis] vaccine, or the measles vaccines. [A recent study from UNICEF] documents the fact that 22 million children have not got their full allotment of DPT shots. Of that, 11 million – half of them – are in India, Pakistan, and Nigeria.'

The emphasis on polio vaccination at the expense of other inoculations is not lost on local villagers. Time and again, they question the emphasis on a disease that places a less burdensome toll on them than other scourges. 'A number of villagers, say, "What is polio? We've never seen it – why are we worried about it?" . . . They say, our children are dying of measles', Henderson said. 'Because of this very intensive effort on polio they stopped administering the other vaccines.'

Henderson has met with Gates, and he came away impressed. He thought Gates seemed as well informed on the science of polio as anyone working in the field – extremely high praise for a scientist to offer a lay individual. Henderson stressed to me that he finds Gates's dedication to fighting polio extremely inspiring. 'Bill Gates has committed himself to make this a very high priority, an exceedingly high priority – he's done exactly that.'

But two years after speaking with Gates, Henderson's reservations were ignited again after seeing evidence that the countries where polio efforts have intensified are the same countries neglecting routine immunization for other infectious diseases – India, Pakistan, and Nigeria. And despite vaccine research funded by the Gates Foundation and elsewhere, the difficulty of fully eradicating vaccine-derived poliovirus, a mutation of the virus contained in the oral vaccine, still lingers. 'I can't see myself how we can satisfactorily eliminate the vaccine-derived strains', Henderson said. 'I just don't think it can be done.'

Henderson's concern seems to irritate Gates rather than raise points for contemplation. 'I've got to get my D. A. Henderson response down better', Gates muttered to one of his aides in 2011, in a remark later reported in the *New York Times*, after the paper interviewed Gates about his polio efforts.[12] Throughout 2013, Gates traversed the globe beseeching rich and poor nations to increase their commitment to polio efforts. His fixation on the problem seems to contradict an outspoken claim from Melinda and Bill: that they choose to invest their money where they can have the most impact in terms of lives saved. 'We literally go down the chart of the greatest inequities and give where we can effect the greatest change', Melinda said in 2008, stressing that two questions shape their decision-making: Which problems affect the most people? And which have been neglected in the past?[13]

In 2012, there were only 223 reported case of polio worldwide – a number that has shrunk from 350,000 in 1988, or a drop of 99 per cent. By any measure, polio eradication efforts have been highly successful even if rare cases continue to persist. And by any measure, polio is not one of the world's greatest killers. Road accidents, for example, kill about 1.25 million people each year. Measles kill about 150,000 children each year.

Sonia Shah, an award-winning journalist, has pointed out similar problems with eradication campaigns against malaria, efforts that, quite counter-intuitively, have caused money to flood to where it is *least* needed: the places where just a handful of cases persist. Five decades ago, more than ninety nations joined a scheme led by the US State Department and the WHO to eradicate malaria. After spending the equivalent of more than $9 billion in today's dollars, the campaign managed to vanquish malaria in a number of rich nations. But it also helped to fuel malaria outbreaks in endemic countries. The World Health Assembly quietly called for the programme's dissolution in 1969. Tibor Lepes, a former director of WHO's malaria control division, called the failed eradication programme 'one of the greatest mistakes ever made in public health'.[14]

Shah has pointed out a paradox of eradication versus control efforts: 'Eradicating a disease is, in several important respects, a goal diametrically opposed to controlling one. When public health leaders want to control a disease, they devote the majority of their resources to the areas of greatest need', she writes. 'When their goal is eradication, then they must spend their resources on areas where eradication is most likely – the areas with the least need.'[15]

Polio is not the only 'donor darling' drawing criticism from global health experts. The Gates Foundation has called loudly and bullishly for national governments to prioritize the inclusion of a number of different high-cost vaccines on national immunization programmes. The problem is not the individual vaccines – although questions over vaccine safety sometimes arise. The problem is that by prioritizing the delivery of expensive vaccines, other proven interventions lose out.

The Gates Foundation's funding of recent HPV trials in India is a good example. A few years ago, the foundation funded the Seattle-based NGO Program for Appropriate Technology in Health (generally referred to by its acronym, PATH) to carry out 'demonstration trials' testing human papillomavirus vaccines in approximately 23,000 girls aged ten to fourteen in the Indian states of Gujarat and Andhra Pradesh. The two HPV vaccines distributed, Gardasil and Cervarix, are manufactured by Merck and GlaxoSmithKline respectively, and are licensed in India for over-the-counter use.

Gardasil has been a top-seller for Merck, earning total global sales of $1.5 billion in 2011, a windfall for the company in the financially lean years that had plagued it since it emerged that the company had manipulated trial data for Vioxx, its bestselling painkiller drug linked to heart failure in tens of thousands of users. Merck pleaded guilty to criminal charges over the marketing and sales of Vioxx, which was pulled from the US market in 2004, after 25 million Americans had been prescribed the drug. When Gardasil was first in production, Merck sales teams reportedly had a catchy unofficial nickname for the HPV vaccine: 'Help Pay for Vioxx.'

PATH received permission to carry out the trials from the Indian Council of Medical Research and the state governments of Gujarat and Andhra Pradesh, and began a two-year vaccination drive in mid-2009. Most of the vaccines were given to girls at *ashram paath-shalas* (boarding schools for tribal children), sidestepping the need to seek parental consent for the shots. A later numerical analysis of 100 consent forms collected in Andhra Pradesh and Gujarat indicated that signatures of witnesses were absent from sixty-nine of the forms.[16]

By 2010, reports of mysterious deaths – four young girls in Andhra Pradesh, and two in Gujarat – fuelled public alarm over the trials. The federal ministry of health suspended the trials and later appointed an expert parliamentary committee to investigate allegations of wrongdoing. News of a seventh death emerged as the committee began its investigation. While none of the deaths have been linked directly to the HPV vaccine (five were deemed conclusively unrelated, and two unlikely), the committee found that PATH had violated ethical guidelines in a number of alarming ways.[17]

Girls selected for vaccination were given 'HPV Immunization Cards' in English, which they couldn't read. Those vaccinated were told the vaccines would offer 'lifelong protection' against cervical cancer – something that was not true. When the trials were underway, health insurance was provided for PATH staff, but not to any participants in the trials. The trials were conducted in impoverished, rural areas where mechanisms for tracking the adverse effects of the vaccines are less robust than in urban areas. Perhaps most alarming of all, PATH did not implement any system for recording major adverse reactions to the vaccines, known technically as Adverse Events Following Immunization, or AEFIs, something legally mandated for large-scale clinical trials.

PATH has justified this omission by insisting that the vaccine trials were 'demonstration trials', and therefore subject to looser safety requirements than a standard clinical trial. A parliamentary report into the vaccine trials lambasted that rationalization, stressing that the HPV trials should have been deemed a clinical trial because it was a 'study of a pharmaceutical product carried out on human participants' and 'four of five primary outcome measures proposed in the study related to evaluation of the safety of the vaccine'.[18] In 2010, the Indian Council of Medical Ethics admitted that its own ethical protocols had been flouted in permitting the trials. In August 2013 a separate parliamentary committee reiterated the severe criticism of PATH, stating that the NGO's 'sole aim has been to promote the commercial interests of HPV vaccine manufacturers who would have reaped windfall profits had PATH been successful in getting the HPV vaccine included in the UIP [universal immunization program] of the Country'.[19]

*   *   *

Vaccine controversies make for colourful news stories. In the United States, few public health controversies have been as inflammatory as recent debates over the safety of HPV vaccines. When US Congresswoman Michele Bachmann, a former presidential hopeful and Tea Party favourite, learned of a recent US campaign to pass state legislation forcing HPV vaccines on pre-teens, she castigated health officials for daring to inject young girls with a toxic cocktail that caused, she alleged, mental retardation and death.

The issue fast evolved into a pulpit-banging campaign crowd-pleaser as Bachmann laid into fellow Republican Rick Perry, who, as Governor of Texas, signed a 2007 executive order requiring all sixth-grade children in the states to receive the vaccine. The order was eventually overturned by the state legislature after a furious conserv-ative backlash over what was seen as a restriction of human liberty.

Bachmann's allegations helped to undermine her own argument. The more outlandish her pronouncements on the vaccine's dangers, the harder it became for more sober voices to call attention to an uncomfortable reality: some of her concerns may be warranted. Recent evidence from the US Centers for Disease Control and Prevention suggests there is a very small, but real, risk of death following Gardasil vaccinations. Data from the US national Adverse Event Reporting System (AERS) indicates that the vast majority of side-effects following HPV vaccination have been mild in nature. But a small number – 6.2 per cent of all reports – were classed as serious, including thirty-two reports of death. Aside from the AERS surveil-lance data, a number of individual case reports, published in reputable journals, have suggested that HPV vaccination can lead in rare cases to serious illnesses, 'with nervous system and autoimmune disorders being the most frequently reported in the medical literature.'[20]

Diane Harper, a professor at the University of Missouri-Kansas City who served as a lead investigator on early HPV vaccine clinical trials carried out by both GSK and Merck, has suggested that the risks of Gardasil need to be better disclosed to US parents, many of whom wrongly presume the vaccination offers lifelong protection against cervical cancer. Once a paid consultant for Merck, Harper grew critical of the company's marketing tactics, and began publicly speaking out against the introduction of the vaccine to US markets despite limited evidence of its effectiveness. 'Ninety-five per cent of women who are infected with HPV never, ever get cervical cancer', she suggested to media. 'It seemed very odd to be mandating something for which 95 per cent of infections never amount to anything.'[21]

Exposing children or adolescents to a toxic substance is always a risk-benefit gamble – is the risk of vaccine-related injury worth staving off the possibility of contracting a fatal illness? With many vaccines – measles for example – the answer is a resounding yes. But in this case, given the vaccine's limited proven benefits (coverage against two strains of HPV for up to five years), there may not yet be sufficient scientific evidence for exposing pre-teen girls to a risky vaccine.

In 2013, two separate groups of health activists and human rights advocates submitted public interest litigation (PIL) petitions calling on India's Supreme Court to investigate the HPV trials and determine whether PATH and other stakeholders responsible for the trials should be held liable for financial damages in relation to the families of the seven girls who died while participating in the studies.

One of the lead petitioners is Amar Jesani, a physician who directs the Centre for Studies in Ethics and Rights in Mumbai. 'Our problem is not with the vaccine per se, because at the moment we don't have enough data to say that it should be prohibited', Jesani said to me by phone from Mumbai. '[The PIL is focused] on what happened in the demonstration project, and the seven girls who died in the project – as well as the girls who had serious adverse events. We're going to talk about their compensation. We're going to talk about the violation of ethics during the project – and demand punishment for those involved.'

Jesani's group has strong legal support – their PIL petition is represented by Anand Grover, a current UN rapporteur on the right to health. Grover successfully represented India's Cancer Patients Aid Association in a recent seven-year legal battle over the pharmaceutical company Novartis's attempt to extend patent life on Glivec, a bestselling cancer drug.

Jesani pointed out to me an inconsistency with PATH's pre-trial ethical approval. Initially, PATH sought and received permission from the Drugs Controller of India to carry out a post-licensing observational study – in other words, a phase IV clinical trial. Despite this regulatory approval, PATH later denied, after the project was underway, that the trial *was* a phase IV study at all. '[PATH insists it was] not a clinical trial – it was a demonstration trial for operations research', Jesani told me, adding:

> I keep asking them – how can you keep denying that there was no clinical trial, when you actually went to the Drugs Controller and took permission from them? . . . It was a clinical trial and one of the objectives was to look at efficacy. Because one of their objectives was to look at efficacy . . . the [Indian parliamentary committee] came to the conclusion that they should have used their own surveillance system, or invested money in improving the governmental system. Because they did not do all these things, when serious adverse events took place . . . there was no mechanism to follow up and provide medical care to those girls.

Jesani and his colleagues debated whether to name the Gates Foundation as a respondent in their writ – potentially rendering it liable if compensation is awarded. They chose not to, primarily because in Indian law, 'the sponsor [in this case, PATH] is the main responsible party for any clinical trial'. But the omission has left Jesani uneasy. 'The ethical guidelines of the Indian Council for Medical Research talks about totality of responsibility. It defines the totality of responsibility in terms of everybody – that means sponsor, funder, the investigator, and any other collaborating organizations involved', Jesani said. 'Under that principle, everyone should be held responsible. There is also no evidence at the moment that the Gates Foundation took any step to discipline PATH for the research it carried out in India . . . I think, to some extent, the Gates Foundation thinks PATH has done nothing wrong. And that is a concern. One needs to get a spotlight on the Gates Foundation.'

Human rights lawyers based at the European Center for Constitutional and Human Rights (ECCHR) agree with the points made by Jesani. In 2013, they submitted an *amicus curiae* brief in support of the second PIL filed in the HPV case.[22] An *amicus* is a legal term for when someone who is not a specific party in a court case offers legal opinion or testimony shedding light on the possible broader implications of a court's decision. In this case, staff at ECCHR felt it was important to call attention to the legal duties of multinational pharmaceutical companies and NGOs carrying out clinical trials. As Carolijn Terwindt, a lawyer and joint author of the *amicus*, has pointed out, the legal obligations of trial sponsors such as PATH are unclear and should be strengthened. The *amicus* calls on the Supreme Court to consider passing legislation which will ensure that 'only clinical trials that could benefit the local population will be approved . . . Adequate compensation in the case of injuries of death is also necessary.'[23]

I contacted the Gates Foundation and PATH for comments on the allegations of misconduct. PATH did not respond. A press officer at the Gates Foundation stated to me via email that public concern over the HPV vaccine trials stemmed from 'misinformation'. Asked to elaborate, he wrote that 'some of the critical press failed to understand how trials are designed and implemented and what makes them effective, but, again, you should really get in touch with the folks that conducted them to get more clarity into details'.

Much of my research as a sociologist is focused on global pharmaceutical regulation and the governance of clinical trials research.

I've published research and comment editorials on this topic in the *Journal of Medical Ethics*, *The Lancet*, and the *American Journal of Bioethics*. I agree with the Indian parliamentary report stating that ethical violations took place, and with Jesani's view that it is problematic for PATH to have first listed the trials as a post-licensing observational study and then to have denied having done so. Given this concern, I pressed PATH for a response but received none. The Supreme Court admitted both public writs; hearings are ongoing, with a decision expected in late 2015 or 2016. PATH's public stance has remained constant, insisting that no ethical violations occurred. In a public statement released on 2 September 2013, PATH referred to the Indian government's parliamentary report as an 'inaccurate characterization' of the trials.

In September 2012, shortly after the PATH vaccine trials were suspended, I visited Scotland to give a workshop presentation at the University of Edinburgh. The theme of the workshop was the global governance of clinical trials research. There were a number of India-based researchers at the meeting, and the recent PATH HPV trials came up time and again during presentations and informal discussion until, after two days, attendees dispersed back to their home cities or towns.

The meeting took place in a spartan seminar room, located in a wing off the University's main library. It was late September. Any flashes of late summer warmth were quickly checked by heavy rains darkening the green courtyard outside. Those in the room – lawyers, physicians, sociologists, anthropologists – seemed inured to the steady barrage of statistics on the global clinical trials industry. They'd heard it all before. In 1990, only a small proportion of experimental clinical trials testing new drugs with the American market in mind were conducted outside the US. Today, an estimated 40 per cent of clinical trials take place outside Western Europe and the US. This number is a 'very conservative' projection; estimates are hard to verify as US regulators have little knowledge of how many experiments take place before a drug application is submitted.[24]

When trials go global, safety risks proliferate – both in the US, the world's largest market for pharmaceuticals, and in poor countries combed for 'treatment naïve' patients corralled onto trials for drugs they have very little chance of being able to afford once the trial is complete. Pharmaceutical companies are literally 'body hunters', to use Sonia Shah's term – a trial's success or failure hangs on having an ample supply of bodies at hand to take part as research subjects. An estimated four out of five clinical trials are delayed because of difficulties recruiting subjects, which can be financially crippling for manufacturers who lose months or years of patent life the longer it takes to complete testing on a new breakthrough drug awaiting approval from regulators.

Those attending the Edinburgh workshop were familiar with the marketing literature on the opportunities for conducting clinical trials research in populous nations such as India. 'Apart from the low cost of field trials', beams a Pfizer press release, 'a billion people means there is never a shortage of potential subjects.'[25] They were also familiar with long-standing ethical debates over the morality of outsourcing trials that mostly benefit western consumers to developing countries. A recent hefty edited collection published by Princeton University Press, featuring chapters with titles like 'Broadly Utilitarian Theories of Exploitation and Multinational Clinical Research', marshalled a half-dozen of the world's leading medical ethicists to weigh in on the morality of trying to shoehorn as many trials as possible into countries with the most lax clinical safeguards in place. The collection might have benefited, one reviewer wryly suggests, from a contribution written by an ethicist hailing from 'those parts of the world most adversely affected by clinical-trial outsourcing'.[26]

Since 2005, the number of clinical trials in India has ballooned to 1,600 studies involving over 150,000 research subjects. Health campaigners in India have mounted a vigorous campaign calling for stricter regulation of an industry that has seen over 2,000 research participants die between 2007 and 2013. Some of those participants likely died of underlying illnesses, not as a result of the experimental treatment. With poor surveillance measures in place, it's often difficult to know whether a new drug or vaccine is the specific cause of death or whether an external factor – disease or an environmental hazard – is responsible. Ironically, this very uncertainty, fomented by companies themselves through poor record-keeping and slack surveillance standards, is legally useful for manufacturers in exonerating them of liability when trials lead to mysterious, unexpected deaths.[27] India's health minister recently reported to the Indian parliament that to date, less than twenty-five family members have received compensation from foreign drug companies for loss of life. Families received an average of about $3,000 per individual – a pittance.[28]

India's human rights community is fighting back, demanding better regulatory protections for research participants. To some extent, they've succeeded. In 2013, India's Ministry of Health and Family Welfare enacted new legislation emphasizing that any sponsors of experimental clinical trials have an unconditional ethical obligation to provide free and comprehensive medical treatment of adverse health reactions during a clinical trial. Spirited public discussion over the legal responsibilities of organizations carrying out clinical trials in India helps to make clear why the Gates Foundation's funding of ethically fraught medical experiments frustrates Indian health activists.

'Whose impact on India's health policies has been *worse*?' one attendee in Edinburgh asked during the second morning of the workshop. 'The Gates Foundation or Rockefeller?' It was not a flippant question. The speaker, her face earnest, wanted answers. There was a momentary silence. Attendees shuffled in their chairs, trying not to glance too obviously at the Indian researchers scattered throughout the room. 'At least Rockefeller built institutions!' one researcher, dressed in a sari, called out eventually. 'The Gates Foundation just leaves chaos. Not only is it changing the ideology of public health – it is deinstitutionalizing public health.'[29]

I glanced around. Most faces were unperturbed. Some nodded in agreement. The anger directed at the Gates Foundation might surprise people living in wealthy nations. Indeed, even vehement critics of the foundation's influence on US public education seem to have a remarkably rose-colored perception of the foundation's good deeds abroad. Michael Klonsky, for example, an outspoken critic of the Gates Foundation's influence on US education, has commended its international pursuits, writing recently that 'if it wasn't for Gates, half of the countries in Africa wouldn't have a medical system.'[30]

I quoted Klonsky's comment during my own presentation at the Edinburgh conference. Chuckles broke out through the room. Why? Because the comment struck the audience as an amusing, if somewhat infuriating example of how the Gates Foundation's work in developing nations is widely perceived by casual observers in the west.

Surprising as it may be, African nations didn't suddenly sprout medical systems the moment the Gates Foundation emerged on the global health scene less than twenty years ago. African communities have been battling to improve community-based infrastructures since before the colonial era.[31] After independence from colonial rule, many incumbent governments treated healthcare as a fundamental goal. Ghana, for example, implemented free public healthcare services to all after gaining independence from Britain in the 1950s. Its health system slowly deteriorated under economic stagnation in the 1970s, compounded by IMF and World Bank lending requirements. Throughout the 1980s and 1990s, these loan conditions led to reductions in government spending. Jobs at publicly funded hospitals were slashed to appease IMF development experts.[32]

Today, Ghana faces similar challenges as other nations in the region: health workers are often lured away from poorly paid jobs in national health services to take on more lucrative positions in clinics run by foreign NGOs, philanthropic organizations, and faith-based organizations. In Ethiopia, staff hired on a contractual basis to implement disease-specific programmes earn salaries *three* times greater than regular government health employees. A hospital in Malawi reported recently that eighty-eight nurses left within an eighteen-month period, tempted by higher salaries with NGOs.[33]

Laurie Garrett pointed out in 2007 that 'decades of neglect' had undermined health infrustructures in poor nations, and as a consequence, a great deal of philanthropic funding was 'leaking away without result' In the aftermath of the Ebola crisis, the Gates Foundation garnered praise for suggesting that more attention to primary healthcare strengthening is needed. And yet for years the foundation has refused to prioritize this very goal. One example is the foundation's Grand Challenge schemes, launched in 2003. On the positive side the initiative helped galvanize leading scientific minds to combat global diseases. Less helpfully, the first Grand Challenge called explicitly excluded grants focused on problems of 'priority, access to health interventions and delivery systems.'[34]

The IMF's international clout expanded during the oil and inflation crises of the 1970s. Many families recall the long petrol lines and crippling interest rates that broke household budgets during the latter half of the decade. The same debt spirals engulfed poor nations, which borrowed money from the US and other lenders at a time when interest rates were low. As the rates spiked, heavily indebted countries fought fiercely against a growing tsunami of debt, imposing tough austerity measures on their populaces at the behest of the IMF.

Like animals in quicksand they just sank further. As the Greek economist and former finance minister Yanis Varoufakis points out, the IMF gamely offered them more loans in order repay existent ones, but at a very steep price. Countries were placed under strict surveillance, forced to dismantle public sector institutions, including public schools and hospital clinics, and transfer lucrative public assets, such as water services and telecommunication providers to private US and European companies. Varoufakis argues that IMF conditions conspired to create the developing world's second brutal historical disaster, leaving countries as enfeebled as they were at the peak of nineteenth-century imperialism and its associated slave trade.[35]

But you don't have to take Varoufakis's word for it. The most damning critics of the IMF, and its sister organization, the World Bank, are people who used to work there. Nobel laureate Joseph Stiglitz was the chief economist at the World Bank during the 1997–98 East Asian crisis, an economic implosion that left countries such as Japan mired in economic malaise for over a decade. Back in 1997, he watched 'in horror' as the IMF and US Treasury imposed policies certain to aggravate the crisis, leaving countries such as Indonesia – facing unemployment rates of 40 per cent in its central island of Java – worse off than before the recession had hit.

Why? Stiglitz's answer is candid: the political interests of western nations trumped those of eastern ones. 'The crisis struck in the developing countries, sometimes called the "periphery" of the global economic system', he writes. 'Those running the global economic system were not so much worried about protecting the lives and livelihoods of those in the affected nations as they were in preserving western banks that had lent these countries money.'[36]

The tendency for political objectives to drive economic decisions – which are then propagated as purely technical policies geared at improving economic growth – is a well-known operating principle within the IMF. The late economist Jacques Polak, a former IMF director of research and one of the longest serving staffers – the IMF honoured him after his death by naming its annual research conference after him – once put it bluntly. 'The proprieties of the Fund', he said, 'contain an unwritten rule that, if at all possible, political arguments be dressed up in economic garb.'[37]

The Gates Foundation, a relatively new arrival on the stage of international development, is obviously not to blame for decades of IMF austerity programmes or resource exploitation by US companies operating in poor nations. But it tends to partner with the companies that are. Investigative reporters from the *LA Times* were the first to report widespread dissatisfaction with the Gates Foundation's endowment investments in companies such as ExxonMobil pointing out that flares from oil plants mushrooming across the Niger Delta are widely believed to have caused epidemics of bronchitis in adults and lowered immunity in children – increasing their susceptibility to measles and polio. Local physicians told the *LA Times* that they felt that unregulated oil extraction was a prime cause of the poor health they faced daily.[38]

Publicly slated in the aftermath of the *LA Times* exposé, Bill and Melinda at first announced that they would rethink their investment policies – and then retracted that decision. For years, with the exception of tobacco companies, the foundation chose to invest in companies offering strong financial returns regardless of negative health effects.

Recently, faced with ongoing criticism of their investment choices – the foundation's stake, for example, in GEO Group, a leader in the for-profit prison industry, drew outrage from human-rights activists – the foundation seems to have shifted its investment policy. Until 2014, the foundation had a large stake in Coca-Cola and McDonald's, both as a direct shareholder and through its investments in Buffett's company, Berkshire Hathaway. In 2006, Buffett pledged to donate the bulk of his fortune to the Gates Foundation before the end of his lifetime. This gift consists mostly of shares in his highly profitable Berkshire Hathaway holding company. Currently, nearly half of the Gates Foundation's endowment is invested in Berkshire Hathaway. Until recently, about 5 per cent of the Gates Foundation's endowment was invested in McDonald's, while over 7 per cent was invested in Coca-Cola. That figure does not include the foundation's further investments in Berkshire Hathaway.

For a number of years, Buffett has been the single largest investor in Coca-Cola, owning 400 million shares valued at approximately $17 billion. In 2011, three highly regarded global health scholars, David Stuckler, Sanjay Basu, and Martin McKee published an article pointing out that once Buffett's donation of stock in Berkshire Hathaway was fully transferred, a process of incremental stages, the Gates Foundation would be poised to become the largest shareholder in Coca-Cola in the world.[39]

During the last quarter of 2014, the foundation sold its shares in Coca-Cola and McDonald's, unloading 10.9 million shares in McDonald's and 21.4 million shares in Coca-Cola, valued respectively at $1 billion and $914.million. Whether the sale was due to growing concern over the Gates Foundation's close links to Coca-Cola, something seen as a conflict of interest given Gates's own extensive personal investments in the company, or whether the divestment was a strategic financial decision driven by vociferous criticism of Coca-Cola's management and executive compensation in 2014, is not publicly known.[40]

The Gates Foundation has a policy of not commenting publicly on its investment decisions. In 2006, partly to accommodate Buffett's gift, the Gates Foundation announced it was reorganizing and establishing itself as two separate entities: an asset trust and a programme foundation. A reported aim of the reorganization was to enable Buffett to avoid accusations of a conflict of interest once he joined Bill and Melinda as a trustee of the Gates Foundation.

Today, more and more philanthropic foundations are embracing what's known as 'mission-related investing', defined as the effort to ensure that one's endowment is invested in ways that are conducive to overarching social missions. Aaron Dorfman, executive director of the US National Committee for Responsive Philanthropy, suggested to me that there are three main channels a foundation can adopt in order to practise mission investing: 'The first 'is what we call "screens", so they can screen into or out of their portfolio investments that are consistent or inconsistent with their mission.' The second channel, he said, is 'shareholder activism . . . we've got a lot of demonstrated cases, especially on environmental concerns where foundations that own shares in certain companies as an activist shareholder have been able to influence the corporate practices of the companies they are invested in and improve their wage policies or their environmental policies'. The third channel is 'proactive investments that directly relate to the foundation's mission but also seek a [financial] return . . . this could be a below market-rate return in which case they would call it a "program-related investment" (PRI), or it could be seeking a regular market-rate return'.

Of these three main channels, the Gates Foundation *does* engage in the third approach: it has a number of PRIs, including a financial stake in biotechnology companies trying to find innovative solutions to healthcare burdens. But when it comes to the first two criteria, the foundation is seen as a laggard.

Mitch Kapor, the billionaire founder of Lotus software, expressed to me his surprise and dismay at Gates's intransigency on the topic of ethical investing: 'The Gates Foundation manages its endowment along conventional lines, i.e., it does not pay attention to mission or impact. I recently spoke to Bill about this and he spoke about this fact as though it were out of his hands and that he didn't have the ability to change the approach to investment.'

In 2009, David McCoy, a London-based physician and global health policy expert, investigated the Gates Foundation's spending on global health and found that out of 659 grants awarded to non-governmental or for-profit organizations, 560 were offered to organizations in high-income countries, mainly in the US. Only thirty-seven grants went to NGOs based in low or middle-income countries. Similarly, of 231 grants given to universities, just twelve were awarded to universities based in developing regions.

A number of researchers have questioned whether this resource allocation is a sound strategy. Robert Black, an international expert in the prevention of childhood mortality and chair of the department for international health at Johns Hopkins University, offered a quietly scathing pronouncement on the foundation's funding priorities:

> The health problems being targeted are in low-income countries and little of the research and development funding is going to capable individuals and credible institutions in these countries. The very limited direct funding to these countries is arguably the most unfortunate imbalance in the research portfolio of the Foundation because it excludes scientists and programme managers who best understand the problems from contributing creative solutions.[41]

Martin Addo (the name is a pseudonym), a young health researcher based at the University of Cape Coast, in western Ghana, echoed the sentiment:

> From my point of view, it's more like [the Gates Foundation] are selling technology than solving problems. Most of their calls have to do with developing some new technology or vaccines . . . What is [the foundation doing] to help those that are always spending their time and energy to look for grants? Not just to look for grants, but to do something to help their country. If you are really interested in a country and its development, develop the human resources that are also interested in bringing solutions to the fore.

'I've stopped writing to the Gates Foundation', he added, explaining he that has twice submitted grant applications. 'They didn't go through.'[42]

In the summer of 2011, I met in Geneva with Joan Awunyo-Akaba, a Ghanaian physician who serves as national vice-chair of

Ghana's Coalition of NGOs in Health, representing over 400 NGOs, and is a current board member of the Global Alliance for Vaccines and Immunisation (GAVI), an organization that received extensive funding from the Gates Foundation. 'I remember the first GAVI board meeting I attended as an observer', she said:

> A board member from the foundation made a passionate inter-jection that the Bill and Melinda Gates Foundation alone contributed 28 per cent of the GAVI funding. That really touched me; that one individual can be so passionate about chil-dren . . . Maybe what they don't realize is that some of us from the civil society in the south do not have the type of wealth that Bill Gates has, but we sacrifice all. We are not paid. I am not paid for what I'm doing . . . so in comparison we sacrifice more from the little that we have. I admire him and especially the global health platform that he has set, but what saddens us, those of us from the south, is that he really resources the CSOs [civil society organiza-tions] in the north . . . and he has never extended this type of support to us.

There are some signs that the foundation is evolving – growing more aware of the need to harness local knowledge and empower regional, country-based organizations in order to meet health objectives. During a visit to Ghana in 2012, I met with Vida Duti, the country director of the IRC International Water and Sanitation Centre. She heads a team of researchers and policy-makers who work with the Ghanaian government in the development of sustainable rural water delivery services; IRC-Ghana is an offshoot of a Dutch-based non-profit that receives substantial funding from the Gates Foundation and other donors.

Before touching specifically on the Gates Foundation, Duti mentioned the importance of the Paris Declaration on Aid Effectiveness, which resulted from a high-level summit on overseas aid held in 2005. The Paris Declaration is a list of guidelines for trying to improve the effectiveness of aid delivery. Core principles include ownership, alignment, and harmonization – all aimed at ensuring that developing nations, and not overseas donors, are able to devise their own strategies for poverty reduction. Although the Declaration is sometimes derided as meaningless policy-speak, paying lip service to ideals rarely reached in practice, Duti told me she has seen a significant shift in how donors approach local organizations. They are more cooperative, far more willing to listen to local NGOs rather than dictate to them – and she sees the Gates Foundation as playing a strong role in bringing that development about. At first, she said, the foundation's objectives seemed unrealistic – but they've gradually changed tack. 'Initially their thinking was, "within a year, you should have a model that can solve the problem of sustainability". That stance is far less visible today. She noted that the foundation 'has helped to better position us to deliver on mandates . . . They are capitalizing on existing good will by leveraging the reputation of existing donors – IRC was already a trusted partner. I think their strategy of using already existing agencies has been very positive. You can fly on their wings.'

Comments such as this are highly promising, suggesting an organization that's learning from early criticism. But so far the numbers don't yet indicate a significant shift in policy. Five years after his first analysis of the foundation's spending on global health, McCoy carried out a follow-up analysis. Preliminary results suggest that the global imblance remains unchanged, with at least as high a proportion of grants directed to US-based research teams than in the years prior to 2009.[43]

At the close of the 2012 Edinburgh workshop on clinical trials, I took a flight from Edinburgh to London's City airport. The flight was delayed, and my seatmate and I chatted during the long lull. He mentioned that he worked as a management consultant with Bain &

Company – he'd landed the job just a year earlier, after finishing an MBA at the London Business School.

He asked me what I did. When I told him I was a sociologist, researching philanthropy and global health, he nodded excitedly. One of his favourite guest speakers at the London Business School, he said, was an Indian physician – an expert in global health – who spoke about the effort to build a strong generic pharmaceutical sector in India. 'I'm of two minds about it', he said. 'This guy said that Indian companies could make drugs for a fraction of the costs of branded drugs. And I get that. The humane, ethical side of me really gets that. But the free-market side of me thinks that of course patents are necessary.'

I nodded and the conversation drifted to other things. But if I had had the energy I probably would have pressed him on the point. Was he taught it at business school – the idea that free markets and patents go hand in hand? And if not at school, then where?

His comment was hardly unusual. In fact, it's a widely held belief, impressed on generations of scholars from at least the eighteenth century onwards, when a convenient reading of Adam Smith helped to propagate the idea that patents are fundamentally economic devices: an integral feature of laissez-faire economies. But patents are not market devices. They are the opposite. They are a government-sanctioned monopoly permitting exclusive sales of a product for a limited period of time, protected by courts of law.

In *The Wealth of Nations*, Smith suggested that, in instances where individuals take huge financial risks to come up with a new invention, it was not unreasonable for a government to grant a 'monopoly of the trade for a certain number of years'. Over a century later, Joseph Schumpeter reiterated Smith's sentiment. 'Long-range investing under rapidly changing conditions, especially under conditions that change or may change any moment under the impact of new commodities and technologies, is like shooting at a target that is not only indistinct but moving – and moving jerkily at that', he wrote. 'Hence it becomes necessary to resort to such a protecting device as patents.'[44]

Both men thought that such privileges should be used sparingly, especially given that, as Smith emphasized, if there's anything worse than unrewarded investment, then it's excessively rewarded investment. At all times, he asserted, governments should guard against the creation of what he called 'perpetual monopolies,' something he viewed as devastating to the public interest – akin to price-fixing among competitors. Patents are often important, and highly useful, in rewarding innovation. Sometimes they help to foster economic growth. Other times they stifle it. But the bottom line is that their magic, their authority, doesn't come from the market. It comes from governments. And that magic can be taken away.

CHAPTER SIX

Forgive Them, Bastiat

To understand Gates's personal views on patent protection, and why health activists fear that his own beliefs may be curtailing access to medicines in low-income countries, we need to look back thirty years, to a time when Microsoft was a fiery upstart challenging the dominance of established players such as IBM.

Gates and Paul Allen, the co-founder of Microsoft, first registered their company in 1976. At that time, software was freely exchanged among a dedicated group of early computer enthusiasts. It was a period when the development of software was 'strictly home-brewed . . . back then, virtually no one paid for software'.[1] Gates was a Harvard student when he and Allen first registered their company; Allen was not. Both made themselves at home in Harvard's Aiken Computer Lab, a base where they logged hundreds of hours in computer time.

In 1975, Gates and Allen had learned that Ed Roberts, president of MITS, a company that sold Altair 8080s, a small microcomputer, was looking for a functioning computer language to go with his new hardware. Gates and Allen were fairly certain they could come up with the right program in a short period of time. They wrote to Roberts, telling him they had just the software he required. Roberts told them the same thing that he told other programmers who had gotten in touch: the first one to show up at his company's headquarters in Albuquerque with a functional version of BASIC would win his business. Allen, who looked older and more mature than Gates, was dispatched to Albuquerque eight weeks later bearing the software he and Gates had hammered out. After checking its compatibility with his Altair machine, Roberts struck a deal, paying Gates and Allen a flat fee of $3,000 for the program, plus a small royalty for every copy that Roberts sold. Gates was just nineteen years old at the time.[2]

Computer hobbyists quickly perceived an easy way to save a buck. It was difficult to come by a bootlegged computer for free – one had to spend money for the hardware – but copies of Altair BASIC could be easily copied and shared free of charge.

Gates grew furious when he learned of the practice, penning an open letter to hobbyists in a MITS newsletter that accused them of theft. He also made a few debatable statements. He claimed, for example, that he and Allen had spent the equivalent of $40,000 in working hours to develop the software, only to have their investment stripped through illegal bootlegs. Hobbyists scrambled to learn more about the little-known sender of the vitriolic letter. When they found out that Gates was a Harvard undergraduate, developing Altair BASIC in a communal lab space that he shared with Allen, not even a registered Harvard student, the irony was a bit much for them. They circulated their own vitriolic notes in return. Considering that Harvard had provided him with his lab space, perhaps university administrators and students vying for lab time were entitled to royalties, too?

The technology reporter Gary Rivlin points out what he calls the 'cruellest irony' facing computer hobbyists frustrated that Gates's attitude was threatening what had been largely been a non-profit environment, populated by aficionados eager to share rather than sell personal copies: It was their unauthorized distribution of pirated copies that helped Altair BASIC to emerge as *the* industry standard. The hobbyist's own anti-commerce stance contributed to Microsoft's emergence as the industry powerhouse it fast became.

Gates and Allen's use of Harvard's lab space would return to haunt them over the years, as their rivals suggested time and again that Microsoft played a rigged business game, forcing competitors to comply with their own business demands regardless of whether those demands were lawful or not. The company was accused of slandering its competition, as well as forcing competitors and consumers to accept unlawful 'tying' practices (requiring a consumer to buy something they don't want in order to procure the thing they do want). Even those sympathetic to Microsoft, as *New Yorker* reporter Ken Auletta points out, have described the company's business practices as 'thuggish'. Former staff at Microsoft stated that it was common practice during negotiations with outside firms to hide 'things even if it would blindside people you were working with'.[3]

As he accumulated his fortune, Gates had little interest in the philanthropic ethos that would later characterize his work at the Gates Foundation. In 1997, Microsoft executives were petrified that the rise of the internet might derail Windows's market strength. When Gates was presented with a proposal from some employees to write for the web rather than simply for Windows, he was incensed, shouting, 'Why don't you just give up your options and join the Peace Corps?'[4]

Gates is known for his verbal combativeness, regularly quipping 'that's the stupidest thing I ever heard!' at Microsoft's product or management meetings. The phrase became much-mimicked by his staff – his underlings reportedly developed the habit of vying to repeat the phrase to *their* underlings whenever possible.

Resentful of negative press attention to the company's business tactics, Microsoft's management adopted a practice of blacklisting journalists. John Dvorak, a columnist at *PC Magazine*, describes how Microsoft management would list reporters on a whiteboard with the comments 'Okay', 'Sketchy', or 'Needs work'. Many reporters believed, Dvorak writes, that if you ended up in the 'needs work' category, Microsoft would take pains to try and have you fired.

Dvorak himself ended up on Microsoft's blacklist, something he only realized because of documents unearthed during the discovery process of the *Comes v. Microsoft* lawsuit in Iowa. Dvorak adds, rather dryly, that while Microsoft failed to completely unseat him, threats from the company did succeed in seeing him removed as a licensed columnist for *PC Magazine Italy*.[5]

By 1995, a trend was sweeping the world of technology. Netscape, a little-known communications company, had launched Netscape Navigator, a browser that gave many Americans access to a phenomenon that had been around for decades: the internet. Navigator became the industry leader, a *de facto* standard used on most Windows platforms. Gates has admitted that he didn't see the internet coming. Until early in 1995, he failed to realize that Navigator, a technology largely free at point of use, was eating into his profits.[6]

He caught up quickly. Microsoft's flagship internet browser, Internet Explorer, was launched in late 1995. At a press conference, Gates quipped that every morning he woke up thinking about browser share. His key weapon in the ensuing browser war with Netscape was product leverage. For years, Compaq, a computer company specializing in hardware, had been selling machines that were preloaded with Netscape Navigator. As Rivlin describes, Compaq sought to honour an earlier deal with Netscape when Microsoft's Internet Explorer came on the market by ensuring that Compaq computers featured Netscape, rather than Explorer, on their opening screens. Microsoft, meanwhile, had packaged Explorer with Windows. Explorer was therefore available on Compaq machines – but not, to the frustration of Microsoft management, featured on each opening screen. Microsoft issued Compaq an ultimatum. The hardware specialist was free to feature whatever browser it liked on its opening page, but if it chose Netscape Navigator, then Compaq would lose the right to sell Windows on any of its machines. The threat piqued the interest of the US Federal Trade Commission and Department of Justice.

Other major hardware firms such as Gateway 2000 and Micro Electronics confirmed to federal investigators that Microsoft had strong-armed them with similar tactics.

When a company has a monopoly on any given market, US federal anti-trust law forbids that company from requiring its customers to buy a second product in order to gain access to the first. Like price-fixing, the practice of product bundling is deemed an illegal abuse of market dominance because it limits the options available to consumers. Complaints from firms such as Netscape and Compaq were at the heart of the Department of Justice's 1998 anti-trust case against Microsoft. In a press release in May, the DOJ announced that it was filing suit against the company for a pattern of anti-competitive acts, including the charge that Microsoft had 'unlawfully required PC manufacturers to agree to license and install its browser, Internet Explorer, as a condition of obtaining licenses for the Windows 95 operating system.'[7]

In November 1999, the presiding judge, Thomas Penfield Jackson, issued initial findings. He stated that Microsoft was a monopoly power. It had deliberately used its market dominance to harm consumers and other companies. He later ruled that Microsoft should be broken into two companies. Microsoft launched a series of appeals. Jackson's proposed solution, to divide the company in two, was retracted during these appeals. Microsoft reached settlements with the Department of Justice and a number of US states which had simultaneously launched lawsuits against the tech giant.

Frustration over Microsoft's tactics was also brewing across the Atlantic. In 2004, in its then-largest fine ever imposed, the European Commission ordered Microsoft to pay nearly €500 million in fines for abusing its monopoly position in the European market, one of the company's largest revenue sources.

Microsoft appealed, issuing a vitriolic rebuke of the European Commission's ruling. In a seven-page response on its website, Microsoft's argued that EC regulations were preventing the company from using its resources to find innovative solutions for its consumers. 'The commission is seeking to make new laws that will have an adverse impact on intellectual property rights and the ability of dominant firms to innovate', Microsoft stated.[8] Microsoft's key argument – that proposed EC regulations impinged upon intellectual property rights – sums up the company's current views on the need for stringent intellectual property protections, a stance which marks a stark divergence from Bill Gates's own early writing on patents, something he once saw as a barrier to Microsoft's competitiveness.

In 1991, in a memo to his senior management, Gates wrote that 'if people had understood how patents would be granted when most of today's ideas were invented, and had taken out patents, the industry would be at a complete standstill today'. He added the worry that 'some large company will patent some obvious thing' and use the patent to 'take as much of our profits as they want'.[9] At the time, Microsoft was a fledgling upstart compared to giants such as IBM. It held only eight patents. Today, the situation could not be more different. The richer Microsoft becomes, the more doggedly Gates has defended strong patent rights. In 2004 alone, Microsoft submitted a total of 3,780 different patent applications.

Why did Gates change tack so dramatically on patents? The short answer is obvious. Once Microsoft grew in size, it needed legal protections to guard its vast product monopoly from upstarts like the company it once was. The longer answer is more complex. Gates's about-face on patents took place during a decade when the primary legal means for software protection changed from copyrights to patents. Prior to the 1980s, software developments were not privy to the vast patent protections enjoyed today. One revolutionary treaty would foment vast changes in the realms of information technology, software development and pharmaceutical innovation: the World Trade Organization's agreement on Trade-Related Aspects of Intellectual Property (TRIPS).[10]

SUING SOUTH AFRICA

TRIPS grew out of the lobbying efforts of a group of North American software, pharmaceutical, and entertainment executives working under the banner of the Intellectual Property Committee (IPC), set up in 1986 by CEOs from companies such as Warner Communications, Bristol-Myers, Johnson & Johnson, Monsanto, Merck, and Pfizer. These CEOs had a simple argument with considerable appeal for the US public. They asserted that the fundamental cause of America's economic woes was lost income as a result of insufficient intellectual property protection. The IPC worked tirelessly to persuade the American public that foreign companies and nation states were benefiting from the innovation of American producers while failing to shoulder their fair share of development costs. They demanded the enactment of global legislation that would enforce US patents throughout the hemisphere.[11]

In 1996, TRIPS was signed by member states of the World Trade Organization (WTO), a Geneva-based organization established in 1995 as a replacement for the early General Agreement on Tariffs and Trade (GATT). TRIPS extended patent, copyright, and trademark protections to previously unthinkable areas such as software, which open-source computer activists had long argued should be universally available in the same way that mathematical knowledge is freely accessible. The treaty also led to sweeping changes in the global market for medicines. It became much harder for patented drugs to be replicated and distributed affordably in poor regions, depriving millions of people of the chance of receiving life-saving medicines in their lifetime.

Before its passing, the treaty was predicted to reap vast windfalls for American corporations. And it has. In 2011, the net surplus in royalties from intellectual property was twice as much as the total revenue from US agricultural exports combined. With a growing monopoly over global innovations comes growing resentment.

Today, as the *Financial Times* reporter Alan Beattie points out, there is a widespread suspicion that global patent laws are 'mainly being written by their beneficiaries'. And nowhere is this frustration more visible than when it comes to global health inequality and access to medicines.[12]

Take the case of South Africa. In the late 1990s, bolstered by the new legal powers afforded them through TRIPS, a team of thirty-nine major pharmaceutical companies sued the South African government after it passed legislation that would enable it to distribute affordable antiretroviral drugs to treat HIV.

The pharmaceutical companies' suit was launched in 1998 with the strong support of the Clinton administration. Clinton's government had placed South Africa on its '301' list, an annual report which identifies countries that are purportedly in violation of intellectual property rights, leading to sanctions if they do not comply with US property norms. In the case of South Africa, the US revoked favourable tariffs for South African imports in order to pressure the country into abandoning the effort to distribute affordable HIV drugs.

Al Gore, vice president at the time, led the US campaign against the South African government. According to a State Department report presented to the US Congress in February 1999, Gore had mounted an 'assiduous, concerted campaign' to overturn the newly passed South African legislation. An aim of the report was to appease members of Congress who thought that the US was acting too complacently in enforcing intellectual property protections.

'History will judge people harshly as to how they acted in this crisis. And it's going to be a harsh judgement on Gore', James Love, a health activist instrumental in building public opposition to the consortium's lawsuit, suggested at the time.[13] He was right. Gore had long been a staunch supporter of strict intellectual property privileges. In 1994, for example, on an official visit to Argentina, he announced that unless Argentina supported US-backed legislation on pharmaceutical patents, it would be included on the '301' list and face trade sanctions by the United States.[14]

Public backlash against Gore's intimidation efforts in countries such as Argentina and South Africa overshadowed his 2000 presidential bid. Gore tried to backpedal, effecting an astonishingly speedy flip-flop on patent issues (he publicly criticized the tendency of pharmaceutical companies to try to extend patent life for trivial modifications, a practice known as evergreening). But the damage was done. While in office, Clinton and Gore massively misgauged how US citizens would respond to their bullying of South Africa and other nations.

In 1997, about 14 per cent of South Africa's population was estimated to have HIV. By 1999, surveys in pregnancy clinics suggested the number had risen to 22 per cent. The decision to sue the South African government under such circumstances led to public outrage. After three years of fighting, the pharmaceutical companies bowed to public pressure and dropped their suit. At global trade talks in Doha in 2001, a declaration was issued that affirmed provisions with TRIPS which secure the right of WTO members to 'adopt measures necessary to protect the public health and nutrition'. The provisions include the right to issue compulsory licenses when needed. A compulsory licence is a legal permit enabling a nation to commission affordable medicines from a third party, such as a generic pharmaceutical manufacturer.

The Doha Declaration confirmed the right of all nations to import or domestically produce affordable versions of patented medicines. But did they have financial means to do so? A niggling question remained: just *how low* could the price of HIV medicine drop? Few people imagined that life-saving HIV drugs, typically costing tens of thousands per patient in the United States, could be supplied for less than one dollar a day by generic drug firms. But that is exactly what the brash CEO of Cipla, then a little-known generics manufacturer, promised.

Cipla was first established in 1935 with the aim of empowering Indian manufacturers to produce drugs at a fraction of the cost of foreign multinationals operating in India. It is something of a family business, founded by Khwaja Abdul Hamied, a nationalist and proud anti-imperialist who saw the company as vital to strengthening India's economic independence from Britain. Following Khwaja, the company was headed for fifty-two years by his son, Yusuf Hamied, a research scientist with a PhD in chemistry from Cambridge University (as of 2013, Yusuf's family owns about 36 per cent of equity shares).

In the late 1990s, a coalition of health NGOs, spearheaded by the health activist James Love, met with Hamied to ask how cheaply he could produce a three-drug combination of HIV antiretroviral medicine. Hamied's reply provoked incredulity. He suggested that, providing a buyer picked up the drugs at Cipla's factory door, saving on transport costs, he could supply the combination treatment for $350 per year. In other words, for less than a dollar a day. Just over a year later, Love announced to Bernard Pécoul, then director of Médecins Sans Frontières's Campaign for Access to Essential Medicines, that Hamied had promised that he could deliver the drug combination for a figure that amounted to less than a dollar per day. Pécoul was sceptical. He had been lobbying for *years* for multinationals to lower the costs of HIV drugs in poor regions – and made only modest progress.

At the time, HIV/AIDS treatment in Africa cost about the same as it did in the United States: about $10,000 or more per patient. After laborious negotiations with Pécoul, a handful of companies agreed to offer special deals, offering to reduce the price of treatment to $1,000 per year for a select number of African sufferers. As a strict provision, companies insisted that the lower prices must be kept secret (they didn't want news of the price reduction to reach US markets, where local HIV activists were calling for sky-high drug costs to be lowered). Even at $1,000 per patient, however, antiretrovirals were priced out of reach of Sub-Saharan Africa where the virus was most virulent.

Hamied presented an unexpected option, one that the multinationals hadn't bargained on. He suggested that low-income nations should invoke the TRIPS provisions enabling them to import generic drugs when facing a health emergency. Few people could honestly say that a nation such as South Africa, with HIV cases hovering at around 20 per cent of the adult population, was *not* in the grips of a pandemic. With Love's encouragement, Hamied sent a letter to four major pharmaceutical companies that held patents on antiretroviral drugs, offering them a 5 per cent royalty in exchange for a licence to manufacture the drugs.[15]

In 2002, the WHO released its first list of manufacturers of safe AIDS drugs. Hamied's Cipla was one of the named companies. Peter Piot, director of the United Nations AIDS agency, said the WHO's decision to include Cipla on its list of approved manufacturers would enable more patients to 'gain greater access to affordable HIV medicines of good quality'.[16]

The WHO announcement chimed with a policy suggestion hailing from the United States, where a group of 128 economists and health specialists based at Harvard University called for rich countries to establish a fund that could procure and distribute HIV drugs at affordable rates. The Harvard-based team called for the establishment of a multibillion trust fund to pay for AIDS drugs in poor regions, managed through the oversight of the WHO. Signatories to the Harvard statement suggested that it was a moral duty for wealthy nations to find affordable ways to help poor nations procure more antiretroviral treatments.[17]

Underpinning the Harvard proposal was a theory that seemed logical but did not yet have significant epidemiological or clinical evidence to support it. Researchers behind the Harvard statement believed that increased treatment would help halt the spread of the disease by reducing transmission rates. They were at the forefront of a ground-breaking idea in HIV research, one challenged for years as too expensive and ethically fraught to undertake on a global scale. That idea is 'treatment as prevention', the belief that because early exposure to antiretrovirals decreases the potency of the 'viral load' in an individual's bodily fluids, the chance of a person transmitting the disease diminishes the sooner they are started on HIV treatments.

In the wake of the Harvard statement, the Gates Foundation announced a surprise press conference. Together with the heads of the Rockefeller and the United Nations Foundations, Gates appeared personally at the press conference. What was their core message? They wanted to make public their strong opposition to the Harvard group's call for increased distribution of HIV drugs. Gates, who was then still heading Microsoft, suggested that the global community simply did not have enough funds to both subsidize HIV treatment in poor regions and to prioritize much-needed emphasis on HIV prevention efforts. When it came to HIV efforts, the Gates Foundation was firmly in the 'prevention' rather than treatment camp – fearful that ramping up immediate distribution efforts would detract funding and political will from the effort to find a HIV cure.[18]

The primary concern of the Gates Foundation, then and today, appears to be financial. Speaking anonymously, a senior scientist at the Gates Foundation suggested to me in early 2012 that, 'If I had all the money in the world to spend, this wouldn't even be a conversation. We'd go out and find everyone we could and treat everyone possible. But we have limited resources.'[19]

Those opposed to the Harvard statement also raised an important medical concern – the danger of rolling out mass drug treatments in poor regions without enough trained health workers for monitoring compliance with drug regimes. Many experts believed that improper administration of antiretroviral combinations might lead to drug-resistant disease strains. 'There's something worse than AIDS in Africa', said William Foege, former director of the US Centers for Disease Control and Prevention and a senior adviser to the Gates Foundation. 'What's worse is AIDS in Africa *and* drug-resistant strains of HIV.'[20]

The Gates Foundation would later emerge as the largest private donor to the Global Fund to Fight AIDS, Tuberculosis, and Malaria, a public-private partnership that works with industry and governmental stakeholders to procure and distribute low-cost treatments for these three global killers. Through the billions he has spent on institutions such as the Global Fund, Gates is often praised for putting his fortune towards combating HIV. But his campaigning against increasing antiretroviral treatment in poor countries infuriates health activists who say that the Gates Foundation has continually lobbied against price reductions for HIV drugs and other medicines. These activists want a more equitable global patent regime, fostering fair competition. They do not want charity handouts.

In 2012, I spoke with a policy analyst who works at a leading humanitarian relief organization (she wished for both her own and the organization's name to remain anonymous). 'Ten years ago, the Gates Foundation, and Bill Gates himself, were very vocal in their support for HIV prevention, and would oftentimes speak against HIV treatment', she said.

> Still, to this day, I can't tell you whether the reason was because he felt that HIV treatment, and the effort to have access to affordable drugs, to ARVs [antiretrovirals], would be a threat to intellectual property, the regime of which he staunchly supports, or whether, through some other analysis, he really felt that HIV prevention should be supported at the expense of HIV treatment – and couldn't imagine a world where we would have room for both . . . Frankly, Bill Gates has been a barrier to getting lifesaving medicines to people.

Many of my informants reiterated this concern. Two examples emerge from the WHO's effort to establish international guidelines on the use of ARVs in HIV-positive individuals. The analyst just quoted – I will call her Anna – described both instances to me. Each was confirmed by separate sources, one a senior scientist who was seconded to WHO, and one based at Human Rights Watch. Both examples concern situations where health practitioners were frustrated by what they saw as lobbying by the Gates Foundation to keep strict treatment thresholds in place.

In the first case, the WHO is believed to have delayed its guidance on the early use of HIV treatment among serodiscordant couples, a term for when one partner is infected and the other is not. In the lead-up to the 2011 International Aids Society meeting in Rome, guidance advocating early use of HIV drugs among infected partners in serodiscordant couples was expected to be released. The WHO abruptly chose to delay the guidance. Many people attributed its reticence to opposition from the Gates Foundation, which was strongly invested in separate studies exploring the medical benefits of pre-exposure prophylactic treatments (PrEP), a new HIV treatment method which involves negative individuals – those who have not tested positive for the virus – taking a combination of drugs.

'There's a struggle between providing treatment to serodiscordant couples to prevent transmission versus providing pre-exposure prophylaxis treatment to high-risk populations . . . there was a sense raised at the [Rome] meeting by people I spoke with that Gates was really supporting pre-exposure prophylaxis', a staff member of Human Rights Watch said to me, adding, 'there's a lot of rumour and it wasn't clear what the picture was [but the Gates Foundation was believed to have] basically stepped into this process which was far along at WHO and when the guidance was about to be released said, "no you can't release this guidance"'.

Treatment Action Campaign, a health policy organization that advocates for price reductions and better access to medicines, circulated an open letter to the WHO following the Rome conference.

'We are writing with alarm following the International AIDS Society conference in Rome, where it seems that the WHO scrapped release of technical guidelines on HIV testing and treatment for discordant couples', the open letter states.

> The evidence for [the technical guidance] came after over a decade of evidence culminating with the HPTN 052 trial, which showed a 96% reduction in HIV transmission through ARV treatment. What was obvious prior to the last few months has now become clear scientific consensus: antiretroviral treatment not only prevents mortality and morbidity, [it also] prevents infection among discordant couples. WHO is now failing in its responsibility to help implementing countries and program managers translate this science into policy.[21]

The letter is signed by seven organizations, including the AIDS and Rights Alliance of Southern Africa; the Global Network of People Living with HIV/AIDS, and the UK Stop AIDS Campaign.

The second example discussed by Anna was a decision taken in Lesotho to flout WHO guidance in order to treat HIV-positive individuals at an early stage. As Anna explained, health practitioners in developing regions generally start treating HIV-positive individuals 'based on two criteria: If their CD4 count – CD4 being a white cell immune system – if it was below a certain threshold. That means your immune system is weakened so we need to build it up. You're sick to the point where you need ARVs. The other indication is clinical status, so, what we see in terms of what a patient is experiencing and what we're told of their symptoms . . . The WHO has a staging classification system: Stage 1, 2, 3, 4.'

Anna suggested that, 'Before WHO changed its guidelines at the end of 2010, most people in the developing world were started out on HIV treatment only if their CD4 count was below 200 or if they were Stage 4 – the last stage', Anna explained, adding:

Some countries went ahead of WHO. This is really important to know. Lesotho, for example, went ahead. They were like, well, we know it's better for patients so we're going to do it.

The reason that Lesotho was more ambitious than WHO is that WHO is essentially accountable to its stakeholders, and most of all to its donors. And what we know – and we know it from people at the highest levels – is that it was Bill Gates himself that made phone calls to WHO to dissuade them from issuing new guidelines that would mean earlier treatment and better drugs.

Lesotho went ahead in 2008. The WHO didn't issue its guidelines until the end of 2010. Lesotho had two full years on the WHO. That is how long the guidelines were suppressed. Even at the last hour Gates tried to intervene.

The Rome example was confirmed to me by a senior policy-maker who had been seconded to the WHO. He emphasized the need to protect his identity due to concerns over a backlash from the Gates Foundation. 'Maybe I'm a paranoid guy', he said. 'But I'm scared out of my mind talking to you right now.'

On the other hand, a number of my sources firmly rejected the idea that the Gates Foundation was steering HIV research in a counter-productive direction or stifling treatment efforts. I spoke with Myron Cohen, the lead author of a ground-breaking 2011 *New England Journal of Medicine* study providing conclusive evidence that early antiretroviral therapy decreases HIV transmission. Cohen stressed that there was much overlap in the 2000s between research focused on PrEP interventions and research exploring the health benefits of early treatment with existent ARVs. 'All the work we did with antiviral agents and pharmacology all relates to PrEP just as much as it relates to treatment. So my lab group was always working on both fields', he said. 'But when we made a decision on what we were going to spend our time doing, we [decided] we were going to treat the infected first.' He added, 'I felt that that had greater public health impact.'

Cohen emphasized that he never felt that the Gates Foundation might be suppressing scientific research that diverged from its own funding investments. 'I have met Mr. Gates; I certainly know the leaders of the Gates Foundation, and I've never got the impression that they were opposed to the research that we were doing . . . I certainly have a good relationship with the Gates Foundation and we are doing a study with them now, a policy study that flows from [study] 052.'

George Rutherford, head of the Division of Preventive Medicine and Public Health at the University of California, San Francisco, reiterated the same points as Cohen. I asked him if he knew of any evidence to suggest that Gates personally intervened at the eleventh hour to try to delay technical guidance advising early access to ARVs. He doubted that such lobbying ever took place, commenting, 'A) I have no knowledge of it and B) it seems so preposterous to me that he would get in at that level . . . it doesn't sound particularly credible to me. It just doesn't ring true.'

Whether or not Gates *did* intervene warrants more media attention, something reiterated to me by those who fear that that Gates Foundation's funding of media outlets leads journalists to censor negative criticism; those in the field refer to the problem as the 'Bill Chill Effect'. Anna made this point:

> You have a foundation that is essentially paying for areas that it wants to pursue, and also supporting otherwise independent international agencies or norm-setting agencies. Once you have them on the payroll, their voices are compromised. That's why you're not going to get anyone to talk on the record . . . [this] reality has to come to light.

A PATENT CONFLICT

In recent years, Frédéric Bastiat, a nineteenth-century French economist, has emerged somewhat unexpectedly as a modern-day
intellectual hero of the Tea Party movement. Bastiat is the author of
'The Candlemaker's Petition', a satire written to underscore Bastiat's
contempt for government protectionism. This pamphlet describes
the case of a group of candlemakers and industrialists in the lighting
sector who petition the French monarchy to ban a foreign stake-
holder who they allege is infringing on their trade interests: the sun.

'Gentlemen', the candlemakers write, 'you are on the right track.
You reject abstract theories and have little regard for abundance and
low prices. You concern yourselves mainly with the fate of the
producer . . . We ask you to be so good as to pass a law requiring the
closing of all windows, dormers, skylights, inside and outside shut-
ters, curtains, casements, bull's-eyes, deadlights, and blinds.' Bastiat's
tongue-in-cheek arguments have become a rallying cry for Tea
Partiers whose anti-subsidies stance is starkly at odds with the
industrial heavyweights funding their grassroots efforts.[22]

Most Tea Partiers tend to share with the Koch brothers, the
deep-pocketed sugar daddies of the far-right movement, a seeming
dislike for big government, high taxes and any intervention smack-
ing of 'state socialism'. The irony – one yet to dawn on Tea Party
stalwarts who take to the streets bearing anti-government placards –
is that the Koch brothers have lobbied for years for the very state
protections that Tea Partiers publicly deplore.[23]

And so has Bill Gates. His current position on intellectual property is clear. Speaking with reporters after giving a keynote address to
the 2011 World Health Assembly in Geneva, Gates said, 'the intellectual property system has worked very well to protect our investments
so that when they are used in rich countries we get a payback and
then we have the control to make sure that it is not creating any financial burden on the countries that are the poorest'.[24]

He voiced the same sentiment at a Microsoft faculty summit in July 2013. In response to a question about how patent privileges affected the work of the Gates Foundation, Gates rejected the idea that patent rights hindered access to medicines: 'In the poor countries we work in, nobody files or enforces patents. It's essentially a transfer of people buying drugs in rich world, who are now enabling these things to be done at marginal cost in the poor world.'[25] He added that 'it's a complex system . . . the mix of commercial with free, without any coercion by countries forcing one model or other, in my view is working very well.'[26]

But twenty years of the current patent system contradicts Gates's claim. The system *has* worked – but only for a very small minority of businesses. Even American citizens lose out thanks to the enormously high price of branded pharmaceuticals in the US, a problem that has led to familiar news reports featuring busloads of senior citizens who cross national borders each year to have their prescriptions filled in Mexico or Canada.

In 2012, Michele Boldrin and David Levine, professors of economics at the University of Washington in St. Louis, published a working paper commissioned by the Federal Reserve Bank of St. Louis. It had a blunt argument: we should abolish the patent system. Drawing on a wealth of statistical data, Boldrin and Levine's argument is simple. They contend that there is simply *no* evidence to support the widespread belief that strong patent protections produce significant gains for the US economy. Some evidence does suggest that a limited amount of patent protection makes nations and industries slightly more innovative. But under the current system, patents have ceased rewarding innovation. Instead, they act as lucrative gifts for established corporations that seek to dominate markets by keeping small players at bay.[27] The system mostly benefits that strata of the international elite that Chrystia Freeland, a former Reuters executive and current Member of Parliament in Canada, terms 'rent-seeking plutocrats – those who owe their fortunes chiefly to favourable political decisions'.[28] The more stringent property rights become, the more serious a toll they take on the US economy, limiting the ability of smaller firms to compete against big guns such as Microsoft or IBM.[29]

Adam Smith once warned of this very problem. He stressed that while a 'temporary' restriction of trade was justifiable in some circumstances, governments must take care to ensure that such restrictions don't infringe upon long-term opportunities for competition. As he wrote, 'By a perpetual monopoly, all the other subjects of the state are taxed very absurdly in two different ways: First, by the high price of goods, which in the case of a free trade, they could buy much cheaper; and, secondly, by their total exclusion from a branch of business which it might be both convenient and profitable from many of them to carry on.'[30]

Boldrin and Levine's manifesto, combined with growing evidence of the ways large pharmaceutical companies tend to exaggerate their research and development costs in order to command increasingly strong patent protections, is winning the minds of an impassioned force. Members of the Tea Party movement seem to have grasped suddenly that patents are form of governmental patronage. Boldrin and Levine's research has caused something of a stir. It's been making the rounds of various patriot-themed websites featuring fatherly headshots of Thomas Paine, Ron Paul, and, of course, Bastiat.

Unquestionably, there is growing animosity on both the American left and right towards a patent system that keeps the prices of life-saving drugs artificially high, both on US soil and abroad. Ultimately, however, it's neither diehard patent protectionists at organizations such as ALEC, nor abolitionists such as Boldrin and Levine, who have advanced the most sensible proposals for patent reform. It's the more moderate voices. These include James Love, who spent years lobbying pharmaceutical manufacturers to drop their suit against South Africa and who today is fighting for a proposal that seems surprisingly modest. He wants wealthy nations to cease bullying less developed nations whenever they enforce the right to issue compulsory licenses. Even though compulsory licences are permissible under international trade regulations, countries are extremely reluctant to issue them. Why? Because doing so would expose them to punitive trade sanctions from the US government and costly lawsuits from pharmaceutical manufacturers.[31]

Today, a growing number of countries are fighting back. In March 2012, India's Patent Controller issued the country's first ever compulsory licence. It licensed the generic manufacturer Natco to produce cheap batches of Nexavar, a kidney and liver cancer medicine crucial in India's fight against escalating cancer rates. Bayer, a German pharmaceutical company, holds the patent for Nexavar. Thanks to India's compulsory licence, Natco is now able to provide the medicine for *97 per cent less* than Bayer did in the past, while paying Bayer 6 per cent in royalties.[32]

While this case suggests that compulsory licences *can* work well to secure access to desperately needed medicines, such examples are rare. Since the early 2000s, the US government has negotiated numerous bilateral trade deals that restrict medicines access. A good example is CAFTA, the US–Central America Free Trade Agreement. Signed in 2005, the treaty overrides safeguards within TRIPS in a number of key ways. For one, the treaty requires CAFTA members to establish specific monopoly protections for regulatory data. In most nations, once a patent expires, generic companies are not expected to repeat drug safety and efficacy tests, thereby hastening medicine access. But provisions within CAFTA stipulate that even *after* a patent expires, new manufacturers may *not* rely on brand-name drug tests for a certain period of time. This is called 'data exclusivity'. In countries such as Guatemala, legislators were forced to change domestic laws in order to offer data exclusivity to large multinationals. CAFTA, in other words, makes TRIPS looks like the lenient parent smiling benignly next to a whip-bearing authoritarian.[33]

Another problem is that CAFTA forces regulators in low-income nations to carry out surveillance tasks traditionally shouldered by pharmaceutical companies themselves. Angelina Godoy, director of the Center for Human Rights at the University of Washington, points out that under previous patent systems, and, indeed, under US law today, it is up to a patent holder to detect patent infringement, and to then litigate accordingly if they wish. Under CAFTA, the responsibility is transferred to states. This burdens drug regulatory authorities with duties they don't have the funding to carry out, exposing states to endless lawsuits by private companies if they're slow in detecting patent infringement.[34]

Somewhat ironically, the US government is far more approving of the use of compulsory licences when it comes to its domestic economy. It has issued compulsory licences to increase the availability of patented cancer treatments, the manufacture of contact lenses, and access to Hepatitis C diagnostic technologies. In 2006, a US court granted Microsoft a compulsory licence to use two patents owned by z4 Technologies that relate to features used in Microsoft Office.[35]

When Gates suggests that the current patent system works well to protect the interests of rich nations – he's right. Where he's misguided is in suggesting that the system also works well for poor nations.

THE BUSINESS OF BRANDING AID

In the early months of 2013, the Gates Foundation hosted a 'strategic media partners' meeting at its headquarters in Seattle – representatives from the *New York Times*, the *Guardian*, NBC, NPR, and the *Seattle Times* all came. The aim of the event, writes Tom Paulson, a Seattle-based reporter, was to 'improve the narrative' of media coverage of global aid and development, highlighting good news stories rather than tales of waste or corruption.[36]

In 2013, the foundation gave Ogilvy, a global public relations firm, a $100,000 grant for a project titled 'Aid is Working: Tell the

World'. Ogilvy PR is part of Ogilvy and Mather, one of the largest marketing companies in the world. That Ogilvy is a beneficiary of Gates Foundation largesse raises the same question as does its grants to Vodacom: why can't a highly profitable company cover its own marketing or business-expansion efforts?

And, secondly, if aid flows *are* working well, why do they need a masterful PR campaign to convey that message effectively? Many observers on the left and right suggest that the problem isn't a marketing failure; it's a failure with the underlying 'product'. Aid, they argue, is not working. And efforts to propagate claims to the contrary only exacerbate its limitations. Tied aid, conditional lending by bodies such as the IMF, and patent privileges which favour wealthy nations: these are just a few of the ways in which current development policies are failing the global south. One particularly egregious example of protectionist policies in the north is the tendency for OECD countries to place tariffs on manufactured goods from poor nations at levels four times higher than duties placed on goods from other wealthy countries.[37]

Also useful for wealthy nations are the considerable subsidies that North American and European governments offer to their own domestic energy, pharmaceutical, and agriculture sectors. These subsidies make it difficult, if not impossible for poor countries to compete with western multinational firms. To give an illustration, in 2000, each cow in the European Union received $913 worth of agricultural subsidies, while each Sub-Saharan human being received about $8 in aid dollars.[38]

And that aid comes with strings. The US government, for example, currently provides about 50 per cent of all global food aid, spending approximately £2 billion per annum in recent years. The vast majority of this US food aid is tied: by law, it's bought exclusively from US suppliers and transported on US ships, even when far cheaper alternatives are available.

In 2010, USAID overhauled its procurement procedures, making it possible for aid providers to buy goods and services from producers in poor countries rather than from US companies, a change praised for fostering aid independence in poor regions. Unfortunately, US-funded food aid and US-patented pharmaceuticals were exempted from the new procedures. In 2010, 40 per cent of US aid was spent buying food from just three US companies: ADM, Bunge and Cargill, and 75 per cent of goods were shipped on US vessels, stifling economic competition in the very countries purportedly boosted by US aid.[39]

Individual country examples offer sobering figures. Owen Barder, a development economist at the Center for Global Development, has called attention to OECD figures indicating that, of the $5 million spent by the US government on food aid to Cambodia in 2010, $3.5 million was spent on freight costs and other logistics. In other words, 70 per cent of the total budget was spent transporting the food. 'Is there really no limit on how much money is spent lining the pockets of our own companies', Barder asks, 'before the OECD refuses to count the spending as aid?'[40]

Perhaps the most glaring challenge facing developing countries is the problem of tax avoidance. A recent new law in Zambia – which loses an estimated £2 billion in tax avoidance annually – now requires mining companies to bring the proceeds of export sales back to Zambia, where the country's tax authorities can examine dividends and other payments in order to determine whether adequate tax has been paid. OECD policy-makers swiftly condemned the actions, warning that rogue actions by individual countries could lead to a fragmented set of rules with no clear standards – and reprimanded countries such as Zambia for not waiting until the leaders of G8 and G20 nations reached an agreement on how to deal with corporate tax avoidance.[41]

A Tanzanian MP recently pointed out that tax avoidance loopholes introduced by the World Bank and IMF in the late 1990s are costing African nations *double* the funding that they receive in foreign aid grants. 'It is killing us, you cannot now explain poverty in

Africa without this and this is the story that has been suppressed for so long', Zitto Kabwe, a former chair of the Tanzania Public Accounts Committee, stated to media.[42]

Zambia and Tanzania are not members of the G8 or G20, and yet they are bound by rules devised by far wealthier member states, and berated for having the temerity to implement national legislation that is not sanctioned by northern nations. When the Gates Foundation exhorts and empowers media outlets to prioritize 'good news' stories of how aid is 'working', his efforts displace stories such as this – attention to the ways that economic development is *not* working thanks to trade policies that benefit US and European multinationals and governments at the expense of poor nations. When observers point this out, Gates has on a number of occasions dismissed such criticism as 'cynical' and even 'evil'. At a talk at the University of New South Wales in May 2013, when asked his opinion about Dambiso Moyo's bestselling *Dead Aid*, Gates criticized the book in the strongest of terms: 'Having children not die is not creating a dependency, having children not be so sick they can't go to school, not having enough nutrition so their brains don't develop. That is not a dependency', he said, adding: 'That's an evil thing and books like that – they're promoting evil.'[43]

Moyo's book *is* prone to overgeneralization. But one of her main objectives is to point out that protectionist policies in the US and Europe can be damaging to African development – and she is right. As development expert Claire Provost argues, flows of aid from wealthy nations to poor ones 'pale in comparison' to the 'tax revenues lost by many African countries. Trade rules and migration policies can have just as large – if not larger – impacts on development.'[44]

Can aid really be said to be working when US and EU subsidies and import controls continue to thwart African growth? Can we be as sanguine as Gates is about current patent rules when poor and middle-income nations are leading the charge to alter them?

Medicines and software are not the only areas where dominant firms such as Bayer and Microsoft invoke patent privileges to fend off smaller rivals. Few industries have seen fiercer battles over intellectual property than the agribusiness sector, where companies such as Monsanto have launched aggressive suits against scores upon scores of small farmers. Today, with the Gates Foundation's support, Monsanto is bringing its business to Africa.

CHAPTER SEVEN

Always Coca-Cola

The Gates Foundation began investing substantially in global agriculture in the mid-2000s – an emphasis that was, at first, widely applauded. It seemed the foundation was moving from a narrow focus on disease eradication to a more holistic approach to global development. The foundation was recognizing that ill health is often rooted in problems that 'pharmaceutical bullets' can't fix; things as basic – and yet frustratingly hard to achieve – as access to better nutrition and clean water.

Since then, a number of the foundation's investments in agriculture have been praised for taking a farmer-centred approach, helping to increase the ability of smallholders in the developing countries to use locally produced seeds and gain a market for their products. One example is Purchase for Progress, a programme launched by the World Food Programme (WFP), the food assistance branch of the UN.

With funding from Gates and other donors, Purchase for Progress aimed to create a market for small farmers by guaranteeing that a certain amount of food would be purchased at a set price. The guarantee makes small farmers more attractive to commercial lenders, enabling them to procure loans. Traditionally, the WFP has relied on food aid shipped to poor regions from wealthy ones, putting cash into the pockets of large US agribusinesses rather than local industries or individual smallholdings.

During the 1960s and 1970s, the WFP tended to procure food aid almost exclusively from US and European food giants, buying surplus food from companies such as Archer Daniels Midland and Cargill, and shipping it overseas. In 2012, researchers at Cornell University published a study indicating that a very small handful of food products, such as processed vegetable oil, are cheaper to ship from the US. For most other foods, it's far cheaper to buy local goods, leading to 50 per cent savings on cereals such as wheat and 25 per cent saving on foods such as lentils.[1]

In the 1990s, the WFP began buying food from regions closer to famine-struck areas, typically from large agribusinesses in Africa and Asia. The Purchase for Progress programme takes a welcome step further: it helps to foster sufficiency among local smallholders, ensuring a stable market regardless of whether yields flounder or flourish in a given year.

Although the programme is not a replacement for overseas food assistance, it helps in a small way to dislodge large US and European multinationals from their dominant position in global food chains. Food exports today are monopolized by a small number of multinationals with strongholds on various markets: Monsanto and seed genetics, for example, or Cargill and grain and poultry exports. Cargill is the world's largest agricultural producer. Based in the US, with a commodities trading operation run from Switzerland, Cargill was founded by a family of grain traders and has been in private hands since. Together with three other food giants, ADM, Bunge, and Louis Dreyfus, Cargill accounts for between 75 and 90 per cent of the global grain trade – the precise percentage is hard to determine as two of the companies, Cargill and Louis Dreyfus, are privately owned and don't offer public market shares.

The concentration of food production in a small handful of companies is financially crippling for farmers in both poor and wealthy nations, as well as burdensome for consumers. One problem is that increased concentration among commodity buyers and food retailers tends to lower the price that primary food producers, smaller-scale dairy farmers, for example, receive for their produce. Often, lowered prices are cited as good for the consumer; in practice this isn't always the case. Even when prices do fall at grocery store check-outs, often that drop is negligible compared to the losses for the majority of producers. A 2011 Oxfam report suggests that growing consolidation enables companies such as Monsanto and Cargill to 'extract much of the value along the chain, while costs and risks cascade down on to the weakest participants – generally the farmers and labourers at the bottom'.[2] Olivier de Schutter, a former UN special rapporteur on the right to food, has suggested that competition law is useful for ensuring that large-scale buyers don't abuse their monopoly power; in the US, the departments of Justice and Agriculture have joined forces to consider new legislative measures, and similar policies are underway in the EU.

In the Gates Foundation's 2012 annual public letter, Gates emphasizes the problem of global hunger and rising food prices. He points out that the foundation has spent almost $2 billion on agricultural initiatives aimed at 'helping people like Christina Mwinjipe, a farmer [who] supports her family by farming cassava . . . for Christina and other small farmers – and for hundreds of millions of extremely poor people living in slums in big cities – getting food is the most pressing concern'.[3]

Throughout the letter, Gates details the foundation's approach to agriculture, including improving sustainable land management and better connecting local farmers to functioning markets. The foundation's earlier investments in companies such as Goldman Sachs and Monsanto, two companies seen as compounding recent spikes in seed and food prices, are, however, not mentioned.

A closer look at the connections between Goldman Sachs, Monsanto and the Gates Foundation will help in understanding why the foundation's investments in global agriculture may be compounding food insecurity rather than mitigating it.

Global food prices began rising sharply in 2006, when the price of staples such as wheat, soybean, rice, and cooking oil rose to levels not seen for three decades. In a number of countries, prices swiftly rose to about 50 per cent above the average for the years 2000–04. In 2008, the cereal price index was 2.8 times higher than in 2000, and the UN's Food and Agriculture Organization's world food-price index reached a record high. In early 2011, the index spiked again, toppling the 2008 record. A number of factors contributed to these price hikes, including global droughts, low agricultural yields, and poor livestock production.[4]

The crisis was not limited to poor nations such as Haiti. Even in the US, the number of people living in 'food-insecure households' jumped from 36.2 million in 2007 to over 49 million in 2008. In the UK, government statistics released in October 2012 showed that the UK's poorest households began buying less food in 2007, just after food prices first started climbing. Since then, the retail price of processed food has risen 36 per cent, including a 15 per cent rise in the year to 2012. Fruit prices have risen by 34 per cent since 2007, and vegetables by 22 per cent.[5]

A number of grain producers profited handsomely from the price hikes. In the third quarter of 2008, Cargill reported an 86 per cent jump in profits; much of the gains flowed from the company's commodities trading division. 'Demand for food in developing economies and for energy worldwide is boosting demand for agricultural goods, at the same time that investment monies have streamed into commodity markets', Cargill's CEO, Greg Page, reported at the time.[6] But why exactly did a tsunami of investment pour into commodities markets back in 2008? And what role do commodities markets play in the price hikes cramping consumer budgets? The answer lies in little-publicized US regulatory decisions hailing from the 1990s, a decade when the US relaxed a number of legal provisions geared at taming wild speculative swings in global commodities markets.

Such markets have a long and in many ways venerable history. Modern commodities trading has its roots in the Panic of 1857, caused when the rapid growth of the US economy began outstripping international demand. In little more than a year, prices per grain bushel dropped nearly two dollars, to the devastation of farmers who scrambled for ways to insure against price drops in future. They found a solution in the forward contract, an agreement to deliver a set amount of grain at a set price in the future. Usually, the price was set lower than whatever a bushel commanded in the present. The farmers willingly sacrificed some profit in exchange for the security of knowing their future yields had a buyer firmly anchored in place. What the farmers *didn't* have was the luxury of spending endless working hours securing future buyers. Hence the entrance of the speculator: the financial middleman happy to match vendors and buyers for a small commission. Speculators also took advantage of price fluctuations, leveraging 'long' positions with 'short', profiting whenever market ebbs and rises caught other investors out of pocket. The system worked well for speculators, but farmers soon suspected a scam.

'As far back as 1892, you have farmers testifying to Congress about this', comments Michael Greenberger, a former director at the US Commodity Futures Trading Commission, an arms-length agency of the US government that regulates futures and options markets. The CFTC has its roots in the Commodity Exchange Act, signed into law by Franklin Roosevelt in 1936. Pointing out that unregulated derivatives trading was a major culprit in the 1929 collapse, Roosevelt insisted on new policies to reign in speculators who engaged in commodities trading for purely speculative ends. His efforts responded to perennial complaints by American farmers frustrated that they had no control over the 'locals', a slang term for the Chicago speculators who would gamble on food prices for the sheer profit of it, not to pin down a future price as farmers did. Roosevelt's solution was simple and effective. He imposed 'position limits' on some of the actors involved in the market. If you were not a direct participant in the food business – as in, if you were not an actual producer of agricultural commodities – then you could trade no more than 5,000 futures contracts. These regulations worked well until the 1990s, when Goldman Sachs negotiated an exemption from position limits.[7]

In 1991, Goldman Sachs created a landmark entity: a financial instrument known as the Goldman Sachs Commodity Index (GSCI). The index was a derivative that tracked the performance of different traded materials, including coffee, cocoa, corn, and wheat, and then reduced the weighed investment value of each material into a simple mathematical formula. Other firms followed suit by creating their own commodities indices.[8] These indices might have been useful financial innovations, improving liquidity and enabling producers to insure themselves against massive price depreciations – had three things not happened.

First, after diligent lobbying, the CFTC agreed to exempt Goldman Sachs from the need to adhere to position limits. Second, this was followed by a wave of further deregulations throughout the 1990s, allowing other market players to also buy as many futures as they liked. Third, the 2008 financial collapse sent major institutional investors flooding back to the 'safer' agricultural commodities arena, as the quotation from Cargill's CEO above points out.

Almost at once, the explosion of speculation in agricultural markets seemed to distort the 'spot' price of actual food commodities – the price paid for physical products on the ground. The commodities had not changed, and while demand for some commodities in the years leading to 2008 *was* greater than supply, boosted in part by growing consumption in emerging economies such as China, the lack of available goods was not marked enough to explain the unprecedented explosion in price. As Frederick Kaufman, a well-regarded food expert and journalist writes, 'it was as if the price itself had begun to generate its own demand'.

In 2008, Michael Masters, a hedge fund manager, testified before the US Congress about the impact of oil speculation. In what came to be known as the 'Masters thesis', he suggested that excess speculative trading in commodities markets has driven up oil and food prices. The price of wheat, to put it simply, often rises as a result of more and more people betting that it *will* rise. Critics attacked *his* attack, suggesting that Masters has a hidden agenda: a number of stocks he invests in, in particular airlines, were hard hit at the time by rising oil prices. But Masters is hardly alone. George Soros has also suggested that institutional investors such as pension funds were inflating a commodities bubble by investing in commodity indices. He offered a number of policy recommendations, including barring US public pension schemes from investing in commodities indices, and reversing the CFTC exemptions granted to Goldman Sachs and other investment banks in the 1990s. Kaufman, Masters, and Soros aren't suggesting that *all* market actors should have caps placed on the number of forward contracts they can purchase, only those who aren't *direct participants*: those who don't produce any agricultural goods themselves.

They have strong support in DC. In 2009, Gary Gensler, former chairman of the CFTC, appeared before the US Senate with a blunt message, 'I believe that increased speculation in energy and agriculture has hurt farmers and consumers.' Under Gensler's leadership, the CFTC turned to provisions within the Dodd-Frank Wall Street Reform and Consumer Protection Act of 2010 in order to once again impose position limits on some players. His efforts, not surprisingly, were hotly contested by trade organizations representing the largest commodities speculators in the US. With strong industry backing, the trade groups launched a legal appeal against the CFTC's regulatory efforts – and they won. In a recent victory for Goldman Sachs and other traders, a US District Court ruled in 2012 that the CFTC does not have the jurisdiction to impose position limits. The CFTC has vowed to fight the ruling, rather sheepishly trying to correct the trading free-for-all that its own policies brought about.

Many leading economists support Masters, Soros, and Kaufman. In 2011, a coalition of 450 economists circulated a letter calling for G20 governments to curb excessive speculation in food markets. Their argument wasn't simply that speculation can drive prices up. It can also send prices spiralling downward, something lamented recently by those hard hit by plummeting oil prices. Abdalla Salem el-Badri, secretary general of OPEC, emphasized this point in late 2014, speaking with CNBC: 'The fundamentals do not really deserve this decline in price. Oversupply in the market is not really that much to deserve a 28 per cent decline . . . We are looking at speculation, that has some effect on it.'[9]

Neil Kellard, professor of finance at the University of Essex, was one of the signatories of the letter. He has emphasized that taming volatility, not simply arresting upward pressure on prices, is essential to ensuring that actual producers, rather than pure speculators, can hedge future risks. Masters and Soros, he told me,

> have really been voices at the forefront in saying, 'no, we need to regulate, we need to limit trading here, we need to cap speculative positions'. One of the difficulties with the whole area has been getting hold of the positions that traders are taking. In Europe, you still can't get that information. And it's only really been collected properly, in a disaggregated way, in the States since 2006 . . . People were saying, well, you know it looks like speculators might be moving prices in some way, but where's the proof?

The proof is fast emerging. Since 2008, numerous studies have confirmed that futures prices can alter spot prices. A study from Stanford University has documented that spikes in futures prices affect the spot price paid by buyers on the ground. A recent analysis from scholars at the New England Complex Systems Institute, peer-reviewed by economists from Harvard University, argues that the 'dominant causes of price increases are investor speculation and ethanol conversion'.[10] In a recent briefing paper, de Schutter suggested that 'a significant portion of the price spike was due to the emergence of a speculative bubble'.[11] His predecessor at the UN, Jean Ziegler, went a step further. In comments widely reported in the media, he called the investment rush on commodities a 'silent mass murder' that has brought 'horror' to global food markets. 'We have a herd of market traders, speculators, and financial bandits who have turned wild and constructed a world of inequality and horror. We have to put a stop to this.'[12]

In 2008, Warren Buffett invested in Goldman Sachs at a bargain price. As of February 2014, his company Berkshire Hathaway had a $2.2 billion position in the firm, which makes it the eleventh-largest in Buffett's portfolio. His stake also makes Buffett one of the top ten shareholders of Goldman stock in the world.The Gates Foundation was, until recently, also a direct investor in Goldman Sachs: in 2010 it purchased 500,000 shares. A few months later, it quietly sold them; later SEC filings did not report holdings in the investment firm. Despite this divestment, the Gates Foundation is still closely connected to Goldman through its shares in Berkshire Hathaway.[13]

The ties go beyond monetary investment. There is a revolving door of expertise between Gates Foundation advisors and Goldman staff. In 2007, in response to criticism over the foundation's lack of accountability beyond its three trustees, the Gates Foundation announced the establishment of two advisory boards, a US Program Advisory Board and a Global Development Advisory Board. Rajat K. Gupta, a then member of Goldman Sachs's board of directors who later served jail time for insider-trading violations, was appointed as the head of the Gates Foundation's Global Development board; he later stepped down in the wake of the insider trading charges.

The Gates Foundation's close connections to Goldman Sachs have led to a smattering of unflattering media articles, including posts on the *Guardian*'s Poverty Matters blog, a development blog that is funded by the Gates Foundation. Writing for Poverty Matters, John Vidal pointed out that the foundation's shares in Goldman Sachs came at a time when many small farmers in developing regions were questioning the foundation's partnerships with agribusiness giants such as Monsanto. Also in 2010, the foundation purchased shares in Monsanto, an investment worth about $23 million, and announced a partnership with Cargill to help with 'developing the soya value chain' in Mozambique. Later the foundation sold its shares in Monsanto, but it continues to collaborate on philanthropic ventures aimed at expanding the company's presence in African markets.

By partnering with companies such as Monsanto, the Gates Foundation is eroding the positive effects of its investment in programmes such as Purchase for Progress, provoking bewilderment and anger from farmers who have seen their livelihoods threatened by Monsanto's strong-arm tactics. Even unlikely figures such as Warren Buffett's son have emerged as vocal critics of the Gates Foundation's work in agriculture. Speaking recently with *60 Minutes*, Howard Buffett, a long-time philanthropic donor to farming programmes in Africa, criticized Bill Gates's emphasis on expensive, US-manufactured fertilizers and engineered seeds as a solution to African agricultural challenges. He suggested that Gates is trying to export US-style industrial agriculture to Africa, and that it won't succeed – something Buffett discovered from his own earlier efforts to launch similar programmes in the past. 'I don't think it will work', he said. 'We need to quit thinking about trying to do it like we do it in America.' Buffett's criticism was offered with a soft touch. He stressed that the Gates Foundation is funding some positive initiatives and suggested that Gates is the 'smartest guy in the world, next to my dad'.[14]

But his message was a clear one: importing expensive engineered seeds and synthetic fertilizers is not the best solution for developing agricultural markets in regions such as Africa. Why? Partly because championing high-tech interventions often leaves developing markets poorly placed to compete with large multinationals, exposing smallholders to interminable patent battles with well-capitalized firms. Policies championed by the Gates Foundation threaten to price African producers out of their own domestic markets.

In 2006, in partnership with the Rockefeller Foundation, the Gates Foundation created the Alliance for a Green Revolution in Africa (AGRA), an initiative aimed at boosting farm productivity across Africa through adopting similar measures to the 'Green Revolution' first launched in India in the 1960s and 1970s. The term itself was coined in the 1960s by an administrator working at USAID. Since then, thanks to the introduction of new, high-yield crop varieties, the volume of world food production has skyrocketed, helping to stave off famines in countries such as India and Mexico. Globally, the amount of food available rose by 11 per cent, and an estimated 150 million people were saved from chronic hunger.[15]

Sadly, as victories go, the revolution in India and Latin America is seen by many farmers as a Pyrrhic one. Its gains have been plagued by unintended ecological implications, condemning many of India's and South America's peasants and smallholders to destitution.[16] The new high-yielding crops required large plots in order to be economically viable. To free up large enough swaths of land, peasants were forcibly displaced from the countryside. Urban slums mushroomed at the edges of cities like sprawling human moats.

State subsidies to Indian smallholder farmers, once a strong bulwark of Green Revolution reforms, have dwindled in recent years – while US subsidies to its domestic farm industry have not. Current US domestic subsidies amount to nearly $20 billion per year, undercutting the price earned by India's exporters even as Indian smallholders are exhorted to consume seeds and fertilizers manufactured by US companies such as Monsanto in order to thrive.

In 2005, Monsanto doubled its sales of genetically modified BT corn in India, flooding village shops with seeds priced at twice the cost of ordinary, non-modified products. To compete, farmers are compelled to buy BT corn, prized for its resistance to bollworm infestation. But the corn has come with a price tag that is literally too high to bear, forcing farmers to take larger and larger loans from unlicensed lenders charging crippling rates.[17]

Suicide rates among Indian farmers have skyrocketed in recent years. In a grim irony, to end their lives, heavily indebted farmers turn to the same implements that failed them. Often with borrowed funds, they secure the $10 or so that it costs to buy a bottle of pesticide, and swallow it whole before settling to sleep.[18] Norman Borlaug, who won a Nobel Peace Prize in 1970 for his pioneering role in the Green Revolution, later acknowledged that the overuse of pesticides was eroding some of the gains of the agricultural revolution. He called for more judicious use of fertilizer and pesticides in future.[19]

Bill Gates has repeatedly suggested that we need to extend the Green Revolution to Africa. His comments have sparked outrage in developing regions. Vandana Shiva, a renowned Indian environmental activist, has condemned the Gates Foundation's links to Monsanto, calling the foundation the 'greatest threat to farmers in the developing world'.[20] In the late 2000s, a group of Seattle-based activists set up an organization called AGRA Watch in order to monitor, as their website puts it, 'the Gates Foundation's participation in the Alliance for a Green Revolution in Africa (AGRA)'.

In 2008, the Gates Foundation partnered with Monsanto to establish the Water Efficient Maize for Africa (WEMA) project, geared at introducing genetically modified drought-tolerant African maize varieties for Sub-Saharan Africa. While Monsanto has offered to provide seeds royalty-free for an indefinite period, critics fear that the gift is rooted in a longer-term economic strategy: gaining a toehold in African markets that have until now mostly resisted GM products, often for clearly articulated economic reasons.

In an interview appearing in IRIN, a news bulletin published by the UN's Office for the Coordination of Humanitarian Affairs, Michael Lulume Bayigga, Uganda's shadow health minister, encapsulated a concern voiced by other African legislators: 'The owners of these GMOs are whites in the US, Europe, and China who are looking for market[s] in Africa. They are creating markets and empowering themselves . . . I will cautiously support GMOs as long as they have been developed, modified, and tested by our own [African] scientists. But this engineering is worrisome.'[21]

The risk of introducing GM crops to Africa is twofold: the financial cost to local producers, and ecological concerns. The long-term safety risks of GM technologies are unknown, in part because companies such as Monsanto have fought against research being conducted on their products. In order to purchase genetically modified seeds, customers must sign an agreement that limits what can be done with the seeds. For over a decade, the user agreements of companies such as Monsanto, Pioneer, and Syngenta have explicitly forbid the use of the seeds for any independent scientific research. Only research approved of or carried out by the companies supplying the seeds may be published in peer-reviewed journals. 'Scientists must ask corporations for permission before publishing independent research on genetically modified crops', the editors of *Scientific American* wrote recently. 'That restriction must end.'[22]

Monsanto controls approximately 90 per cent of seed genetics in the world. Because genetically engineered seeds are a proprietary technology, farmers must pay royalties to use them and new seeds must be purchased every season, regardless of how steep the price hikes are. Historically, since ancient times, farmers have tended to save their seeds, storing unused ones for future seasons. Monsanto's user agreements insist that farmers must sign contracts agreeing not to reuse or sell GE seeds. Economists suggest that the financial gain to US farmers for introducing transgenic seeds has been negligible in comparison to the gain to patent holders. Diana Moss of the Anti-Trust Institute notes that in the US, from 2000 to 2008, the 'real seed costs [for farmers] increased by an average annual rate of five per cent for corn, almost 11 per cent for cotton, and seven per cent for soybeans.'[23]

Even conservative news outlets such as *Forbes* have condemned the tactics employed by Monsanto to evade compliance with environmental sanctions and enforce patent protections. *Forbes* contributor Nathaniel Flannery points out that Monsanto has failed to adopt globally recognized best-practices when it comes to environmental oversight and reporting, and refuses to report its greenhouse gas or carbon dioxide emissions levels.

In 2009, *Forbes* listed Monsanto as 'company of the year' because of its impressive stock gains. A year later, the magazine offered a *mea culpa*, suggesting that '*Forbes* was wrong on Monsanto. Really wrong.'[24] In the previous year alone, 'super-weeds' resistant to Monsanto's Roundup weed killer had emerged; new bioengineered corn had been unimpressive in its first harvest; and the US Justice Department launched an anti-trust investigation into the company. Two years later, in 2012, the Justice Department quietly dropped the investigation. But something worse hit the company. Research from the University of Caen in France found that rats fed a diet of Monsanto's 'Roundup ready' genetically modified NK603 corn over a two-year period developed more cancerous tumours than a test group fed with regular corn. In the wake of the study, the Russian government suspended the import and use of genetically engineered corn, and the French government announced it had directed its foodsafety agency to swiftly review the study, promising to implement a ban on imports of the strain if the study's finding were deemed robust. France has also curtailed growth of a separate Monsanto crop, its MON 810 insect-resistant maize which, to date, is one of the very few GMO crops permitted for cultivation within EU nations (other products may be imported, but not directly planted). France passed new legislation banning its cultivation within its own national borders.[25]

Legal challenges to Monsanto have yielded mixed results. In April 2004, a US Court of Appeal upheld Monsanto's right to forbid farmers from saving seed for replanting.[26] In another closely watched legal battle, a group of US plaintiffs, including family farmers and small businesses, took Monsanto to court in 2011 in an effort to prevent the company from suing them if seeds accidentally blow onto their land. A New York federal court dismissed the case. The plaintiffs have promised to appeal. A similar battle is underway in Brazil, where a case representing five million Brazilian farmers was launched against Monsanto for collecting profits on royalties from renewal harvests. In 2012, a Brazilian court ruled in favour of the Brazilian farmers. Monsanto is fighting the ruling.

In the winter of 2012, I spoke by phone with Daryll Ray and Harwood Schaffer, eminent agricultural policy analysts based at the University of Tennessee. They emphasized similar concerns to those raised by Howard Buffett – in particular the financial risk of increasing Monsanto's presence in Africa at a time when food markets are in still in their infancy. 'What we fear is the tendency to jump from where farmers are now – not being able to feed their family – to move them directly into a market-based economy . . . If that did happen, it would essentially be condemning the farmers that exist there to poverty in cities. Even if they got paid for the land, that would be a short-term benefit', Ray said. '[We need] to take farmers exactly where they are at the moment, and help them be more productive using their knowledge, and technology that would be appropriate to add to it, and then gradually move them into a higher rate of production. Rather than talking about them buying Monsanto products, or other kinds of products that they can't afford and have to buy every year, as in the case of hybrid seed.'

'It increases the risks farmers face. If they've either taken out a loan, or used all of their money to pay the tech fee', Schaffer added, 'and they have a crop failure, they're in deep trouble. If they use their traditional crop . . . they don't have this financial overburden to a local lender that may be charging 50 per cent interest between planting and harvest.'

When the Gates Foundation first invested in Monsanto, critics pointed out that the foundation had a stake, albeit a small one, in Monsanto's own success, creating a possible pressure to ensure that its philanthropic practices advance the seed giant's financial goals. An article in the *Seattle Times* emphasized this conflict of interest: 'Our biggest concern is that the foundation is invested in Monsanto so they're looking for Monsanto to make a profit', Travis English of AGRA told reporters. 'What they're doing is opening up new markets in Africa for Monsanto to monopolize the seed market.'[27]

The same concern arises when it comes to the Gates Foundation's championing of Coca-Cola, a company that it upholds as a close partner in its efforts to improve the global burden of disease.

Both Gates and Buffett are Coca-Cola men. Vending machines offering free cokes were a feature of Microsoft's company headquarters in the heyday of the 1990s. Today, Buffett is the single largest shareholder in Coca-Cola. In 2013, the Omaha-based financial giant made a surprise appearance at Coca-Cola's annual general meeting, sharing the floor with CEO Muhtar Kent and offering anecdotes about his youth in Omaha, Nebraska, where he'd collect and sell bottles of Coke, pocketing a nickel for each six-pack.

Kent asked Buffett for tips on leading a Fortune 500 company in today's climate of economic instability. 'You basically have to be accepted in countries around the world and bring them something that makes their lives better', Buffett replied. 'If you can do it at a popular price, you can go to the masses of the world and say you're going to live better because I'm going to be here – and then behave that way – you've got a winning formula.'[28]

Buffett's advice is already well heeded by Coca-Cola. Poor and middle-income nations are the company's biggest growth markets. Throughout Asia and Africa, customer loyalty is nurtured with the same marketing panache that triumphed in America – before North America's love affair with one of the world's best-known brands began to lose its bloom. Growing recognition of the health risks of sugared drinks and sweetener substitutes has led sales of Coca-Cola to stagnate in countries such as the US and Canada. The company's greatest hope today is Africa, where it aims to bump consumption levels closer to the region where they are highest: South America. In Mexico, astonishingly, consumption is more than 665 *servings* a year per person. In Kenya, meanwhile, the figure was a mere thirty-nine servings per head in 2010. Coca-Cola has ramped up its African sales and marketing efforts – aiming to double its spending in Africa to $12 billion over the next ten years.[29]

As more and more peasants and smallholders are displaced from their land, in part by high-yield agricultural techniques pioneered through the Green Revolution, they have flooded the cities. Access to cheap, sugary foods is displacing fresh food as the main source of nutrients. In recent years, non-communicable diseases (NCDs) – mainly stroke, heart disease, cancer, diabetes, and chronic respiratory disease – have become the biggest cause of death in poor and middle-income countries, outstripping deaths from infectious diseases such as tuberculosis, malaria, and HIV/AIDS.[30]

Despite the staggering cost of deaths from chronic diseases worldwide, the vast majority of philanthropic donors, including the Gates Foundation, have shown scant interest in tackling the problem. To date, the Gates Foundation has invested less than 4 per cent of funding into research on non-communicable diseases (NCDs). Tikki Pangestu, a former WHO director of the Research Policy and Cooperation Department, explained this problem during an interview in his WHO office in the early summer months of 2011. Gates 'has particularly focused on problems in Africa. Morally, you can't argue with that – HIV/AIDS, TB, and malaria remain very much a problem in Africa . . . by pouring in all this money, he creates visibility, there's no two ways about it', Pangestu said to me. 'But, of course, on the downside, it's very much, let's say, adding to the imbalance of where the funding needs to be. It's a no-brainer that the major problem in the future is not infectious diseases, including in Africa. It's chronic diseases.'

Pangestu pointed out that thirty years ago, over 70 per cent of WHO 'came from assessed contributions from the member states, so we were free to use that funding in the way that we saw fit', Pangestu told me. 'It's shifted . . . to the extent that 70 per cent to 80 per cent now are voluntary contributions.'

Voluntary, or extra-budgetary contributions as they are termed, are earmarked for *specific* interventions stipulated by donors such as the Gates Foundation. As leading global health scholar Devi Sridhar has emphasized, studies show that voluntary contributions to the WHO are far less aligned with the actual global burden of disease than assessed contributions. In 2008–09, for example, most of the WHO's extra-budgetary funding, about 60 per cent, was allocated to infectious diseases, with only negligible allocations for noncommunicable diseases (under 4 per cent).[31]

To be fair to Gates, he is by no means the only person misjudging where the world's largest health burden lies. The sheer speed at which the death toll from cancer and diabetes has outpaced infectious diseases has caught the global health community off guard. The failure to combat obesity, cancer, and heart disease epidemics in poor nations has been one of the most glaring mistakes of global development efforts in recent years, a point reiterated time and again by global health scholars David Stuckler and Martin McKee. They have pointed out that, 'overall there is little or no correlation between global health funding and the [global] disease burden, suggesting factors other than need are driving the global health agenda. This inconsistency comes in spite of donors' commitments to align aid flows with national health needs.'[32] Stuckler, McKee, and their colleagues don't mince words when it comes to attributing blame for this disproportion. They argue that 'global health is ruled by a few private donors who make decisions in secret. The capacity to decide what is relevant and how it will be addressed is in the hands of very few, who ultimately are accountable to their own interests.'[33]

Companies such as Coca-Cola, Kraft, and Nestlé have vigorously resisted government campaigns to reduce sugar intake, challenging regulatory and taxation efforts that would see them better advertise the content of their products. In 2003, for example, the WHO released a report on diet and physical activity that recommended reducing sugar intake. In response, the sugar industry threatened to lobby the US government to cease its financial support for the UN agency. More recently, when asked why Michelle Obama's childhood obesity programmes were not being proposed as a model for developing countries, a US official replied that such a programme could harm US exports.[34]

Robert Reich, a former Secretary of Labor in Bill Clinton's administration, has detailed lobbying efforts among US-based multinationals to pre-empt restrictive regulations by voluntarily 'self-regulating' harmful practices. He points out that 'General Mills, McDonald's, and Coca-Cola [have committed] to dedicate at least half of their child-oriented advertising to messages that encouraged "healthy lifestyles". And yet exactly how healthy lifestyles are defined is 'conspicuously vague'. Reich suggests that displays of 'corporate virtue may lull the public into thinking that a company can be trusted to do what's good for society even if costly to customers or shareholders.'[35]

Despite the fact that large food and beverage manufacturers have long lobbied against any regulations that could lead to mandatory reductions in the amount of sugar and sodium in processed food, these companies are being embraced as partners in the fight against obesity and other chronic diseases. Publicly, WHO Director-General Margaret Chan has rebuffed the lobbying efforts of companies such as Coca-Cola, stating, 'Today, many of the threats to health that contribute to NCDs come from corporations that are big, rich, and powerful, driven by commercial interest, and far less friendly to health. Today, more than half of the world's population lives in an urban setting. Slums need corner food stores that sell fresh produce, not just packaged junk with a cheap price and a long shelf life.'[36]

More quietly, the WHO has been revisiting the rules that prevent it from accepting cash donations from food and beverage companies. A little bit like teenagers frustrated by parental decrees, the WHO's six regional offices spread throughout South America, Africa, and Asia have long rebelled against diktats from WHO headquarters. The Pan American Health Organization (PAHO), the WHO's regional office in Central and South America, for example, has recently chosen to flout a longstanding WHO policy against accepting direct corporate gifts or donations from private donors. Starting in 2012, as Reuters reported, it began taking cash grants from large corporations: $50,000 from Coca-Cola, the world's largest beverage company; $150,000 from Nestlé, the world's largest food company; and $150,000 from Unilever donations.[37] Why? Because PAHO is desperate. Government contributions to UN organizations such as PAHO have dropped in recent years. In 2011, the WHO chopped 300 jobs at its Geneva headquarters after financial constraints in donor countries forced it to slash its budget. In 2012, Reuters reported that Jorge Casimiro, a senior executive from the Coca-Cola Company, had been invited to serve on an Advisory Steering Group for the WHO's Pan American Forum for Action on Non-Communicable Diseases, a group that helps shape governmental health policy in Central and South America. On its website, the WHO forum even touted the benefits of membership of the Pan-American Forum on NCDs as helping businesses to 'avoid regulation' and to 'influence regulatory environments'.[38]

Under Chan's leadership, the WHO has employed 'partnership advisors' to develop closer relationships with food and beverage companies. In 2011, the WHO organized a conference in Moscow for government health ministers. One session was chaired by Casimiro, from Coca-Cola. Representatives from PepsiCo, Nestlé and the World Federation of Advertisers gave talks at the conference. Chan praised their comments, provoking an attendee to stand up and ask whether the relationship presented a conflict of interest for the WHO. Chan, never a wallflower, responded by launching into song – a show tune from the musical *The King and I*, 'Getting to Know You'.[39]

The Gates Foundation has championed the idea that Coca-Cola should be upheld as a key partner in global health policy-making. In 2010, Melinda Gates gave a TED talk titled 'What Non-profits Can Learn from Coca-Cola,' where she exhorted development experts to adopt the beverage giant's distribution strategies. On its own, the suggestion seems fairly commonplace, even commendable. Gates pointed out that Coca-Cola is able to supply its beverages in highly remote areas where health practitioners often have difficulty transporting medicines. But her suggestion ignores a history of objectionable labour practices that made Coca-Cola's distribution strategies more competitive, including suggestions that the company's subsidiaries hired a far-right paramilitary group to intimidate and murder union members at the company's Colombian bottling plants. During the 2000s, a number of high-profile universities, including New York University and Rutgers, forbade the corporation from selling its products on campus in the aftermath of the allegations.[40]

The foundation has also partnered with Coca-Cola in a number of partnerships encouraging communities in developing nations to become business affiliates of Coca-Cola. In 2010, for example, the Gates Foundation provided a $7.5 million grant to TechnoServe, a non-profit organization that works to expand business opportunities for multinational firms in developing regions. TechnoServe, founded in 1968, is rated by the *Financial Times* as 'one of the top five NGOs for corporate partnerships.' Its main partners include Cargill, Kraft, Nestlé-Nespresso, and Unilever. The Gates Foundation's $7.5 million grant was intended, as a 2010 TechnoServe press release stated, to 'create new market opportunities for local farmers whose fruit will be used for Coca-Cola's locally-produced and sold fruit juices.'[41]

Through its shares in Berkshire Hathaway, the Gates Foundation is heavily invested in Coca-Cola. As Stuckler and his colleagues have asked, when a philanthropic foundation that is heavily invested in Coca-Cola chooses to set up a charitable initiative that enlists poor farmers in cultivating fruit for Coca-Cola, the question is – does this still count as philanthropy? And if *not*, then why should the Gates Foundation continue to receive the generous tax exemptions it currently enjoys?[42]

TAMING THE DONORS

In 2014, the Alliance for Food Sovereignty in Africa (AFSA), a pan-African platform composed of different farmers organizations throughout the continent, submitted an 'open letter' to the Gates Foundation and Iowa State University expressing concern over human feeding trials of GM bananas taking place at the university. The results of the trials were aimed at supporting the release of GM bananas into Ugandan farming and food systems although Uganda has resisted efforts to increase the use of GM crops in the nation. Signatories to the open letter included 127 different NGOs and human rights organizations throughout the world. The response from the Gates Foundation was the same response that most concerned stakeholders receive when they question the foundation's funding priorities: silence.[43] The foundation did, however, reply to inquiries from US media: when staff at the *Des Moines Register* investigated a delay in the start of the feeding trials – reportedly due to difficulties in shipping the bananas that had been developed in Australia – the Gates Foundation sent a prepared comment stating, 'The Gates Foundation continues to support the Banana21 project, which is helping find ways to tackle vitamin A deficiency. We look forward to seeing the Iowa trial move forward after the project has completed the necessary due diligence.'[44]

Is there any way for civil society organizations to put a halt to the Gates Foundation's efforts to increase Coca-Coca and Monsanto's presence in the region? The answer is: not really. The foundation is mostly free to spend its endowment however it likes, as long as it's not breaching domestic laws or regulations in the US or in the countries where it operates. Even then, when the foundation underwrites projects that appear to breach domestic laws, as India's parliament found in the case of the PATH HPV trials, it's difficult to hold the funding organization to account.[45]

For years, critical observers have proposed different measures for increasing the transparency and public accountability of philanthropic foundations. At the forefront of this struggle are US-based philanthropy experts such as Ray Madoff, Michael Edwards, Mark Dowie, Rob Reich, based at Stanford University, Robert B. Reich, based at the University of California, Berkeley, and Pablo Eisenberg, to name just a few key figures. There's also no shortage of outspoken voices in developing and middle-income countries most affected by Gates Foundation's grants in the area of global health and agriculture, including Arundhati Roy and Vandana Shiva, both of whom have criticized the lack of transparency, tax allowances and lack of accountability at large foundations such as the Gates Foundation, calling for radical reform of the philanthropic sector.

In a recent article, Eisenberg, a senior fellow at Georgetown University and a founder of the National Committee for Responsive Philanthropy, offers a list of specific proposals – all of which are worth heeding by policy-makers. US foundations currently have to spend 5 per cent of their endowments each year. Eisenberg has suggested that the figure should be increased to at least 8 per cent, and that restrictions should be implemented forcing foundations to invest in areas of the greatest social need. More investment in family or youth shelters for the homeless, for example, may do more good than funding another named chair at Harvard. Eisenberg's second proposal is to reduce the tax incentives for setting up philanthropic foundations, something that would increase the amount of federal money available for spending on social programmes. His third suggestion is to limit the size of large foundations, as well as rethink board representation. In his view, there's no reason why some of the largest and most powerful foundations in the world, including the Gates Foundation and the Walton Family Trust, should be composed of a tight nucleus of family members. 'At family foundations over a certain size', he suggests, 'at least two-thirds of board members should be non-family representatives of the public.'[46] Dowie has reiterated this point as well: a portion of each 'foundation's endowment really belongs to the public, whose state and federal treasuries would hold that portion of any large estate not left to a foundation,' he notes. 'It would seem fair, therefore, for 45 per cent of a foundation's trustees to represent ordinary citizens.'[47]

Reich, now a professor of public policy at Berkeley after serving as labour secretary under Bill Clinton, has pointed out that in 2007 alone, charitable deductions came to a total of $40 billion. 'I see why a contribution to, say, the Salvation Army should be eligible for a charitable deduction. It helps the poor', he writes. 'But why, exactly, should a contribution to the already extraordinarily wealthy Guggenheim Museum or to Harvard University (which already has an endowment of more than $30 billion)?'[48]

It's a sentiment shared by his nominal doppelganger, the well-regarded philosopher Rob Reich, who co-directs Stanford's Center on Philanthropy and Civil Society. He argues that there needs to be more attention to whether generous subsidies for philanthropic donations are warranted or not.

'[It is] very important to figure out empirically whether or not the tax incentive for charitable giving actually stimulates greater giving than would happen in the absence of the subsidy . . . the best evidence so far [is that] giving to religion is basically insensitive to the tax incentive. People will give to religion the same amount independent of whether there's a tax incentive or not', he said to me. 'On the other hand, giving to universities like Stanford or cultural institutions like the opera house are very sensitive, evidence shows, to the tax incentive.'

Given this reality, Reich suggests that we need to think more deeply about what the tax incentive is for. 'What are we trying to accomplish if we're going to subsidize charitable giving? If you think that charitable giving should be for redistributive purposes [which is] the usual understanding of the word charity . . . then the evidence . . . is not going to provide you much support for the tax subsidies that now exist because so relatively little charitable money goes to support the disadvantaged or the poor. So if you thought that that was a justification for the tax subsidy, you're going to wind up very disappointed.'[49]

Reich suggests that governments have an obligation to ensure that philanthropic grants are being used in a way that helps to alleviate some of the harms of increased inequality. So far, there's little evidence that US philanthropy is meeting that goal. One of his key arguments is that 'public policy does not do enough to encourage philanthropic behaviour that aims at greater equality. Worse, public policy currently rewards some philanthropic behaviour – in the form of tax concessions – that worsens social inequalities and causes harm. The state is therefore implicated in these philanthropic harms.'[50]

Madoff, an expert on trust and estate law based at Boston College Law School, has suggested we need to question whether the current law is doing enough to ensure that charitable dollars reach those organizations that are doing charitable work in a timely fashion. She is particularly concerned with the failure of the US Congress to address the surge in donor-advised funds, a vehicle where cash or other assets such as stocks are set aside in accounts that are to be dispersed to public charities over time. Contributions to donor-advised funds are given all of the same tax benefits as contributions to a food bank or other operating charity. Yet, there is no time period during which the funds must be distributed since donor-advised funds are not subject to the minimum payout requirements imposed on private foundations. Madoff has suggested that the growth of donor-advised funds in the US (they now account for about 7 per cent of all individual charitable donations) might have actually *reduced* the amount of funds available to operating charities. While aggregated donations have stayed at about 2 per cent of the GDP since the 1970s, the surge in new organizational vehicles that stash money rather than distributing it suggests that, as the journalist Kelley Holland writes, 'the effect on the rate of overall giving is negative.' Donor-advised funds are widely seen, Holland notes, as 'financial holding pens for the assets of people who want to grab a tax deduction but have no immediate plans for any actual charitable giving.'[51]

I spoke with Madoff in 2015. She emphasized that the problem isn't limited to donor-advised funds and that there is a broader need to recognize the significant public contribution to charitable giving provided by tax incentives, and to evaluate whether the public is getting an adequate return on its investment.

'In the United States, the tendency is for the public to respond to a large charitable gift by saying: "Oh, that's great – isn't that rich person nice for giving to charity."' She stressed that while there's no doubt charitable gifts can create public value, it's also important to recognize the tremendous public investment that these charitable gifts entail. When an individual commits $100 million of their business or other appreciated property to charity, the foregone taxes from the government are often far greater than the after-tax cost to the donor. Had the donor *not* given that $100 million, the donor would have had an additional tax liability of up to $66 million just based on the foregone capital gains tax and the savings from the income tax charitable deduction. If one adds in estate taxes, the tax savings may be as much as $75 million. Given the size of the tax subsidy, it is important to ask what society is getting in return.

Another concern is that the 1969 Tax Reform Act – the last major overhaul of US charity law – is out of step with the proliferation of new charitable vehicles that work in practice to circumvent the principles that underpinned the Tax Reform Act in the first place. Madoff pointed out that at the heart of the 1969 Act was an attempt to draw distinctions between grant-making organizations funded by a small number of individuals, called private foundations, and organizations directly engaged in charitable work, called public charities. The Act was established to strengthen public oversight over private foundations, subjecting them to limitations on self-dealing and the introduction of the 5 per cent payout rule. 'Our whole edifice is that we're going to treat private foundations differently from public charities,' Madoff said – and yet today the distinction is easily breached. First, though public charities are supposed to represent organizations that have broad public support, due to the niceties of the tax rules, a single individual can create a public charity simply by funneling the funding of the organization through a donor-advised fund. The distinctions are less meaningful in another way as well. Though private foundations purportedly have a 5 per cent payout to ensure that they make regular contributions to the public good, the payout rule can be met by administrative expenses (including salaries for the donor and donor's family) and by making contributions to a donor-advised fund, from which there is no payout requirement! What is the point of having a complex statutory structure that draws essentially meaningless distinctions?

Philanthropic donors don't like being told how to spend their money, and to some extent they have robust grounds for defensiveness: freedom from political intervention is what makes philanthropy a check on rather than a handmaiden to political power. But when philanthropy is used as a loot bag for well-financed hedge funders and private equity buccaneers, as in the case of US education, then more restrictions are warranted. If the donors kick up a fuss, one could easily repeat back to them what they often stipulate to their own grantees: a close watch on how dollars are spent is essential to ensuring the creation of 'social value'. And if you don't like the rule, then don't give the money. Pay the taxes instead.

The proposals above might seem restrictive. And yet, they pose fewer constraints than the atmosphere in Congress over a century ago, when those across the political spectrum questioned the value of permitting philanthropic foundations at all.

Eisenberg is a respected doyen of US philanthropy, something of a folk hero for grassroots non-profit groups. His scrappy admonishments of the concentration of philanthropic resources in the hands of a few elite figures are almost identical to the public concerns that compelled Woodrow Wilson to establish the Walsh Commission. But today, in the post–Citizens United era of unlimited political campaign financing, suggestions from pro-grassroots activists such as Eisenberg are increasingly *non grata* in DC power circles.

On the one hand, articulate criticisms of the 'new' philanthropy are growing louder, a pushback that, as Benjamin Soskis suggests, 'can be traced to the nation's mounting uneasiness with income inequality and to the spread of an economic populism that refuses to regard the concentration of wealth charitably.'[52]

On the other hand, legislators don't seem to have yet taken enough notice. 'If I was a betting man', Aaron Dorfman of the National Committee for Responsive Philanthropy said to me, 'I would not be putting money on the idea that there would be any [major legislative] changes implemented soon.'

The Selfish Gift

One of the most acute ironies concerning the size of today's philanthropic foundations is that the emergence of well-financed, politically powerful behemoths is rooted in a political philosophy that cautioned against using the centralized power of states to plan or develop economic growth.

Take the example of J. Howard Pew, who first established the Pew Charitable Trusts in 1948, not long after first reading Friedrich Hayek's *The Road to Serfdom*. As the historian Olivier Zunz describes, Pew's interest in philanthropy stemmed from meetings with Hayek at gatherings of the Mont Pelerin Society.

In *The Road to Serfdom* and influential essays such as 'On the Use of Knowledge in Society', Hayek, inspired by Michael Polanyi's work on tacit knowledge and Karl Popper's work on the open society, made an argument that was then radical for its time. He believed that much formal economic theory represented 'only the visible tip of the vast submerged fund of tacit knowledge, much of which is entirely beyond our powers of articulation'.[1] Because of the inaccessibility of the 'tacit knowledge' that affects individual decision-making, it is impossible, he argued, for a central planner to respond to the needs of different market actors.

Much of Hayek's criticism was directed at his own discipline.

Building on work by Karl Popper, he used the word 'scientism' to criticize what he saw as the unthinking tendency of economists to model their own discipline on the physical sciences. The reason why economics is *not* like the natural sciences, Hayek believed, is because economic transactions are rooted in human motivations, and human motivations are too ephemeral to ever be understood through the same tools used to understand physical laws of nature. Hayek's understanding of the limits of economic knowledge was essential to his criticism of state planning. In place of a central planner, he argued, what are needed are autonomous market actors – those capable of responding swiftly, through pricing mechanisms, to the fleeting decisions of countless individuals separated by space and time. In Hayek's words, 'the most significant fact about this system is the economy of knowledge with which it operates, or how little the individual participants need to know in order to be able to take the right action.'[2]

Hayek's *Serfdom* helped to inspire populist reactions against the evils of 'big government' even as, quite ironically, he embarked on a spirited campaign of 're-education' through invitation-only meetings launched at the resort of Mont Pelerin sur Vevey in 1947, high in the Swiss Alps, with funding from the Volker Fund, an American philanthropic organization. Attendees at the first Mont Pelerin meeting included over two dozen leading proponents of laissez-faire policies, many of them inspired by the writings of the Austrian economist Ludwig von Mises. The Mont Pelerin Society's aim was to 'clarify' the basic principles of a new, reconstructed economic liberalism fit for the twentieth century – a project that Hayek was adamant must start with a small, exclusive group who, in his words 'shared the same basic philosophy'. The meeting featured a contingent of scholars loosely affiliated with the University of Chicago, including, in his first trip outside the United States, Milton Friedman, as well as George Stigler, Frank Knight, and Aaron Director.

In setting up the new society, Hayek was outspoken about the need to avoid direct association with any one specific political party. His decision to avoid direct engagement with politics didn't stem from indifference to political power, but from his realization that his ideology could flourish far more successfully if he steered clear of any one partisan affiliation. This goal is attributable to Hayek's love of the writing of Alexis de Tocqueville, an admiration so profound that Hayek first proposed to call the Mont Pelerin Society the Acton-Tocqueville Society after its 'two most representative figures'. The economist Frank Knight was the fiercest dissenting voice, spluttering 'You can't call a liberal movement after two Catholics!'[3]

In *Democracy in America*, Tocqueville offers a nuanced insight into the power of religion in America, one that Hayek would later apply to his own political machinations. During his travels, Tocqueville was surprised to find that none of the many Catholic priests he encountered during his travels held any public appointments – unlike the clergy in France. Even more astonishingly for Tocqueville, each priest pointed to this lack of a government role as *the* fundamental reason for his own power: 'all thought the main reason for the quiet sway of religion over their country was the complete separation of church and state'. By avoiding direct association with the failures and scandals of fleeting political incumbents, religion achieved an immortality that no political party could engender. 'By diminishing the apparent power of religion', Tocqueville writes, 'one increased its real strength.'[4]

Throughout the twentieth century, the new priests of laissez-faire economic policy exemplified the perceptiveness of Tocqueville's insight. They grasped that in order to wield lasting power it was important to make sure their efforts appeared as non-political as possible. Unfailingly, whenever confronted with a choice between *overt* political engagement and more surreptitious political lobbying, Hayek would recommend the second strategy. Shortly after the

Second World War, Hayek cautioned Antony Fisher, an Old Etonian who would earn a fortune introducing factory poultry production in Britain, against a career in politics, suggesting that positive reform would be impossible without 'first effecting a change in the climate of ideas'.[5] Hayek urged Fisher to establish a 'scholarly research organization' that would supply intellectuals in the academy and journalism with studies of the free market and its application to current affairs. Fisher launched the Institute of Economic Affairs in 1955, and later the Atlas Economic Research Foundation, which spawned over 150 individual think-tanks. By the mid-1970s, the IEA had become Britain's leading free-market think-tank, an organization Margaret Thatcher turned to for regular guidance. Thatcher's devotion to Hayek is well known: she once slammed *The Constitution of Liberty* on the table of the Conservative Party's research department and declared, 'This is what we believe!'[6]

Implementing Hayek's laissez-faire policy meant capturing and augmenting government authority, not weakening it, through quietly ensuring the political structures were in place to allow the 'free' market to flourish. As the economic geographer Jamie Peck writes, 'while the Mont Pelerinian's trek to the mountaintop may have been seen as a metaphor for a certain kind of ethereal contemplation, far removed from the suffocating politics of statism . . . in the final analysis it was state power – *used to different ends* – that mattered most'.[7]

The historian Kevin Phillips has reiterated the same point. As he writes, 'The glaring assemblages of wealth during the Gilded Age, the 1920s, or the 1980s and 1990s have themselves come from assertiveness, not passivity. Laissez-faire is a pretense. Government power and preferment have been used by the rich, not shunned.'[8] The conservative political theorist Michael Oakeshott is another rare voice on the right to underscore this point. In blunt criticism of Hayek's theories, Oakeshott has suggested that, 'This is perhaps the main significance of Hayek's *Road to Serfdom* – not the cogency of his doctrine, but the fact that it is a doctrine.' As Oakeshott empha-sized: 'A plan to resist all planning may be better than its opposite, but it belongs to the same style of politics.'[9] Since the 1940s, when Hayek first brought together a group of like-minded men in Switzerland, his followers have become even more evangelically attached to a convenient interpretation of Hayek's ideas than Hayek was himself. While Hayek's *Serfdom* called for a limited amount of state regulation, over the years his disciples have become more and more attached to a Manichean perception of the state's supposed limitations and the market's supposed strengths: the belief that private actors are *inherently* less constrained by the same temporal or cognitive limits as facing government planners. Where the state is a bureaucratic goliath, market actors are nimble. Where the state is limited by future unknowns, market actors are free to respond swiftly to unexpected events. Where the state's cardinal sin is to *plan*, the market's saving grace is that it simply *responds*. Or so the theory goes.

Free-market enthusiasts such as Hayek are not the sole observers to question the effectiveness of state planning. From a starkly differ-ent ideological camp than Hayek (his most recent book is titled *Two Cheers for Anarchism!*) the left-leaning Yale anthropologist James Scott has advanced a remarkably similar theory for why government planners often fail to realize development goals that appear to be scientifically sound in theory. His book *Seeing like a State*, first published in 1998, has become something of a bible for scholars across the political spectrum. Casting his gaze over a dumbfounding array of state failures, from Prussian 'scientific' forestry to Stalin's agricultural policies, Scott eviscerates the nearsightedness of what he terms 'state simplifications', the tendency for state planners to apply rigid blueprints for economic development. He calls it the 'imperialism' of high modernism: the refusal to incorporate the know-how of local communities into planning processes, fuelled by the assumption that state planners, armed with the latest scientific methodologies or techniques, obviously possess superior methods. Time and again, by failing to embrace local knowledge, state planners inadvertently orchestrate their own failure. Science becomes pseudo-science as the method of discovery that fuels scientific advance is subverted in favour of purposefully myopic strategies, those blind to the changing needs of different communities. Actual progress is undermined *by* proclamations of progress.[10]

In a recent book, technology writer Evgeny Morozov calls such pseudo-scientific fixes 'solutionism' and offers an impressive list of thinkers who criticized solutionist thinking: Jane Jacobs's writing on urban planning, Michael Oakeshott on rationalism, Hayek on central planning, to name just a few.[11] One good recent example of the shortcomings of 'solutionist' thinking is the proficiency targets set by No Child Left Behind legislation, where many schools have been held to strict improvement standards without additional funds offered to meet those standards. After a decade of failure, NCLB is now being 'whittled down' in the wake of widespread complaints over 'what some regard as an obsessive focus on test results, which has led to some notorious cheating scandals. Critics have also faulted the law's system of rating schools, which they say labelled so many of them low-performing that it rendered the judgment meaningless.'[12]

Today, 'solutionism' is alive and well at the Gates Foundation, where most policies seem eerily close to those depicted by Scott. The failures of Prussian forestry read like a litmus test for the failures of the Green Revolution in India, just as today Gates obstinately champions the same ecological policies that have failed in the past. And yet, the Gates Foundation does not simply see like a state. It sees like a *blind, dumb, and deaf* state, one that is not beholden to any sort of social contract obliging it to engage with voices less powerful than its own.

The foundation is a purposefully transient presence, with no pretensions to entrenching itself in the regions it visits and then decamps from. Much like the Rockefeller-funded Harvard researchers in Khanna who showed remarkably little interest in the livelihoods of Indian men and women, the Gates Foundation is there to impart knowledge – they are not there to understand. Recall that offhand comment by an Indian researcher in Edinburgh, 'At least Rockefeller built institutions.'

It's easy to see why Hayek's and Scott's theories of state failure have been so convincing to generations scarred by the memory of what a state could accomplish (or fail to accomplish) through a muscular overconfidence in its own strength. Nazi Germany, Stalinist Russia – each evinced the same horrific, misplaced hubris in their ability to mould nature to their requirements, and each, like Icarus, became the harbinger of their own doom.

It might be tempting, too, to respond to the Gates Foundation's own muscular over-confidence with a solution similar to Hayek's or Scott's. Introduce *more* competition; *more* localism; *more* local knowledge – and the need for philanthropic reform will be tamed. To some extent, encouraging more competition in the philanthropic sector might help a little bit. It would be helpful to return to a time when grants were not increasingly of a 'limited purpose' or 'closed door' nature. Michael Edwards has pointed out that over 73 per cent of America's 1.4 million registered non-profits have budgets of less than $500,000. 'The real work of civil society', he suggests, 'takes place down here, where the majority of America's million volunteers are active.'[13] He is right: better financing these small non-profits would do considerable good.

But will introducing more competition alone act as a panacea for the shrinking government resources available to small non-profit organizations or the low-income communities they serve? The answer is no. Not as long as tax and regulatory structures remain in place that deplete the funds available for government spending, tax structures that are vigorously engineered and defended by the same philanthropists purporting to redress economic inequality.

This is the main irony of the TED Head world. While TED Heads often proclaim that 'market'-oriented strategies and opportunities are necessary for filling the gap left by a receding state – as if they have little control over the state's dwindling coffers – in reality, diminished spending on welfare has been carefully orchestrated by the same individuals bemoaning the state's purported ineffectiveness.

A good example is Eric Schmidt of Google, who, as Morozov points out, lambasts Washington as 'an incumbent protection machine [where] laws are written by lobbyists' at the same time as Google dramatically expands its own lobbying operations in Washington, DC.[14]

Peter Thiel, the PayPal billionaire, is another good illustration of the double-mindedness rife in the TED world, loudly insisting that government intervention should be minimized while spending vast sums formulating legislation to his advantage. Thiel's philanthropic gambits have gained a degree of notoriety thanks in part to some of his more imaginative claims – like his professed disbelief in the 'ideology' of human mortality. Although he is highly educated himself, with a BA in Philosophy from Stanford and a graduate degree from Stanford Law School, he has denounced the value of higher education, offering to pay 'Thiel Fellows' $100,000 each to pursue an entrepreneurial venture of their choice – as long as they forgo or drop out of college.

His personal creed was outlined in a 2009 Cato Institute article, in which Thiel launches with something of a biological puzzler: 'I stand against confiscatory taxes, totalitarian collectives, and the ideology of the inevitability of the death of every individual.' He goes on to argue that the 1920s were the last time it was possible to have any optimism in politics, before a number of political decisions, such as the extension of the vote to women (Thiel disapproves), began to undermine sound economic policies. 'Since 1920', he complains, 'the vast increase in welfare beneficiaries and the extension of the franchise to women – two constituencies that are notoriously tough for libertarians – have rendered the notion of "capitalist democracy" into an oxymoron.'[15]

He also has his reservations about pot smokers. In comments much parodied on the internet, Thiel blasted the management at Twitter, suggesting that while the company has a lot of potential, its performance is hard to gauge because, 'it's a horribly mismanaged company – probably a lot of pot smoking going on there'. In response, Dick Costolo, Twitter's CEO, weighed in on Twitter, 'working my way through a giant bag of Doritos. I'll catch up with you later.'

Thiel's dismissal of politics has not, of course, compelled him to disengage politically. Thiel bankrolled much of the Tea Party darling Ron Paul's 2012 presidential campaign, and he serves as chair of the board of Palantir, a firm specializing in intelligence-gathering and data-mining solutions for the US government's defence community. Thiel is also a steering committee member of the Bilderberg Group, the crown jewel of elite international meetings – a Bilderberg invitation makes a Davos invite look like coffee at the local Walmart.[16]

Thiel and his fellow philanthrocapitalists exhibit the same cognitive dissonance, the same double-mindedness, as the Mont Pelerin enthusiasts who succeeded in shaping government policies in the name of laissez-faire non-interference. They wilfully entrench the market dominance of actors shown to have been complicit in market distortions, such as Goldman Sachs, even as they lament the way that 'marketplace imperatives' direct health investment where it is least needed. They defend protectionist patent policies even as they exhort developing nations to open up their own borders. They exploit tax loopholes that deplete government financial reserves even as they complain about the seeming inability of states to enforce measures to combat global hunger or poverty. They are today's liminal pioneers, or more accurately, liminal profiteers. They are as brash and entitled as the nineteenth-century confidence men determined to sell their ideology to governments and their constituents 'at almost any price you've got the guts to ask'. They are here to save the world – as long as the world yields to their interests.

Gates, despite receiving accolades from across the political spectrum, is no different. His foundation could choose to practise mission investing through screening for companies whose environmental impact and human rights record contravene the foundation's health goals – but it largely does not. The foundation could try to invest a larger portion of its grants directly in developing regions – but so far it has not.

In 2014, Melinda was invited to address the annual World Health Assembly. Hosted each year in Geneva at the WHO, the event is the global epicentre of high-end policy deliberations over global health; it's the health equivalent of the UN General Assembly, which brings streams of chauffeured heads of state to New York each September. During her talk (widely criticized by NGOs who circulated a petition asking the WHO to reconsider the prestigious invitation as it was the third time in less than a decade that either Bill or Melinda had received the honour), Melinda offered a throwaway remark, one that at first glance doesn't seem particularly noteworthy – and yet it is. 'Since you first heard about our foundation', she said, 'our core values haven't changed – and they never will. We will always do this work because we despise inequity, and because we believe in the power of innovation to solve problems.'

Implicit in this remark is something of a cautioning: don't ask us to change. Don't expect us to change. Because we won't.

I have pondered her comment about inequity many times. I believe it to be sincere. I believe it to be heartfelt. And I believe it to be profoundly short-sighted, not, or at least not simply, when it comes to peering outwardly, trying to gauge where the largest global burdens lie, but when it comes to looking inwardly, at the foundation's own practices. How else to account for the failure to appreciate the importance of investing directly in the human resources of the global south?

True equity should entail offering money directly to capable health teams based in the global south, better resourcing of their universities, their access to scientific research, and their ability to publish more extensively in leading journals. Their research could then better inform northern policies: we could certainly use the help.

While his own scorn for philanthropy was marked by unnerving elitism, there is something enduringly relevant about Emerson's suggestion that a dollar given in charity is a 'wicked dollar', one that places its recipients under a boot rather than recognizing their equal right to foster their own independence, to realize their individuality. Against the egotism of Thiel, Balsillie, or the Gateses, individuals who eponymously stamp their mark on their endowments, the best donations are those that extend as far as possible the courtesy of indifference. By indifference I mean, quite literally, gifts offered with a *lack* of self-involvement. Because if a gift is to be actually given – that is, if it's actually meant to be surrendered by a donor, preventing her or him from further claims on that gift – then a donor has no *right* to involvement. Recipients deserve their own independence. They don't deserve sympathy, which suggests a sort of false rapport with recipients, which crushes grantees under the taxing weight of a donor's good will. They don't deserve pity, which demeans as much as it empowers. If the real motivation is to avoid embroiling others in chains of enduring dependency or obligation, then true gifts should offer the respite of autonomy.

The Gateses live in a 40,000 square-foot home set over five acres of wooded land in the Seattle suburb of Medina. It's reported to feature a 100-visitor reception hall, an arcade, a bowling alley, a shooting range, a volleyball court, a hockey ring, a basketball court, a football stadium, and a garage reported to accommodate up to thirty cars, including a 1988 Porsche 989 coupe, which, due to its emissions and questionable crash record, was not deemed street legal in the US until 1999, when a bill championed by Gates was signed into law by Bill Clinton.

Labourers, of course, would have built the house. Perhaps they were well paid; perhaps they weren't. And some of them, spiritual descendants, maybe, of housepainters such as Robert Noonan, would have been put to work inside the library. For there, engraved on the large domed ceiling, there's a quote from *The Great Gatsby*: 'He had come a long way to this blue lawn, and his dream must have seemed so close that he could hardly fail to grasp it.'

Steve Jobs once suggested that the problem with Microsoft, the reason why Apple seem to produce more visually pleasing products, is that Gates is, first and foremost, a 'businessman . . . Microsoft never had the humanities and liberal arts in its DNA'.[17]

That seems a bit harsh. But it is possible to suggest that Gates might not have the strongest grip on irony. Because the tragedy of Fitzgerald's story is that Gatsby never did manage to grasp his dream. His lavish spending could not secure him Daisy's loyalty. If anything, his money was the root of his dashed ambition, a worm marring the sick rose, the source of his untimely death. It's in *The Great Gatsby* that Fitzgerald offers one of his most widely quoted epithets about the wealthy in the Jazz Era. 'They were careless people, Tom and Daisy – they smashed up things and creatures and then retreated back into their money or their vast carelessness or whatever it was that kept them together, and let other people clean up the mess they had made.'

What would Robert Noonan have made of Fitzgerald's comment? Who *was* Noonan? He was a former housepainter who died in 1911 at the age of forty-one, buried in a pauper's grave in Liverpool.[18] When he wrote *The Ragged-Trousered Philanthropists*, he chose a pen name, Robert Tressell, because he was worried that he might be blacklisted for his socialist sympathies. The book was never published in his lifetime. He never lived to see it become a bestseller, credited with helping to bring about Labour's shock victory in the British elections of 1945. He never lived to see his story rouse the anger of future generations of workers, labourers determined *not* to act with good will, determined *not* to feign gratitude. As Wilde once remarked, why should they?

Unlike Tom and Daisy Buchanan, you couldn't call today's elite careless. These are earnest people. They mark off their attendance at global summits with the diligence of boy scouts sifting through merit badges after a hard day's work. But as long as they retain the power to devise the rules of national and global governance, others will forever be left to clean up the mess they have made, a global army of dutiful, working-class philanthropists relinquishing the wealth that is theirs.

Acknowledgements

I carried out dozens of interviews for this book and I'm grateful to the many activists, charity volunteers, scholars, journalists, and NGO staff who spoke with me. Those who agreed to speak on the record are named throughout the text. In instances where a source requested anonymity, I have used pseudonyms. Particular thanks to Thiru Balasubramaniam, Greg Bernarda, Nancy Hamm, Amos Laar, Harold Lockwood, John Mahama, and Alex Nicholls for their time, including putting me in touch with fieldwork contacts.

This book was initiated during separate fellowships at the University of Oxford's School of Geography and Saïd Business School. Thanks to Andrew Barry, Javier Lezaun, Steve Rayner, and Steve Woolgar for their support. While at Oxford, I received fieldwork support from the Skoll Centre for Social Entrepreneurship. The University of Essex also provided generous travel support.

I'm grateful to Michael Power for hosting me during a visiting stay at the London School of Economics' Centre for the Analysis of Risk and Regulation in 2012, and to staff and colleagues at the Brocher Foundation in Geneva in 2011.

Sections of Chapter 3 draw on my earlier article, 'The Philanthropic State: Market-State Hybrids in the Philanthrocapitalist Turn', *Third World Quarterly*, vol. 35, no.1 (2014), 109–25, reprinted by permission of Taylor & Francis.

Jon Elek found the right home in Verso, where Leo Hollis and Mark Martin offered much support and insight throughout.

Additional thanks to Nick Allum, Vanessa Biller, Victoria Bovaird, Anne Cobbett, Troy Cochrane, Will Davies, Jennifer Dickie, Michael Halewood, Sophie Harman, Amy Hinterberger, Paul Hunt, Emily Jackson, Ann Kelly, Diedrah Kelly, Monika Krause, Lee-Ann Leander-Pehrson, Noortje Marres, Teri Murphy, Jennifer Palmer, Lynne Pettinger, Barbara Prainsack, Lydia Prior, Nikolas Rose, Róisín Ryan-Flood, Simon Rushton, Yasemin Soysal, Lisa Stampnitzky, Jackie Turton, Ayo Wahlberg, Robin West, Catherine Will, and Lindsay Wotherspoon.

Particular thanks to Scott Vrecko, who has been a wonderful reader and friend.

Thanks to Diedrah, Sule, and Rastko for their hospitality in Ghana. Much love and thanks to my family, including Darren Thiel, Linda and Bob Sommerville, and Jordan, Gerry, and Kathy McGoey. Thanks also to Darren's family in Clacton. Our friends in Toronto, London, Brighton, and Lewes offered helpful ideas. Darren made incisive comments on the text. My love and deepest thanks to him.

Notes

INTRODUCTION

1   Charles Kenny and Andy Sumner, 'How 28 Poor Countries Escaped the Poverty Trap', *Guardian*, 12 July 2011. For a critical analysis of World Bank classification schemes, see Lorenzo Fioramonti, *Gross Domestic Problem: The Politics Behind the World's Most Powerful Number* (London: Zed Books, 2013).

2   Susan Lederer, *Subjected to Science: Human Experimentation in America Before the Second World War* (Baltimore: Johns Hopkins University Press, 1995), 84.

3   Olivier Zunz, *Philanthropy in America* (Princeton, NJ: Princeton University Press, 2012), 21.

4   See Ron Chernow, *Titan: The Life of John D. Rockefeller Sr.* (New York: Vintage, 2004), 471–2, and Christopher Levenick, 'The Rockefeller Legacy', *Philanthropy Magazine* (Winter 2013).

5   See J. Gordon Frierson, 'The Yellow Fever Vaccine: A History', *Yale Journal of Biology and Medicine*, vol. 83 (2010), 77–85, and 'Funny Noguchi', *Time*, vol. 17, no. 20 (1931), 44.

6   The description is drawn from Bill Gates's reflections in his blog article 'Seeing Ghana's Health Care System in Action', 29 March 2013, at impatientoptimists.org.

7   Quoted in M. J. Smith, 'Bill Gates the Unknown Explores Ghana's Health Progress', *Agence-France Press*, 27 March 2013.

8   Matthew Bishop and Michael Green, *Philanthrocapitalism: How the Rich Can Save the World* (London: Bloomsbury, 2008), 194.

9   See the FAQs at philanthrocapitalism.net.

10 Bishop and Green, *Philanthrocapitalism*, x. (London: A&C Black, 2010).

11 See Charles Clift, 'What's the World Health Organization For?', Chatham House Report (2014), at chathamhouse.org. That following year, 2014, contributions to WHO by the U.S. government slightly outpaced the Gates Foundation.

12 Michael Edwards, *Small Change: Why Business Won't Change the World* (New York and London: Demos, 2010); see also Lisa Ann Richey and Stefano Ponte, *Brand Aid: Shopping Well to Save the World* (Minneapolis, MN: University of Minnesota Press, 2011); Gavin Fridell and Martijn Konings, eds., *Age of Icons: Exploring Philanthrocapitalism in the Contemporary World* (Toronto: University of Toronto Press, 2013); Robin Rogers, 'Why Philanthro-policymaking Matters,' *Society*, vol. 48, 376–81; and Iain Hay and Samantha Muller, 'Questioning Generosity In The Golden Age of Philanthropy: Towards Critical Geographies of Super-philanthropy', *Progress in Human Geography*, vol. 38, no. 5 (2014), 635–53.

13 Email interview with author.

14 The description of Frick's three-mile fence comes from Howard Zinn, *A People's History of the United States* (New York: Harper Perennial, 1980); see also David Nasaw, *Andrew Carnegie* (Harmondsworth: Penguin, 2007), and Kevin Phillips, *Wealth and Democracy: A Political History of the American Rich* (New York: Broadway Books, 2002).

15 Nasaw, *Andrew Carnegie*, 456–7.

16 Quoted by David Nasaw, 'Introduction', in Andrew Carnegie, *The 'Gospel of Wealth' Essays and Other Writings* (Harmondsworth: Penguin, 1996), xiii.

17 Ralph Waldo Emerson, *Self-Reliance and Other Essays* (New York: Digireads Books, 2013 [1841]), 31.

18 Oscar Wilde, *The Soul of Man Under Socialism and Other Essays*

(Harmondsworth: Penguin, 2001 [1891]), 130. Occasionally, Wilde has received more accolades for his insights in this essay than seem warranted. His views on slave resistance and apathy towards abolitionism, while typical of their time, have proved historically wrong. For a corrective to Wilde's suggestion that slaves resisted their own freedom, and that slavery's demise stemmed from agitators and not slaves themselves, see Robin Blackburn's account of the Haitian Revolution. As he points out, abolition inroads were first made not by English or American abolitionists but by Jacobin revolutionaries and the black peasantry of Saint Domingue (later Haiti). Robin Blackburn, 'Haiti, Slavery, and the Age of Democratic Revolution', *William and Mary Quarterly*, vol. 63, no. 4 (2006), 643–74.

19   Quoted in Michael Lopez, 'The Conduct of Life: Emerson's Anatomy of Power', in Joel Porte and Saundra Morris, eds., *The Cambridge Companion to Ralph Waldo Emerson* (Cambridge, UK: Cambridge University Press, 1999), 246.

20   Baudelaire's short story, 'Counterfeit Money', first published in 1869, is excerpted in full as an appendix in Jacques Derrida's *Given Time: 1. Counterfeit Money* (Chicago: University of Chicago Press, 1992).

21   Mareike Schomerus; Tim Allen, and Koen Vlassennott, 'Kony 2012 and the Prospect for Change' *Foreign Affairs* (March 13, 2012).

22   Michael E. Porter and Mark R. Kramer, 'Philanthropy's New Agenda: Creating Value', *Harvard Business Review* (November/December 1999), 22.

23   Nicolas Guilhot, 'Reforming the World: George Soros, Global Capitalism and the Philanthropic Management of the Social Sciences', *Critical Sociology*, vol. 33 (2007), 451.

24   Interview with the author.

25   Stanley Katz, 'What Does it Mean to Say That Philanthropy Is "Effective"?', *Proceedings of the American Philosophical Society*, vol. 149, no. 2 (2005), 126; see also Paul Schervish, 'The Spiritual Horizons of Philanthropy: New Directions for Money and Motives', *New Directions for Philanthropic Fundraising*, vol. 29 (2000), 17–32.

26   Edwards is one of the rare few who have pointed out the relevance of Smith to Bishop and Green's notion. See Edwards, *Small Change*.

27   Adam Smith, *The Wealth of Nations, Books 1–3* (Harmondsworth: Penguin, 1982 [1776]), 292.

28   Felix Salmon, 'Philanthropy Can't be Outsourced to the Profit Motive', Reuters, 16 June 2011, at blogs.reuters.com.

29   Slavoj Žižek, 'The Liberal Communists of Porto Davos', *In These Times*, 11 April 2006.

30   Ray Madoff, '5 Myths About Payout Rules for Donor-Advised Funds', *The Chronicle of Philanthropy*, 13 January 2014.

31   David Moore and Douglas Rutzen, 'Legal Framework for Global Philanthropy: Barriers and Opportunities', *The International Journal of Not-for-Profit Law*, vol. 13, no. 1–2 (2011), icnl.org.

32   Emmanuel Saez, 'Striking it Richer: The Evolution of Top Incomes in the United States' (2012), at eml.berkeley.edu. Updated version of 'Striking it Richer: The Evolution of Top Incomes in the United States', *Pathways Magazine*, Stanford Center for the Study of Poverty and Inequality (Winter 2008), 6–7.

33   See Rob Reich, 'Philanthropy and Caring For the Needs of Strangers', *Social Research*, vol. 80, no. 2 (2013), 517–38.

34   Heidi Blake, 'Carlos Slim: Profile of the World's Richest Man', *Telegraph*, 11 March 2010.

35   See Alan D. Schrift, ed., *The Logic of the Gift: Toward an Ethic of Generosity* (London and New York: Routledge, 1997); see also Jacques Derrida, *Given Time: Counterfeit Money* (Chicago: University of Chicago Press, 1992).

36   Pierre Bourdieu, 'Marginalia – Some Additional Notes on the Gift', in Schrift, *The Logic of the Gift*, 231–2.

37   Mark Dowie, *American Foundations: An Investigative History* (Cambridge, MA: MIT Press, 2001), ix.

38   Barry Ellsworth, 'Koch Brothers' Lies Tear at Very Fabric of American Society', 2 August 2014, allvoices.com.

39   Liza Featherstone, 'On the Wal-Mart Money Trail', *The Nation*, 21 November 2005.

40   Foundation Center, 'Top 100 US Foundations by Asset Size', at foundationcenter.org.

41   Clare O'Connor, 'Report: Walmart's Billionaire Waltons Give Almost None of Own Cash to Foundation', *Forbes*, 6 March 2014.

42   Interview with James Love, available at fireintheblood.com.

43   Francesca Sawaya, 'Philanthropy, Patronage, and Civil Society: Experiences From Germany, Great Britain and North America', *American Quarterly*, vol. 60, no. 1 (2008), 203.

CHAPTER ONE

1   Alec MacGillis, 'Scandal at Clinton Inc', *New Republic*, 22 September 2013.

2   Quotes from www.clintonfoundation.org.

3   Branson's shortfall was described in Naomi Klein's compelling book, *This Changes Everything: Capitalism vs. the Climate* (London: Allen Lane, 2014). The CGI does maintain what they term a "commitment to action" webpage listing how many pledges have been fulfilled or not, but there is no penalty if a pledge is not carried out.

4   Nicholas Confessore and Amy Chozick, 'Unease at Clinton Foundation Over Finance and Ambitions', *New York Times*, 13 August 2013.

5   'Integrated Activist Defense', teneoholdings.com.

6   My description is indebted to Andy Hoffman's National Magazine Award–nominated analysis of Clinton and Guistra's partnership. See 'Renaissance Man', *Globe and Mail*, 27 June 2008.

7   Jonathon Gatehouse, 'Peter Munk's Final Play: Barrick Gold Founder Fends off Revolt and Fights for a Legacy', *Maclean's*, 1 October 2013.

8   Jo Becker and Don Van Natta Jr., 'After Mining Deal, Financier Donated to Clinton', *New York Times*, 31 January 2008.

9   Hoffman, 'Renaissance Man'.

10   See Rena Lederman, 'Big Men, Large and Small? Towards a Comparative Perspective', *Ethnology*, vol. 29, no. 1 (1990); and Rena Lederman, 'Big Man, Anthropology of', in *International Encyclopedia of the Social and Behavioural Sciences* (Amsterdam: Elsevier, 2001), 1162–5.

11   Bronisław Malinowski, *Argonauts of the Western Pacific* (London: Routledge, 2014 [1922]), 91.

12   Marcel Mauss, *The Gift: The Form and Reason for Exchange in Archaic Societies* (New York and London: W. W. Norton, 1990), 41, 18; see also Erika Bornstein, 'The Impulse of Philanthropy', *Cultural Anthropology*, vol. 24, no. 4 (2009), 622–51.

13   Mary Douglas, 'Foreword' in Mauss, *The Gift*, xiv.

14   Avner Offer, 'Between the Gift and the Market: The Economy of Regard', *Economic History Review*, vol. 50, no. 3 (1997), 450–76.

15   Chris Gregory, *Gifts and Commodities* (London: Academic Press, 1982), 51.

16   Dambisa Moyo, *Dead Aid: Why Aid is Not Working and How There is a Better Way for Africa* (New York: Farrar, Straus and Giroux, 2009). For further reading on the stengths and limits of contemporary international aid efforts, see Radhika Balakrishnan and Diane Elson eds., *Economic Policy and Human Rights: Holding Goverments to Account* (London and New York: Zed Books, 2011); Monika Krause, *The Good Project: Humanitarian Relief NGOs and the Fragmentation of Reason* (Chicago: University of Chicago Press, 2014), 204; William Easterly, *The Tyranny of Experts: Economists, Dictators, and the Forgotten Rights of the Poor* (New York: Basic Books, 2014); and Angus Deaton, *The Great Escape: Health, Wealth, and the Origins of Inequality* (Princeton, NJ: Princeton University Press, 2013).

17   Jeffrey Sachs, 'Aid Ironies', *Huffington Post,* 24 June 2009.

18   For a comprehensive discussion of dependency theory, see Ilan Kapoor, 'Capitalism, Culture, Agency: Dependency versus Postcolonial Theory', *Third World Quarterly*, vol. 23, no. 4 (2002), 647–64. Lant Pritchett's work demonstrates that, in contrast to sanguine accounts of increased global prosperity, the last century saw an ever-widening gulf between living standards in 'less developed' countries and 'developed' ones, something he terms 'divergence, big time'. See Lant Pritchett, 'Divergence, Big Time', *Journal of Economic Perspectives*, vol. 11, no. 3 (1997), 3–17. Easterly's *Tyranny of Experts* offers an excellent analysis of this divergence.

19   Andy Beckett, 'Inside the Bill and Melinda Gates Foundation', *Guardian*, 10 July 2010.

20   Jackson Lears, 'Money Changes Everything', *New Republic*, April 2, 2007.

21   See Dowie, *American Foundations*.

22   Carnegie, *The 'Gospel of Wealth' Essays*, 11.

23   Ibid., 12.

24   Lears, 'Money Changes Everything'.

25   Ibid.

26   Carnegie, *The 'Gospel of Wealth' Essays*, 12.

27   Zinn, *A People's History*, 270.

28   Phillips, *Wealth and Democracy*, 238.

29   Zinn, *A People's History*, 271.

30   Phillips, *Wealth and Democracy*, 238.

31   Carnegie, quoted in Nasaw, *Andrew Carnegie*, 459.

32   Zinn, *A People's History*, 252.

33   ibid., 254.

34   Ralph McGill, 'W. E. B. Du Bois', *Atlantic Monthly* (November 1965).

35   Ibid.

36   Zinn, *A People's History*, 272.

37   Nasaw, 'Introduction', xii.

38   Herbert Spencer, *Social Statics, Abridged, Together With Man versus the State, Revised* (1896), 150.

39   Nasaw, Andrew Carnegie, (London: Penguin, 2007), 331.

40   Ibid., 522.

41   Ibid., 703.

42   Lester Frank Ward, 'Plutocracy and Paternalism', *Forum* (November 1895), 303.

43   For a comprehensive account of Ludlow and its effects on American business practices, see Andrea Tone, *The Business of Benevolence: Industrial Paternalism in Progressive America*, (Ithaca, NY: Cornell University Press, 1997), 19.

44   Quoted in Inderjeet Parmar, *Foundations of the American Century* (New York: Columbia University Press, 2012), 38.

45   Tone, *The Business of Benevolence,* 117.

46   Inaugural address (1913), see millercenter.org; Wilson's 'first message to Congress', quoted in Phillips, *Wealth and Democracy,* 47.

47   Robert Arnove and Nadine Pinede, 'Revisiting the "Big Three" Foundations', *Critical Sociology,* vol. 33 (2007), 390.

48   Ibid., 391.

49   Max Weber, *The Protestant Ethic and the Spirit of Capitalism* (London: Routledge, 2001), 159–63.

50   Chernow, *Titan,* 191.

51   Levenick, 'The Rockefeller Legacy'.

52   Steve Weinberg, *Taking on the Trust: How Ida Tarbell Brought Down John D. Rockefeller and Standard Oil* (New York: W. W. Norton, 2008), 225.

53   Ibid., 233.

54   Chernow, *Titan,* 468.

55   Ibid.

56   Quoted in Samuel Crowther, 'Henry Ford: Why I Favour Five Days' Work with Six Days' Pay', *World's Work* (October 1926), 613–16.

57   See Tone, *The Business of Benevolence.*

58   Corporate release quoted in Neil Baldwin, *Henry Ford and the Jews: The Mass Production of Hate* (New York: Public Affair Books, 2001), 37.

59   Quoted in Thomas Conley, *Toward a Rhetoric of Insult* (Chicago: University of Chicago Press, 2010), 104.

60   Baldwin, *Henry Ford and the Jews,* 172–3 see also Victoria Saker Woester, *Henry Ford's War on Jews and the Legal Battle Against Hate Speech* (Stanford: Stanford University Press, 2012).

61   Pankaj Mishra, 'Watch This Man: Review of *Civilisation: The West and the Rest',* *London Review of Books,* 3 November 2011, 10–12.

62   Peter Frumkin, 'He Who's Got It Gets to Give It', *Washington Post,* 3 October 1999, B01; See also Joel Fleishman, *The Foundation: A Great American Secret–How Private Money is Changing the World* (New York: Public Affairs Books, 2007).

63   Dowie, *American Foundations*, 12.

64   Zunz, *Philanthropy in America*, 198.

65   Ibid.

66   Dowie, *American Foundations*, 13.

67   Quoted in Chrystia Freeland, *Plutocrats: The Rise of the New Global Super-Rich and the Fall of Everyone Else* (London: Penguin, 2012), 263.

68   Ibid.

69   Dowie, *American Foundations*, 13.

70   John Simon, 'The Regulation of American Foundations: Looking Backward at the Tax Reform Act of 1969', *Voluntas*, vol. 6, no. 3 (1995), 243–4.

71   There have been some important developments in the field of US charity regulation, but none on the same scale as the 1969 Tax Reform Act. One change was the introduction of the Treasury Department's Anti-Terrorist Financing Guidelines, in 2002. Congress also considered but failed to pass a bill that would increase the minimum spending amount by private foundations. For a comprehensive examination of recent shifts in the US non-profit and philanthropic sector, see William Damon and Susan Verducci, eds., *Taking Philanthropy Seriously: Beyond Noble Intentions to Responsible Giving* (Bloomington, IN: Indiana University Press, 2006), in particular Leslie Lenkowsky, 'The Politics of Doing Good'. See also Kerry O'Halloran, *The Profits of Charity* (Oxford: Oxford University Press, 2012).

CHAPTER TWO

1   James Wallace and Jim Erickson, *Hard Drive: Bill Gates and the Making of the Microsoft Empire* (New York: HarperCollins, 1993).

2   See Simon Atkinson, 'Hedge Fund Hippies Have Trip Out', BBC, 8 June 2006, news.bbc.co.uk.

3   Quoted in Freeland, *Plutocrats*, 58.

4   Simon Johnson, 'The Quiet Coup', *The Atlantic*, May 2009.

5   Quoted in Freeland, *Plutocrats*, 67.

6   Zoe Williams, 'Philanthro-Capitalism May Sound Ugly, But It Could Be the Future', *Guardian*, 30 March 2012.

7   John Elkington and Pamela Hartigan, *The Power of Unreasonable People: How Social Entrepreneurs Create Markets That Change the World* (Cambridge, MA: Harvard University Press, 2008), 3.

8   Ibid., 12.

9   Barry Malone, 'We Got This, Bob Geldof, so Back Off', Al Jazeera, 18 November 2014, aljazeera.com.

10 Jeffrey Skoll, 'Preface', in Alex Nicholls, ed., *Social Entrepreneurship: New Models of Sustainable Social Change* (Oxford: Oxford University Press, 2006), vi.

11 Quoted in Nicholls, *Social Entrepreneurship*, 45.

12 Roger Martin and Sally Osberg, 'Social Entrepreneurship: The Case For Definition', *Stanford Social Innovation Review* (Spring 2007), 38.

13 Ruth McCambridge, 'Social Entrepreneurship and Social Innovation: Are They Potentially in Conflict?', *Nonprofit Quarterly*, 25 December 2011, nonprofitquarterly.org.

14 Ibid.

15 Quoted by Jason Reid, '"The Ayn Rand School for Tots": John Dewey, Maria Montessori, and Objectivist Educational Philosophy During the Postwar Years', *Historical Studies in Education/Revue d'histoire de l'éducation*, vol. 25, no. 1 (2013), 87.

16 Geoff Mulgan, S. Tucker, Rushanna Ali, and Ben Sanders, 'Social Innovation: What It Is, Why it Matters and How It Can Be Accelerated?' Report of the Young Foundation (2007), eureka.bodleian.ox.ac.uk.

17 David Stuckler and Sanjay Basu, *The Body Economic: Why Austerty Kills* (London: Penguin, 2014), 133.

18 Transcript of a speech by the prime minister on the Big Society, 19 July 2010, gov.uk.

19 Celosia Mendes, 'Is the "Big Society" Just a Big Joke?', *Guardian*, 29 December 2010.

20 Quoted in James Meek, 'Worse than a Defeat', *London Review of Books*,

18 December 2014. My point here is indebted to Thiel's forthcoming study of UK welfare reform.

21   Linda McQuaig and Neil Brooks, *The Trouble with Billionaires* (London: Oneworld, 2013), 10.

22   Martin and Osberg, 'Social Entrepreneurship: The Case For Definition', 35.

23   In his excellent undergraduate dissertation, my former student Gerald Palmer first introduced me to susu collections.

24   See Alicia Herbert and Elaine Kempson, *Credit Use and Ethnic Minorities* (London: Policy Studies Institute, 1996); Darren Thiel, *Builders: Class, Gender and Ethnicity in the Construction Industry* (London: Routledge, 2012).

25   David Bornstein and Susan Davis, *Social Entrepreneurship: What Everyone Needs to Know.* (Oxford: Oxford University Press, 2010), 17. See also Berhanu Nega and Geoffrey Schneider 'Social Entrepreneurship, Microfinance, and Economic Development in Africa', *Journal of Economic Issues*, vol. 48, no. 2 (2014), 367–76, 369.

26   David Roodman, *Due Diligence: An Impertinent Inquiry into Microfinance* (Washington, DC: Center for Global Development, 2012), 176, also quoted in Nega and Schneider, 'Social Entrepreneurship', 369. See also Abhijit Banerjee, Esther Duflo, Rachel Glennester, Cynthia Kinnan, 'The Miracle of Microfinance?: Evidence from a Randomized Evaluation', Poverty Action Lab Working Paper (2009), and Hugh Sinclair, *Confessions of a Microfinance Heretic: How Microlending Lost Its Way and Betrayed the Poor* (San Francisco: Berrett-Koehler Publishers, 2012).

27   'Microfinance: Leave Well Alone', *Economist*, 18 November 2010.

28   My comments on the study and David Roodman's response draw on Tyler Owen's blog post from the Centre for Financial Inclusion, at cfi-blog.org. For more on Roodman's measured views on microfinance, see Roodman, *Due Diligence.* Another compelling analysis is Ananya Roy's *Poverty Capital: Microfinance and the Making of Development* (London: Routledge, 2010).

29   Emerson and Bugg-Levine's comment is from an interview with Alex Goldmark, 'Social Impact Investing', 20 October 2011.

30   Harvey Koh, Ashish Karamchandani and Robert Katz, 'From Blueprint to Scale: The Case for Philanthropy in Impact Investing', Monitor Group report (April 2012), 10.

31   See 'Safaricom: Managing Risk in a Frontier Capital Market', at fletcher.tufts.edu; the figures on Gates Foundation grants are drawn from the foundation's Form 990 reports, publicly available on its website.

32   Koh et al., 'From Blueprint to Scale', 16.

33   Eleanor Whitehead, 'Africa: Aiding Business', *All Africa*, 5 January 2012; my discussion in this section is drawn from Linsey McGoey, 'The Philanthropic State: Market-State Hybrids in the Philanthrocapitalist Turn', *Third World Quarterly*, vol. 35, no. 1 (2014), 109–25. Comments on Vodafone's tax avoidance drawn from Richard Brooks, *The Great Tax Robbery* (London: Oneworld, 2014).

34   Katie Collins 'Africa's First Bitcoin Wallet Launches in Kenya', *Wired*, 9 July 2013.

35   William Lazonick and Mazzucato Marinna "The Risk-Reward Nexus in the Innovation-Inequality Relationship: Who Takes the Risks? Who Gets the Rewards?', *Industrial and Corporate Change*, 22, no. 4 (2013), 1093–128, 1099; see also Mariana Mazzucato, *The Entrepreneurial State: Debunking Public vs. Private Sector Myths* (London: Anthem Press, 2013). For an excellent analysis of the new social investment landscape, see Alex Nicholls, 'The Institutionalization of Social Investment: The Interplay of Investment Logics and Investor Rationalities', *Journal of Social Entrepreneurship*, no. 1 (2010), 70–100.

36   Lazonick and Mazzucato, 'The Risk-Reward Nexus', 1095.

37   Koh et al., 'From Blueprint to Scale', 8.

38   Ward, 'Plutocracy and Paternalism'.

39   Georgia Levenson Keohane, 'The Rise and (Potential) Fall of Philanthrocapitalism,' *Slate,* 13 November 2008.

40   See Vinay Nagaraju, 'SkolWorld Forum: Awards and Closing Ceremonies Set the High Points for the Venue', 31 March 2009, nextbillion.net.

CHAPTER THREE

1   As Stephen Kresge notes, it is in the writing of 'Dr. Bernard Mandeville where Hayek finds "the definite breakthrough in modern thought of the twin ideas of evolution and of the spontaneous formation of an order", an order which is the result of human action, but not of human design.' See Kresge's 'Introduction' to F. A. Hayek, *The Trend of Economic Thinking: Essays on Political Economics and Economic History* (London: Routledge, 1999).

2   See Harold J. Cook, 'Bernard Mandeville and the Therapy of "The Clever Politician"', *Journal of the History of Ideas*, vol. 60, no. 1 (1999), 101–24.

3   Ibid.

4   R. B. Kaye, 'The Influence of Bernard Mandeville', *Studies in Philology*, vol. 19, no. 1 (1922), 90.

5   Ibid., 95.

6   Albert Hirschman, *The Passions and the Interests: Political Arguments for Capitalism Before its Triumph* (Princeton, NJ: Princeton University Press, 1997 [1977]), 18.

7   Viviana Zelizer, *Pricing the Priceless Child: The Changing Social Value of Children* (Princeton, NJ: Princeton University Press, 1994); see also Albert Hirschman, 'Rival Interpretations of Market Society: Civilizing, Destructive, or Feeble?', *Journal of Economic Literature*, vol. 20 (1982), 1463–84.

8   Christine Letts, William Ryan, and Allen Grossman, 'Virtuous Capital: What Foundations Can Learn From Venture Capitalists', *Harvard Business Review* (March–April, 1997), 36–44; see also Michael Moran, *Private Foundations and Development Partnerships: American Philanthropy and Global Development Agendas* (London: Routledge, 2013).

9   Porter and Kramer, 'Philanthropy's New Agenda', 121–30.

10 Zunz, *Philanthropy in America*, 21.

11 Michael E. Porter and Mark R. Kramer, 'The Competitive Advantage of Corporate Philanthropy', *Harvard Business Review* (December 2002), 5–16.

12   Michael Porter and Mark Kramer, 'Strategy and Society: The Link Between Competitive Advantage and Corporate Social Responsibility', *Harvard Business Review* (December 2006). For a critical analysis of their argument, see Mark Aakhus and Michael Bzdak, 'Revisiting the Role of "Shared Value" in the Business-Society Relationship', *Business & Professional Ethics Journal*, vol. 31, no. 2 (2012), 231–49.

13   Steve Denning, 'Why "Shared Value" Can't Fix Capitalism', *Forbes*, 20 December 2011. See also David Cargill, 'The General Electric Superfraud', *Harper's* (December 2009), 41–51.

14   Aakhus and Bzdak, 'Revisiting the Role of "Shared Value"', 231–46. See also Alix Rule, 'Good-as-Money', *Dissent* (Spring 2009), 86–9.

15   Garry Jenkins, 'Who's Afraid of Philanthrocapitalism?', *Case Western Reserve Law Review*, vol. 61, no. 3 (2011), 753–821.

16   Crutchfield et al., 11.

17   Katz, 'What Does it Mean to Say That Philanthropy is "Effective"?', 128.

18   Louise Armitstead, 'Children's Investment Fund Foundation Feels the Pain as City Power Couple Divorce', *Telegraph*, 9 June 2014.

19   See James Meek, *Private Island: Why Britain Now Belongs to Someone Else* (London: Verso, 2014).

20   Sumit Moitra, 'TCI Withdraws Case Against Coal India, Quits Battle to Change Government Ways', 24 December 2014, dnaindia.com.

21   Latha Jishnu, 'A Treaty Too Many', *Down To Earth*, 15 May 2013.

22   Nina J. Crimm, 'The Global Gag Rule: Undermining National Interests by Doing Unto Foreign Women and NGOs What Cannot be Done at Home', *Cornell International Law Journal*, vol. 40, no. 587 (2007); see also Melinda Cooper, 'The Theology of Emergency: Welfare Reform, US Foreign Aid and Faith-Based Initiative', *Theory, Culture and Society* (2014), 588–92.

23   See Julian Savulescu, 'Thalassaemia Major: The Murky Story of Deferiprone', *British Medical Journal*, vol. 328 (2004), 358–9.

24   Norman Goldfarb, 'Review of *The Drug Trial: Nancy Olivieri and the Science Scandal that Rocked the Hospital for Sick Children*', *Journal of Clinical Research Best Practices*, vol. 5, no. 22 (2009).

25   Jeanne Lenzer, 'Manufacturer Admits Increase in Suicidal Behaviour in Patients Taking Paroxetine', *British Medical Journal*, vol. 332 (2006), 1175.

26   See Marilyn Elias, 'Psychiatrist: Company Hid Prozac Suicide Link', *USA Today*, 5 January 2005, usatoday30.usatoday.com.

27   David Roodman, 'An Index of Donor Performance', Center for Global Development, Working Paper No. 67 (October 2009).

28   Eduardo Galeano, *The Book of Embraces* (New York: W. W. Norton, 1993); also quoted in Paul Farmer, *Pathologies of Power* (Oakland: University of California Press, 2005).

29   Jenkins, 'Who's Afraid of Philanthrocapitalism?'.

30   Tristan Hopper, 'York University Rejects RIM Co-founder Jim Balsillie's $60-million Deal', *National Post*, 3 April 2012.

31   Freeland, *Plutocrats*, 14–15; see also Phillips, *Wealth and Democracy*, and Claudia Goldin and Robert Margo, 'The Great Compression: The Wage Structure in the United States at Mid-Century', *The Quarterly Journal of Economics*, vol. 107, no. 1 (1992), 1–34.

32   Joseph Stiglitz, *The Price of Inequality* (London: Penguin, 2013); see also James Galbraith, *Inequality and Instability: A Study of the World Economy Just Before the Great Crisis* (Oxford: Oxford University Press, 2012). Hacker's comment is quoted in Judith Warner's 'The Charitable-Giving Divide', *New York Times*, 20 April 2010.

33   Freeland, *Plutocrats*, 246–7.

34   David Futrelle, 'Was Nick H. Hanauer's TED Talk on Income Inequality too Rich for Rich People?', *Time*, 18 May 2012.

35   See Warner, 'The Charitable-Giving Divide'.

36   Zunz, *Philanthropy in America*, 122.

37   Lears, 'Money Changes Everything', *New Republic,* 2 April 2007, newrepublic.com.

38   Zunz, *Philanthropy in America*, 125.

39   Paul Krugman, 'The Mellon Doctrine', *New York Times*, 31 March 2011.

40   Bishop and Green, *Philanthrocapitalism*, 14.

41   John Kenneth Galbraith, *The Affluent Society* (New York: Houghton Mifflin Harcourt, 1998 [1958]).

CHAPTER FOUR

1   Phillips, *Wealth and Democracy*, 39.

2   'The Perverse Incentives of Private Prisons', *Economist*, 24 August 2010.

3   Michel Foucault, *Discipline and Punish: The Birth of the Prison* (New York: Random House, 1995 [1978]), 276–7.

4   Abbe Smith, 'Undue Process, "Kids for Cash" and "The Injustice System"', *New York Times*, 29 March 2013.

5   Henry George, *Progress and Poverty* (Memphis, TN: General Books: 2012 [1880]), 4.

6   Michael Hudson, 'Veblen, Capitalism and Possibilities for Rational Economic Order', speech given in Istanbul, Turkey, 6 June 2012.

7   Quoted in Bishop and Green, *Philanthrocapitalism*, 54.

8   Jean Strouse, 'How to Give Away $21.8 Billion', *New York Times*, 16 April 2000.

9   See Timothy W. Martin, 'Atlanta School Scandal Sparks House Cleaning', *Wall Street Journal*, 13 July 2011; Diane Goldstein, 'How High-Stakes Testing Led to the Atlanta Cheating Scandal', 21 July 2011; see also Diane Goldstein, *The Teacher Wars: A History of America's Most Embattled Profession* (New York: Doubleday, 2014).

10   John Cannell, 'Lake Woebegone, Twenty Years Later', *Third Education Group Review*, vol. 2, no. 1 (2006), 2.

11   Duncan's comments were made during an interview on NBC News on 30 September 2011; see also Motoko Rich, '"No Child" Law Whittled Down by White House', *New York Times*, 6 July 2012.

12   Author interview, January 2012.

13   Jeffrey Young, 'A Conversation with Bill Gates About the Future of Higher Education.' *Chronicle of Higher Education*, 25 June 2012; Bill Gates, 'How Good Schooling Matters', *Washington Post*, 28 January 2009.

14   Bishop and Green, *Philanthrocapitalism*, 58.

15   Sanford is no longer with the Gates Foundation – a few months after our interview, she took up a position at the College Board, a non-profit education institution.

16 Diane Ravitch, *The Death and Life of the Great American School System* (New York: Basic Books, 2011); see also Diane Ravitch, *Reign of Error: The Hoax of the Privatization Movement and the Danger to America's Public Schools* (New York: Vintage, 2014); and Frederick Hess, ed., *With the Best of Intentions: How Philanthropy is Reshaping K–12 Education* (Cambridge, MA: Harvard Education Press, 2005).

17 Jack Buckley and Mark Schneider, *Charter Schools: Hope or Hype?* (Princeton, NJ: Princeton University Press, 2007).

18 Bob Tourtellotte, 'Bill Gates Goes to Sundance, Offers an Education', Reuters, 23 June 2010.

19 Reported by Sean Coughlan, 'Charter Schools: Winning Tickets?', BBC, 14 April 2010, news.bbc.co.uk.

20 Diane Ravitch, 'The Myth of Charter Schools', *New York Review of Books*, 11 November 2010.

21 Davis Guggenheim, 'Repeat After Me: We Can't Have Great Schools Without Great Teachers', *Huffington Post*, 9 June 2010.

22 Dan Goldhaber and Roddy Theobald, 'Managing the Teacher Workforce in Austere Times: The Implications of Teacher Layoffs', University of Washington, CEDR Working Paper 2011–1.3, 32.

23 Bill Gates, 'How Teacher Development Could Revolutionize Our Schools', *Washington Post*, 28 February 2011.

24 See Sharon Otterman, 'Lauded Harlem Schools Have Their Own Problems', *New York Times*, 12 October 2010.

25 See, for example, Ronald Ehrenberg et al., 'Class Size and Student Achievement', *Psychological Science in the Public Interest*, vol. 2, no. 1 (2001), 1–30. US Department of Education Institute of Education Sciences, National Center for Education Evaluation and Regional Assistance, 'Identifying and Implementing Educational Practices Supported by Rigorous Evidence: A User-Friendly Guide' (December 2003).

26 Michael Powell, 'A Mayor Sure of Himself, if Nothing Else', *New York Times*, 5 December 2011.

27 Paul Tough, 'Teachers Aren't the Problem', *Slate*, 5 September 2011.

28   Michael Winerup, 'Teachers Get Little Say in a Book About Them', *New York Times*, 28 August 2011.

29   Stephanie Saul, 'Profits and Questions at Online Charter Schools', *New York Times*, 12 December 2011.

30   Ibid.

31   On the prison industry, see in particular Cindy Chang, 'Louisiana Incarcerated: How We Built the World's Prison Capital: An Eight-Ppart Series', *Times-Picayune* (May 2012).

32   Stephanie Mencimer, 'Jeb Bush's Cyber Attack on Public Schools', *Mother Jones* (November/December 2011).

33   Mike McIntire, 'Conservative Nonprofit Acts as a Stealth Business Lobbyist', *New York Times*, 21 April 2012.

34   Colin Woodward, 'The Profit Motive Behind Virtual Schools in Maine', *Portland Press Herald*, 2 September 2012.

35   Stephanie Simon, 'Private Firms Eyeing Profits From US Public Schools', Reuters, 2 August 2012.

36   See Valerie Strauss, 'Privacy Concerns Grow Over Gates-funded Student Database', *Washington Post*, 9 June 2013.

37   Joanne Barkan, 'Got Dough?: How Billionaires Rule Our Schools', *Dissent* (Winter 2011).

38   Jason Riley, 'Was the $5 Billion Worth it?', *Wall Street Journal*, 23 July 2011.

39   Daniel Golden, 'Bill Gates's School Crusade', *Bloomberg Businessweek*, 15 July 2010.

40   Michael Klonsky, 'Power Philanthropy', in Philip E. Kovacs ed., *The Gates Foundation and the Future of U.S. Public Schools* (New York: Routledge, 2011), 26.

41   Ibid. 29.

42   Lyndsey Layton, 'How Bill Gates Pulled off the Swift Common Core Revolution', *Washington Post*, 7 June 2014.

43   See 'A. G. Schneiderman Secures $7.7 Million Settlement With Pearson Charitable Foundation To Support Recruitment, Training And Hiring Of K–12 Teachers', press release, 13 December 2013, ag.ny.gov.

44   Quoted in Golden, 'Bill Gates's School Crusade'.

45   Jason Felch, 'Study Backs "Value-Added" Analysis of Teacher Effectiveness,' *LA Times,* 11 December 2010.

46   Jesse Rothstein, 'Review of *Learning About Teaching*: Initial Findings from the Measures of Effective Teaching Project' (2011), National Education Policy Center, nepc.colorado.edu.

47   Peter Schochet and Hanley S. Chiang, 'Error Rates in Measuring Teacher and School Performance Based on Student Test Score Gains,' National Center for Education Evaluation and Regional Assistance, Institute of Education Sciences, US Department of Education (2010).

48   Bill Gates, 'Shame Is Not the Solution,' *New York Times,* 22 Feb 2012.

49   David Labaree, 'Targeting Teachers,' *Dissent* (Summer 2010), 10; see also Kenneth Zeichner and César Peña-Sandoval, 'Venture Philanthropy and Teacher Education Policy in the U.S. The Role of the New Schools Venture Fund,' *Teachers College Record,* vol. 117, no. 6 (2015).

50   Michael Cieply, 'Bill Gates Stirs Up the Education Debate in Toronto,' *New York Times,* 11 September 2012.

51   Kurt Eichenwald, 'Microsoft's Lost Decade,' *Vanity Fair,* (August 2012), vanityfair.com.

52   Joanne Barkan, 'Firing Line: The Grand Coalition Against Teachers,' *Dissent,* 29 June 2011.

53   Michael Chandler, 'Md. Teacher Evaluation Redesign Bogs Down,' *Washington Post,* 5 June 2011.

54   Caroline Preston, 'Gates Reorganizes Global Staff and Listens to School Critics,' *Chronicle of Philanthropy,* 16 October 2012.

55   Valerie Strauss, 'Gates Foundation Backs Two-Year Delay in Linking Common Core to Teacher Evaluation, Student Promotion,' *Washington Post,* 10 June 2014.

56   Paul Wells, 'Why Bill Gates is Stephen Harper's Favourite American,' *Maclean's,* 4 March 2015.

57   Peter Singer, 'The Why and How of Effective Altruism' (TED talk, March 2013), ted.com.

58   Valerie Strauss, 'An Educator Challenges the Gates Foundation,' *Washington Post,* 8 October 2010. See also Anthony Cody, *The Educator*

and the Oligarch: A Teacher Challenges the Gates Foundation (New York: Garn Press, 2014).

59   I first make this point in Linsey McGoey, 'Philanthrocapitalism and Its Critics', *Poetics*, vol. 40, 185–99, drawing on work by Michael Power and James Ferguson. See James Ferguson, *The Anti-Politics Machine* (Minneapolis, MN: University of Minnesota Press, 1990) and Michael Power, *The Audit Society: Rituals of Verification* (Oxford: Oxford University Press, 1997).

CHAPTER FIVE

1   Jeremy Youde, 'The Rockefeller and Gates Foundations in Global Health Governance', *Global Society*, vol. 27, no. 2 (2013), 139–58; See also Anne-Emanuelle Birn, 'Backstage: The Relationship Between the Rockefeller Foundation and the World Health Organization, Part I: 1940s–1960s', *Public Health*, vol. 128, no. 2 (2014), 129–40; Anne-Emanuelle Birn and Elizabeth Fee, 'The Rockefeller Foundation and the International Health Agenda', *The Lancet*, vol. 381 (2013), 1618–19; and – a seminal article on the parallels between the Gates and Rockefeller foundations – Anne-Emanuelle Birn, 'Philanthrocapitalism, Past and Present: The Rockefeller Foundation, the Gates Foundation, and the Setting(s) of the International/Global Health Agenda', vol 12, no. 1(2014), e8.

2   Lederer, *Subjected to Science*, 80–3.

3   Matthew Connolly, *Fatal Misconception: The Struggle to Control World Population* (Cambridge, MA: Harvard University Press, 2008), 171; see also Rebecca Williams, 'Rockefeller Foundation Support to the Khanna Study: Population Policy and the Construction of Demographic Knowledge, 1945–1954', rockarch.org.

4   Connolly, *Fatal Misconception*, 173.

5   Institute for Health Metrics and Evaluation, *Financing Global Health 2012: The End of the Golden Era?*, report available at healthdata.org.

6   Piot quote from Jon Cohen, 'Gates Foundation Rearranges Public Health Universe', *Science*, vol. 295 (2002).

7   Arthur Caplan, 'Is Disease Eradication Ethical?', *The Lancet*, vol. 373, no. 9682 (2009), 2192–3.

8   Neetu Vashisht and Jacob Puliyel, 'Polio Programme: Let us Declare Victory and Move on', *Indian Journal of Medical Ethics*, vol. 9, no. 2 (2012), 114–17.

9   Orin Levine and Laurie Garrett, 'The Fallout from the CIA's Vaccination Ploy in Pakistan', *Washington Post*, 15 July 2011.

10   Neil Tweedie, 'Bill Gates Interview: I Have No Use for Money. This Is God's Work', *Telegraph*, 18 January 2013.

11   The following quotations are from a phone interview and email exchange with Henderson, conducted in April 2013; see also William Muraskin, *Polio Eradication and Its Discontents: A Historian's Journey Through an International Public Health (Un)Civil War* (Telegam, India: Orient BlackSwan, 2012).

12   Donald McNeil, 'Can Polio Be Eradicated? A Skeptic Now Thinks So', *New York Times*, 14 February 2011.

13   Patricia Sellers, 'Melinda Gates Goes Public', *Fortune*, 7 January 2008.

14   Sonia Shah, 'Live with It', *Le Monde Diplomatique*, October 2010; see also Ann H. Kelly and Uli Beisel, 'Neglected Malarias: The Frontlines and Back Alleys of Global Health' *BioSocieties*. vol. 6, no. 1 (2011), 71–8.

15   Sonia Shah, 'Learning to Live With Malaria', *New York Times*, 8 October 2010.

16   Nadimpally Sarojini, Anjali Shenoi, Sandhya Srinivasan, and Amar Jesani, 'Undeniable Violations and Unidentifiable Violators', *Economic and Political Weekly*, 11 June 2011.

17   Priya Shett, 'Vaccine Trial's Ethics Questioned', *Nature*, vol. 474 (2011), 427–8; see also I. Mattheij, A. M. Pollock and P. Brhlikova, 'Do Cervical Cancer Data Justify HPV Vaccination in India?: Epidemiological Data Source and Comprehensiveness', *Journal of the Royal Society of Medicine*, vol. 105 (2012), 250–62.

18   Sarojini et al., 'Undeniable Violations,' 17.

19   Quoted in Carolijn Terwindt, 'Health Rights Litigation Pushes for Accountability in Clinical Trials in India', *Health and Human Rights Journal*, vol. 2, no. 16 (2014), 84–95.

20   Barbara A. Slade et al., 'Postlicensure Safety Surveillance for Quadrivalent Human Papillomavirus Recombinant Vaccine', *Journal of the American Medical Association*, vol. 302, no. 7 (2009), 750–7. Case report data drawn from Lucija Tomljenovic et al., 'HPV Vaccines and Cancer Prevention, Science Versus Activism', *Infectious Agents and Cancer*, vol. 8, no. 6 (2013).

21   Quoted in Richard Knox, 'The Science Behind the HPV Controversy', National Public Radio, 19 September 2011.

22   *Amicus curiae* brief concerning non-state actor responsibility in clinical trials, November 22, 2013, submitted to the Supreme Court of India by the European Center for Constitutional and Human Rights and the University of Essex Business and Human Rights Project in Writ Petition (Civil) No. 558 of 2012, on file with ECCHR.

23   Terwindt, 'Health Rights Litigation Pushes for Accountability', 91; see also Kaushik Sunder Rajan, 'Experimental Machinery of Global Clinical Trials: Case Studies from India', in Aiwha Ong and Nancy Chen, eds., *Asian Biotech: Ethics and Communities of Fate* (Durham, NC: Duke University Press, 2010), 55–80.

24   Adriana Petryna, 'Clinical Trials Offshored: On Private Sector Science and Public Health', *BioSocieties*, vol. 2 (2007), 21–40.

25   Quoted in Sonia Shah, *The Body Hunters: Testing New Drugs on the World's Poorest Patients* (New York: New Press, 2006), 8.

26   Sheldon Krimsky, 'Help, Harm and Human Subjects', *American Scientist* (January–February 2010).

27   On the capitalization of uncertainty, see Linsey McGoey, 'The Logic of Strategic Ignorance', *British Journal of Sociology*, vol. 63, no. 3 (2012), 553–76; and Emily Jackson, *Law and the Regulation of Medicines* (Oxford: Hart Publishing, 2012).

28   Andrew Buncombe and Nina Lakhani, 'Without Consent: How Drugs Companies Exploit Indian "Guinea Pigs"', *Independent*, 14 November 2011.

29   Quoted with permission.

30   Klonsky, 'Power Philanthropy', 32.

31   For an introduction to the history of public health in African nations, see Ruth Prince and Rebecca Marsland, *Making and Unmaking Public Health in Africa: Ethnographic and Historical Perspectives* (Cambridge, UK: Cambridge University Press, 2013).

32   See also David Goldsborough, 'Does the IMF Constrain Health Spending in Poor Countries?: Evidence and an Agenda for Action', Report of the Working Group on IMF Programs and Health Spending, Center for Global Development (2007); Gopal Garuda, 'The Distributional Effects of IMF Programs: A Cross-Country Analysis', *World Development*, vol. 28 (2000), 1031–51; and James Raymond Vreeland, 'The Effect of IMF Programs on Labor', *World Development*, vol. 30 (2001), 121–39.

33   Kammerle Schneider and Laurie Garrett, 'The End of the Era of Generosity?: Global Health Amid Economic Crisis', *Philosophy, Ethics, and Humanities in Medicine*, vol. 4, no. 1 (2009); see also Laurie Garrett, 'The Challenge of Global Health,' *Foreign Affairs*, January–February 2007, 14–38; Sophie Harman, 'Innovation and the Perils of Rebranded Privatisation: The Case of Neoliberal Global Health', in Anthony Payne and Nicola Phillips, eds., *Handbook of the International Political Economy of Governance* (Cheltenham: Edward Elgar Publishing, 2014); and Simon Rushton and Owain Williams, eds., *Partnerships and Foundations in Global Health Governance* (Basingstoke: Palgrave, 2011).

34   Laurie Garrett, 'The Challenge of Global Health,' *Foreign Affairs*, January–February, 2007; the Grand Challenges scheme is discussed in A. E. Birn, 'Gates's Grandest Challenge: Transcending Technology as Public Health Ideology', *Lancet*, March 11, 2005.

35   Yanis Varoufakis, *The Global Minotaur: America, Europe and the Future of the Global Economy* (London: Zed Books, 2013).

36   Joseph Stiglitz, *Freefall: America, Free Markets, and the Sinking of the World Economy* (London: W. W. Norton, 2010), xiv.

37   See 'Survey: The IMF and World Bank', *Economist*, 12 October 1999, 46.

38   Charles Piller, Edmund Sanders, and Robyn Dixon, 'Dark Clouds Over

Good Works of Gates Foundation,' *LA Times,* 7 January 2007; see also Alex Park and Jaeah Lee, 'The Gates Foundation's Hypocritical Investments' *Mother Jones,* 6 December 2013.

39   David Stuckler, Sanjay Basu and Martin McKee, 'Global Health Philanthropy and Institutional Relationships: How Should Conflicts of Interest Be Addressed?' *PLoS Med,* vol. 8, no. 4 (2011).

40   In 2015, the *Guardian* took the unusual step of launching a public campaign calling for both the Gates Foundation and the Wellcome Trust to divest from fossil fuel investments. The Wellcome Trust publicly refused to alter its position. The Gates Foundation declined to make any comment to the *Guardian,* stipulating that all investment decisions are taken by its separate asset trust which 'never makes public comments'. See Daniel Carrington and Karl Mathiesen, 'Revealed: Gates Foundation's $1.4 bn in Fossil Fuel Investments' *Guardian,* 19 March 2015.

41   Robert Black et al., 'Accelerating the Health Impact of the Gates Foundation', *Lancet,* vol. 373 (2009), 1584–5; see also Grieve Chelwa, 'Economics Has an Africa Problem', on *Africa Is a Country* (10 Febuary 2015), africasacountry.com, in which Chelwa criticizes the 'expulsion of Africa from the debates that concern it'.

42   The interview took place in April 2012. I have used a pseudonym at the researcher's request.

43   Personal communication.

44   Smith, *Wealth of Nations,* 490. Joseph Schumpeter, *Capitalism, Socialism and Democracy* (New York: Harper & Row, 1975 [1942]), 88.

CHAPTER SIX

1   Gary Rivlin, *The Plot to Get Bill Gates* (New York: Three Rivers Press, 1999), 27.

2   My discussion of Gates's early years at Microsoft draws on a number of sources, in particular Rivlin, *The Plot to Get Bill Gates*; Ken Auletta, *World War 3.0: Microsoft and its Enemies* (New York: Random House,

2001); James Wallace and Jim Erickson, *Hard Drive*; Bill Gates, *The Road Ahead* (New York: Viking, 1995). Knowledge Ecology International also has a useful timeline on its website exploring important patent rulings in relationship to the work of both Microsoft and the Gates Foundation; see keionline.org/microsoft-timeline.

3   Rivlin, *The Plot to Get Bill Gates*, 98.

4   David Bank, *Breaking Windows: How Bill Gates Fumbled the Future of Microsoft* (New York: The Free Press, 2001).

5   John Dvorak, 'Microsoft, the Spandex Granny', *PC Magazine*, 17 July 2008.

6   Mitchell Kapor, '*The Road Ahead* Traverses Hollow Path', *USA Today*, 12 February 1999.

7   'Justice Department Files Antitrust Suit Against Microsoft', press release, 18 May 1998, justice.gov.

8   See Catherine Rampell, 'Microsoft Yields to European Regulators', *Washington Post*, 23 October 2007.

9   Quoted in Timothy Lee, 'A Patent Lie', *New York Times*, 9 June 2007.

10   Jerome Reichman, 'The Know-How Gap in the TRIPS Agreement: Why Software Fared Badly, and What Are the Solutions', *Hastings Communications & Entertainment Law Journal*, vol. 17 (1995), 763–94.

11   Melinda Cooper, *Life as Surplus: Biotechnology and Capitalism in the Neoliberal Era* (Seattle: University of Washington Press, 2008); Stefan Ecks, 'Global Pharmaceutical Markets and Corporate Citizenship: The Case of Novartis' Anti-cancer Drug Glivec', *BioSocieties*, vol. 3 (2008), 165–81.

12   Alan Beattie, 'Intellectual Property: A New World of Royalties', *Financial Times*, 23 September 2012. For a comprehensive history of the TRIPS agreement, see Ellen 't Hoen, *The Global Politics of Pharmaceutical Monopoly Power* (Netherlands: AMB Publishers, 2009).

13   Love's comment, and the State Department report, are quoted in Meredith Wadman, 'Gore Under Fire in Controversy Over South African AIDS Drug Law', *Nature* (June 1999).

14   See James Love, 'Patents vs. People', *Multinational Monitor*, vol. 15, no. 6 (1994).

15   The story of Hamied's meeting with Love is drawn from Daniel Pearl and Alix Freedman's excellent account of Cipla's efforts to slash HIV drug costs: 'Altruism, Politics and Bottom Line Intersect at Indian Generics Firm', *Wall Street Journal*, 12 March 2001.

16   Quotes from Donald MacNeil, 'New List of Safe AIDS Drugs, Despite Industry Lobby', *New York Times*, 21 March 2002.

17   J. Cohen, 'A Call for Drugs', *Science Now*, 6 April 2001.

18   Tom Paulson, 'Prevention vs. Treatment: Gates Fights Group Pushing U.S. to Buy AIDS Drugs for Africa', *Seattle Post-Intelligencer*, 8 April 2001, seattlepi.com.

19   At the request of the Gates Foundation staff member, our phone interview was not recorded. This quote is a paraphrase of the speaker's comments, drawn from notes.

20   Quoted in Paulson, 'Prevention vs. Treatment'.

21   Treatment Action Campaign, 'Open Letter to WHO on Delayed Testing and Treatment Guidelines for Discordant Couples', available at tac.org.

22   Frédéric Bastiat, 'A Petition', in *Economic Sophisms* (Irvington, NY: Foundation for Economic Education, 2010), 56–60.

23   Frank Rich, 'The Billionaires Backing the Tea Party Movement', *New York Times*, 8 August 2010.

24   Quoted in William New and Catherine Saez, 'Bill Gates Calls For "Vaccine Decade"; Explains How Patent System Drives Public Health Aid', *Intellectual Property Watch*, 17 May, 2011.

25   Dan Farber, 'Bill Gates on Education, Patents, Microsoft Bob, and Disease', *CNET*, 16 July 2013, cnet.com.

26   Ibid.

27   Michele Boldrin and David Levine, 'The Case Against Patents', Federal Reserve Bank of St. Louis Working Paper Series (2012); see also Michele Boldrin and David Levine, *Against Intellectual Monopoly* (Cambridge, UK: Cambridge University Press, 2010).

28   Freeland, *Plutocrats*, xiv; see also Joseph Stiglitz, 'How Intellectual

Property Reinforces Inequality', *New York Times,* 14 July 2013; and Peter Moser, 'Patents and Innovation: Evidence from Economic History', *Journal of Economic Perspectives,* vol. 27, no. 1, 23–44.

29 See Jordan Weissmann, 'The Case for Abolishing Patents (Yes, All of Them)', *The Atlantic,* 27 September 2012.

30 Smith, *Wealth of Nations,* 490.

31 See Ruth Lopert and Deborah Gleeson, 'The High Price of "Free" Trade: U.S. Trade Agreements and Access to Medicines', *Journal of Law, Medicine and Ethics,* vol. 41, no. 1 (2013), 199–223. For a country-based example, see the experiences of Thailand, which issued compulsory licences for two HIV drugs between November 2006 and November 2007, and subsequently faced prolonged rebuke from the US government, at keionline.org.

32 Leena Menghaney, 'India's Patent Law on Trial', *British Medical Journal,* 27 September 2012.

33 Angelina Godoy, *Of Medicines and Markets: Intellectual Property and Human Rights in the Free Trade Era* (Stanford, CA: Stanford University Press, 2013).

34 Ibid., 60; see also Ellen Shaffer and Joseph Brenner, 'A Trade Agreement's Impact on Access to Generic Drugs', *Health Affairs* (August 2009).

35 James Love, 'Will the UN Backtrack on Available Medicines?', Al Jazeera, 16 September 2011, aljazeera.com.

36 Tom Paulson, 'Behind the Scenes', Humanosphere.com, 14 February 2013; see also Robert Fortner, 'How Ray Suarez Really Caught the Global Health Bug', *Columbia Journalism Review,* 7 October 2010.

37 Alastair Greig, David Hulme, and Mark Turner, *Challenging Global Inequality: Development Theory and Practice in the 21st Century* (Basingstoke: Palgrave Macmillan, 2007).

38 Ibid., 160.

39 Claire Provost, '$500m of US Food Aid Lost to Waste and Company Profit, Says Oxfam' *Guardian,* 20 March 2012.

40 See Barder's blog post, 'Wasting Food Aid', 19 November 2012, owen.org.

41   See Michael Robinson, 'Tax Avoidance: Developing Countries Take on Multinationals', BBC, 24 May 2013, bbc.co.uk. Work by Prem Sikka, Richard Murphy, and John Christensen offers most rigorous academic scholarship on tax avoidance and its social costs. See Prem Sikka, 'Smoke and Mirrors: Corporate Social Responsibility and Tax Avoidance', *Accounting Forum*, vol. 34 (2010), 153–68; John Christensen and Richard Murphy, 'The Social Irresponsibility of Corporate Tax Avoidance: Taking CSR to the Bottom Line', *Development*, vol. 47, no. 3 (2004), 37–44; and Nicholas Shaxson and John Christensen, *The Finance Curse: How Oversized Financial Sectors Attack Democracy and Corrupt Economics* (Margate: Commonwealth Publishing, 2013).

42   Nikolaj Nielsen, 'EU Multinationals Scamming Africa out of Billions, Tanzanian MP Says', *EU Observer*, 31 October 2013, euobserver.com.

43   See Joshua Keating, 'Feud Watch: Dambiso Moyo Responds to Being Called "Evil" by Bill Gates', *Foreign Policy*, 5 June 2011.

44   Claire Provost, 'Bill Gates and Dambisa Moyo Spat Obscures the Real Aid Debate', *Guardian*, 31 May 2013.

CHAPTER SEVEN

1   Erin C. Lentz, Simone Passarelli and Christopher B. Barrett, 'The Timeliness and Cost Effectiveness of the Local and Regional Procurement of Food Aid', Cornell University Working Paper, January 2012.

2   Oxfam, 'Growing a Better Future,' Oxford International, July 2011, 34. See also Felicity Lawrence, 'The Global Food Crisis: ABCD of Food – How the Multinationals Dominate Trade', *Guardian*, 2 June 2011.

3   Gates Foundation, 'Annual Letter 2012', (January 2012), gatesfoundation.org.

4   Marc Lacey, 'Across Globe, Empty Bellies Bring Rising Anger', *New York Times*, 18 April 2008; see also *The Global Social Crisis: Report on the World Social Situation 2011*, Department of Economic and Social Affairs, United Nations Secretariat, un.org.

5   Patrick Butler, 'Britain in Nutrition Recession as Food Prices Rise and Incomes Shrink', *Guardian*, 18 November 2012.

6   Cargill media release, 'Cargill Reports third-quarter Fiscal 2008 Earnings', 14 April 2008, cargill.com.

7   Greenberger's comment is from Frederick Kaufman, 'Want to Stop Banks Gambling on Food Prices? Try Closing the Casino', *Guardian*, 10 May 2012. Preceding paragraphs are indebted to Frederick Kaufman, 'The Food Bubble: How Wall Street Starved Millions and Got Away With It', *Harper's* (July 2010), 27–33; see also Frederick Kaufman, 'How Goldman Sachs Created the Food Crisis', *Foreign Policy*, 27 April 2011.

8   Kaufman, 'The Food Bubble'.

9   Catherine Boyle, 'Oil Price Falls? Why You Should Relax: OPEC Head', CNBC, 7 November 2014.

10   Kenneth Singleton, 'Investor Flows and the 2008 Boom/Bust in Oil Prices', Graduate Business School, Stanford University, Working Paper, 2011; Marco Lagi, Yavni Bar-Yam, Karla Z. Bertrand, and Yaneer Bar-Yam, 'The Food Crises: Predictive Validation of a Quantitative Model of Food Prices Including Speculators and Ethanol Conversion', Working Paper, New England Complex Systems Institute, 2012.

11   Olivier de Schutter, 'Food Commodities Speculation and Food Price Crises', UN Briefing Note (September 2010), 3.

12   'Do Speculators Take Food from the Starving?', (20 July 2010), *This Is Money*, thisismoney.co.uk,.

13   Steve Schaefer, 'Where Will Goldman Sachs Rank Among Buffett's Biggest Holdings?', *Forbes*, 26 March 2013.

14   Thomas Philpott, 'Warren Buffett's Son Schools Bill Gates on African Ag', *Mother Jones* 14 December 2011; Buffett's children have been remarkably outspoken about the limitations of large-scale giving. In 2013, Peter Buffett, Howard's younger brother, published an eviscerating criticism of what he calls 'the charitable-industrial complex', where 'people (including me) who had very little knowledge of a particular place would think that they could solve a local problem'. It's a candid and important article. Peter

Buffett, 'The Charitable-Industrial Complex', *New York Times*, 26 July 2013.

15   Raj Patel, Eric Holt Gimenez, and Annie Shattuck, 'Ending Africa's Hunger', *The Nation*, 21 September 2009.

16   Raj Patel, *Stuffed and Starved: Markets, Power and the Hidden Battle for the World's Food System* (London: Portobello Books, 2013).

17   Somini Sengupta, 'On India's Farms, a Plague of Suicide', *New York Times*, 19 September 2006.

18   See Patel, *Stuffed and Starved*.

19   Justin Gillis, 'Norman Borlaug, Plant Scientist Who Fought Famine, Dies at 95', *New York Times*, 13 September 2009. See also Patel et al., 'Ending Africa's Hunger', and Dowie, *American Foundations*, esp. 128–33.

20   Quoted in David Rieff, 'A Green Revolution for Africa?', *New York Times Magazine*, 10 October 2008.

21   'Is Africa Ready for GM?', *IRIN*, 27 November 2013; Friends of the Earth International recently published a lengthy report detailing concerns over the Gates Foundation's role in GM expansion in Africa; see 'Who Benefits From GM Crops?: The Expansion of Agribusiness Interests in Africa Through Biosafety Policy', FOEI report, February 2015, foei.org.

22   The Editors, 'Do Seed Companies Control GM Crop Research', *Scientific American*, 20 July 2009.

23   Diana Moss, 'Transgenic Seed Platforms: Competition Between a Rock and a Hard Place?', Executive Summary, American Anti-Trust Institute, 23 October 2009.

24   Robert Langreth, '*Forbes* was Wrong on Monsanto. Really Wrong', *Forbes*, 10 December 2010.

25   Michael Haddon and Ian Berry, 'Russia Suspends Use of Genetically Modified Corn', *Wall Street Journal*, 25 September 2012.

26   Janice M. Mueller, 'Patent Controls on GM Crop Farming', *Santa Clara Journal of International Law*, vol. 4 (2006).

27   Maureen O'Hagan and Kristi Heim, 'Gates Foundation Ties with

Monsanto Under Fire from Activists', *Seattle Times*, 28 August 2010.

28   Duane Stanford and Noah Buhayar, 'Buffett Steals Coke's Show Telling CEO to Study Failure', *Bloomberg Businessweek*, 25 April 2013.

29   Duane Stanford, 'Africa: Coke's Last Frontier', *Bloomberg Businessweek*, 28 October 2010.

30   See David Stuckler, Sanjay Basu, and Martin McKee, 'Commentary: UN High Level Meeting on Non-communicable Diseases: An Opportunity for Whom?', *British Medical Journal*, 23 August 2011; David Stuckler and Marion Nestle, 'Big Food, Food Systems and Global Health', *PLoS Medicine*, vol. 9, no. 6 (2012); and Felicity Lawrence, 'Alarm as Corporate Giants Target Developing Countries', *Guardian*, 23 November 2011.

31   Devi Sridhar and Larry Gostin, 'Reforming the World Health Organization', *Journal of the American Medical Association*, vol. 305, no. 15 (2011), 1585–6.

32   David Stuckler et al., 'Politics of Chronic Disease', in David Stuckler and Karen Siegel, eds., *Sick Societies: Responding to the Global Challenge of Chronic Disease* (Oxford: Oxford University Press, 2011), 136.

33   Ibid.

34   Stuckler et al., 'Commentary: UN High Level Meeting on Non-communicable Diseases', 2.

35   Robert Reich, *Supercapitalism: The Battle for Democracy in an Age of Big Business* (London: Icon Books, 2007), 191.

36   Margaret Chan, 'The Rise of Chronic Noncommunicable Diseases: An Impending Disaster', Opening remarks at the WHO Global Forum, 27 April 2011, who.int.

37   Duff Wilson and Adam Kerlin, 'Special Report: Food, Beverage Industry Pays for Seat at Health-Policy Table', Reuters, 20 October 2012.

38   Wilson and Kerlin, 'Special Report'.

39   The description of the Moscow meeting is taken from Wilson and Kerlin, 'Special Report'.

40   Elizabeth Woyke, 'How NYU chose Colombia over Coke'. *BusinessWeek*, 23 January 2006.

41   TechnoServe press release, 'The Coca-Cola Company, Technoserve and the Gates Foundation Partner to Boost Incomes of 50,000 Small-Scale Farmers in East Africa', 20 January 2010, at technoserve.org.

42   See Stuckler et al., 'Global Health Philanthropy and Institutional Relationships'.

43   Bridget Mugambe, an AFSA policy advocate, confirmed to me in March 2015 that they never received a response from the foundation.

44   Tony Leys, 'Iowa Trial of GMO Bananas is Delayed', *Des Moines Register*, 12 January 2015.

45   The foundation's non-accountability has been strongly criticized in India. See, for example, Arundhati Roy, *Capitalism: A Ghost Story* (Chicago: Haymarket Books, 2014). Currently, there's a dearth of scholarship on the tax and legal constraints facing cross-border philanthropy, although evidence suggests that regulatory constraints have increased significantly in recent years, a change that is lauded and condemned in equal measure. In 2000, scholars at the Centre for Civil Society at LSE and the Center for Civil Society Studies at Johns Hopkins published a report presenting 'the first attempt to make systematic survey of the ways in which charitable funding is distributed from one country to another.' See Helmut K. Anheier and Regina List, eds., *Cross-border Philanthropy: An Exploratory Study of International Giving in the United Kingdon, the United States, Germany and Japan* (Kent: Charities Aid Foundation, 2000); more recently, editors at the *International Journal of Not-for-Profit Law* devoted a special issue to the subject. See Douglas Rutzen, 'Aid Barriers and the Rise of Philanthropic Protectionism,' *The International Journal of Not-for-Profit Law*, vol. 17, no. 1 (March 2015).

46   Pablo Eisenberg, 'Less Elitism, More Equity', *Boston Review* (March–April 2013).

47   Dowie, *American Foundations*, 266.

48   Robert Reich, 'Is Harvard Really a Charity?', *LA Times*, 1 October 2007.

49   Interview with author. See also Reich, 'Philanthropy and Caring For the Needs of Strangers,' and Benjamin Soskis, 'The Importance of Criticizing Philanthropy', *Atlantic Monthly*, 12 May 2014.

50   Rob Reich, 'Philanthropy and its Uneasy Relation to Equality,' in Damon and Verducci, *Taking Philanthropy Seriously,* 28.

51   Both quotes from Kelley Holland, 'The Pros and Cons of Donor-advised Funds', CNBC, 15 December 2015; see also Madoff, '5 Myths about Payout Rules'.

52   Soskis, 'The Importance of Criticizing Philanthropy'.

CONCLUSION

1   See John Gray, *Hayek on Liberty* (London and New York: Routledge, 1998), 15; see also Jeffrey Friedman, 'Popper, Weber and Hayek: The Epistemology and Politics of Ignorance', *Critical Review*, vol. 17 (2005); and Annelise Riles, *Collateral Knowledge: Legal Reasoning in Global Financial Markets* (Chicago: University of Chicago Press, 2011).

2   Friedrich Hayek, 'The Use of Knowledge in Society', *American Economic Review*, vol. 35, no. 4 (1945), 527; see also Will Davies and Linsey McGoey, 'Rationalities of Ignorance: On Financial Crisis and the Ambivalence of Neo-liberal Epistemology', *Economy and Society*, vol. 41, no. 1 (2012), 64–83.

3   Quoted in an Alan O. Ebenstein, *Friedrich Hayek: A Biography* (Chicago: University of Chicago Press, 2003), 146.

4   Alexis de Tocqueville, *Democracy in America* (New York: Harper & Row, 1966), 295–7.

5   Quote from 'Founder's Story', atlasnetwork.org.

6   Lee Edwards, 'Right on the Money', *Philanthropy* (Spring 2009).

7   Jamie Peck, 'Remaking Laissez-faire', *Progress in Human Geography*, vol. 32, no. 1 (2008), 30.

8   Phillips, *Wealth and Democracy*, xiv.

9   Michael Oakeshott, *Rationalism in Politics and Other Essays* (Indianapolis, IN: Liberty Fund, 1991), 26.

10   James Scott, *Seeing Like a State: How Certain Schemes to Improve the Human Condition Have Failed* (Princeton, NJ: Princeton University Press, 1998), 4; the relevance of Scott's work to large-scale donors today

is also discussed by Timothy Ogden. See Timothy Ogden, 'Living with the Gates Foundation: How Much Difference Is it Making?', *Alliance* 16 (2011), 29–45.

11   Evgeny Morozov, *To Save Everything, Click Here: The Folly of Technological Solutionism* (London: Allen Lane, 2013)

12   Rich, '"No Child" Law Whittled Down by White House'.

13   Edwards, *Small Change*, 25.

14   Morozov, *To Save Everything, Click Here*, 133.

15   Peter Thiel, 'The Education of a Libertarian', *Cato Unbound*, 13 April 2009.

16   See Morozov, *To Save Everything, Click Here*.

17   Quoted in Eichenwald, 'Microsoft's Lost Decade'.

18   Tressell's biographer, F.C. Ball, discovered that Noonan – Tressell's name while alive – was itself an earlier pseudonym. He was likely born Robert Croker. I refer to him as Noonan as it was his chosen name.

Index